Christopher S. Celenza is Assistant
Professor of History, Michigan State
University.

Renaissance Humanism
and the Papal Curia

PAPERS AND MONOGRAPHS

OF THE

AMERICAN ACADEMY IN ROME

VOLUME XXXI

Renaissance Humanism and the Papal Curia

Lapo da Castiglionchio the Younger's
De curiae commodis

Christopher S. Celenza

Ann Arbor

THE UNIVERSITY OF MICHIGAN PRESS

Copyright © by the University of Michigan 1999
All rights reserved
Published in the United States of America by
The University of Michigan Press
Manufactured in the United States of America
⊚ Printed on acid-free paper

2002   2001   2000   1999   4   3   2   1

A CIP catalog record for this book is available from the British Library.

Library of Congress Cataloging-in-Publication Data

Celenza, Christopher S., 1967–
     Renaissance humanism and the Papal Curia : Lapo da
Castiglionchio the Younger's De curiae commodis / Christopher S.
Celenza.
        p.   cm. — (Papers and monographs of the American Academy in
Rome ; v. 31)
     Includes bibliographical references and index.
     ISBN 0-472-10994-4 (alk. paper)
     1. Castiglionchio, Lapo da, d. 1381. De curiae commodis. 2.
Catholic Church. Curia Romana—History—To 1500. 3. Catholic Church
and humanism—History—To 1500. I. Title. II. Series.
BX1818.C45   1999
262'.136—dc21   99-6686
                                                                               CIP

For Louis S. and Nancy Celenza, in gratitude

Preface and Acknowledgments

This study began life as a Duke University dissertation in the History Department, where I intended to write on the fate of the pre-Socratic tradition in the Renaissance. In the course of research into this field in the Vatican Library, I happened, through the suggestion of Prof. David Wright, on something only very tangentially related to that field (if at all), the unedited will of Cardinal Giordano Orsini. Through studying Orsini and his sociocultural environment I came upon Lapo, whom Orsini patronized, and Lapo's prose *capolavoro,* the *De curiae commodis.* Even though it was unrelated to my primary field of interest, I decided to devote time to studying the work and its author. I was originally naive enough to think it was a project I could complete on the side. Time proved otherwise and it eventually seemed prudent to change dissertation topics, even as I have continued research into my original area of interest.

My hopes for this work are twofold. First, I hope that it broadens, if only modestly, the evolving and growing canon of Italian Renaissance Neo-Latin literature, whose vitality and interest Paul Oskar Kristeller and many others have signaled. If one considers Italian Renaissance studies from the perspective of the availability of primary sources (especially Latin ones), my sense is that the discipline is now approximately where classics was at the turn of the twentieth century: many important authors have been edited once, many have not, few are translated into more than one language, and the large majority of secondary but nonetheless interesting figures (like Lapo) perforce receive only cursory consideration. No series for Renaissance authors have reached the levels of popularity and completeness of the Loeb, Teubner, or Belles lettres series in classics or the Patrologia Latina and Patrologia Graeca and the Corpus Christianorum (and its Continuatio medievalis) in patristics and medieval studies. This lack of availability of basic sources makes it hard to profit from welcome theoretical developments in other disciplines. It is difficult to write

about the sociology of Renaissance intellectuals, for example, without having fairly complete and easy access to the majority of their extant writings.

Second, I hope that my introductory monographic discussion of Lapo and his cultural environment contributes in some degree to our understanding of the inner workings of Renaissance humanism during what was one of its most interesting phases. Lapo's liminal status is of primary importance here, I think. He was a talented and highly qualified humanist who before his death could not break into the inner circles of important patron/client relationships. Instead of looking at the world of early- to mid-Quattrocento humanism from the inside, we see it from the perspective of an outsider who desperately wanted to break in.

This study has benefited greatly from the time, energy, and patience of many. I thank especially Profs. Ronald G. Witt and Francis Newton of Duke University, Prof. John M. Headley of the University of North Carolina at Chapel Hill, and Prof. John Monfasani of the State University of New York at Albany, all of whom, through careful readings and rereadings, improved this work considerably. I owe extra thanks to Professors Monfasani and Witt for their generous support and mentoring throughout my undergraduate and graduate career. What I have learned, I owe to them. I also thank Profs. Walther Ludwig and Dieter Harlfinger of the University of Hamburg; both made many sagacious contributions to this work. They also helped guide me through a second, related graduate career in the study of the transmission of ancient texts. *Die Forschung-geht immer weiter!* Prof. Riccardo Fubini of the University of Florence has been kind to share conversations on Lapo with me on a number of occasions. The two readers for this press offered a number of extremely helpful suggestions and criticisms, without which this would be a much poorer work. Thanks also to Marcello Simonetta, for timely suggestions. Even a modest project such as this could never have been completed without the *Iter Italicum* of Paul Oskar Kristeller. I pay tribute to that great work and thank Professor Kristeller for kindly responding to my inquiries and providing encouragement for this and other projects. I thank also the staffs of all of the European libraries in which I worked gathering manuscript information on Lapo, especially those of the Biblioteca Nazionale and the Biblioteca Riccardiana in Florence and the Biblioteca Apostolica Vaticana in Vatican City. Thanks to my parents, Louis S. and Nancy Celenza, to whom I dedicate this work, and to my sister,

Mary-Frances. And thanks to my wife, Anna Harwell Celenza, for everything.

For financial support, it is a pleasure to thank Duke University, for a graduate fellowship in medieval and Renaissance studies for 1989–92; the Fulbright Foundation, for a Fulbright to Florence in 1992–93; the American Academy in Rome, both for a Rome Prize in postclassical humanistic studies in 1993–94 and for accepting this book into their Occasional Monographs series; and the Deutsche Forschungsgemeinschaft along with the Frei- und Hansestadt Hamburg, for a graduate fellowship at the University of Hamburg's Graduiertenkolleg Textüberlieferung for 1994–96. Since 1996 I have enjoyed generous financial and intellectual support as well as fruitful working conditions as a faculty member of Michigan State University, which I gratefully acknowledge.

Contents

Abbreviations

Works other than those listed here are cited in full the first time they occur in the book and thereafter by short author-title abbreviations for which full publication information can easily be found in the bibliography. Classical texts are cited according to either the most recent Oxford Classical Text edition or the most recent Teubner edition. Their titles are abbreviated according to the abbreviations in *The Oxford Classical Dictionary*, 3d ed., ed. S. Hornblower and A. Spawforth (Oxford, 1996), xxix–liv.

BAV	Biblioteca Apostolica Vaticana
BN	Biblioteca Nazionale, Bibliothèque Nationale
Bresslau	H. Bresslau. *Handbuch der Urkundenlehre für Deutschland und Italien*. 3d ed. 2 vols. Berlin, 1958.
Celenza, "Parallel Lives"	C.S. Celenza. " 'Parallel Lives': Plutarch's *Lives,* Lapo da Castiglionchio the Younger (1405–1438), and the Art of Italian Renaissance Translation." *Illinois Classical Studies* 22 (1997): 121–55.
CHRP	*The Cambridge History of Renaissance Philosophy*. Ed. C.B. Schmitt and Q. Skinner. Cambridge, New York, 1988.
D'Amico	J. D'Amico. *Renaissance Humanism in Papal Rome: Humanists and Churchmen on the Eve of the Reformation*. Baltimore and London, 1983.
Fubini	R. Fubini. "Castiglionchio, Lapo da, detto il Giovane." *Dizionario biografico degli Italiani* 22 (1979): 44–51.

Hoffman	W. von Hoffman. *Forschungen zur Geschichte der kurialen Behörden vom Schisma bis zur Reformation.* 2 vols. Rome, 1914.
Iter	P.O. Kristeller. *Iter Italicum: A Finding List of Uncatalogued or Incompletely Catalogued Humanistic Manuscripts of the Renaissance in Italian and Other Libraries.* 6 vols. Leiden and London, 1963–95.
Luiso	F.P. Luiso. "Studi su l'epistolario e le traduzioni di Lapo da Castiglionchio iuniore." *Studi italiani di filologia classica* 8 (1899): 205–99.
Müllner, *Reden*	K. Müllner. *Reden und Briefe italienischer Humanisten.* Vienna, 1899. Reprint, with an introduction by H.B. Gerl, Munich, 1970.
O	MS Vatican City, BAV Ottob. Lat. 1677
Par. Lat. 11,388	MS Paris BN Lat. 11,388

CHAPTER 1

Lapo's Life and Work

In the years that preceded the more or less permanent reentry of Pope Eugenius IV into Rome, the Renaissance humanist movement was in the middle of an interesting phase. At that time a large component of its members consisted of intellectuals who lacked fixed institutional places. Humanism—this new *ars* whose curricular focus was the *studia humanitatis*—had still to find its place in society and was dependent largely on patrons. One practitioner of this new art was the Florentine Lapo da Castiglionchio the Younger, who died in 1438 at the age of thirty-three. One of his most interesting cultural bequests to us is a treatise that he wrote in the year of his death, entitled *De curiae commodis,* or *On the Benefits of the Curia.* In this dialogue, Lapo offers us a portrait of the papal curia that is written elegantly, learnedly, earnestly, and even angrily. It is a human document that is alive with information not only for intellectual historians but for social and cultural historians as well. The goal of this study is to discuss this dialogue in its intellectual and social contexts. A critical edition of the Latin text along with an annotated English translation follows the discussion.

This first chapter offers an examination of Lapo's life and work, followed by a brief look at the historiography on the dialogue. Chapter 2 deals with the literary context of the dialogue and examines a complicated passage on the virtues, which I believe can serve as an interpretive key for the piece as a whole. Chapter 3 has a twofold theme: Lapo's self-presentation as a papal propagandist and, linked to this, his defense of wealth in the *De curiae commodis.* Chapter 4 presents concluding thoughts, and chapter 5 offers an introduction to the text and translation.

Lapo was born in 1406 into a family of the feudal aristocracy, whose name remained intact but whose financial situation was not what it once

had been.[1] The family's most famous fourteenth-century member was Lapo the Elder, an acquaintance of Petrarch, noted jurist, and major participant in the events leading up to the 1378 revolt of the Ciompi.[2] His lifelong defense of the rights and privileges of the aristocracy led during that crisis to the burning of the family estate and to his exile.[3] Although Lapo the Elder died in 1381 in Rome, Lapo the Younger must have grown up in the shadow of his family history.

Most of the data of Lapo's life have to be reconstructed from his self-collected letters and the prefaces of his various works,[4] where the preponderance of what we find consists of references to his humanistic career. The 1430s, consequently, are the years about which we know the most.

At some point in the early 1430s he spent time in Bologna, perhaps working for a family-owned banking concern.[5] Humanistic studies, however, were without doubt his first love; what little we know of Lapo's life has to do for the most part with his continuous search for humanistic employment. For Lapo, as for most humanists, this type of search was conducted on the basis of what would today be called networking.

---

1. This overview relies, but is not exclusively based, on Fubini. For the date of Lapo's birth, see Fubini, 44.

2. See M. Palma, "Castiglionchio, Lapo da," *Dizionario biografico degli Italiani* 22 (1979): 40–44; P.J. Jones, "Florentine Families and Florentine Diaries in the Fourteenth Century," *Papers of the British School at Rome* 24 (1956): 182–205, at 191–92; M. Becker, *Florence in Transition* 2 vols. (Baltimore, 1967–68) 2:136–37, 144–46, and *ad indicem*; G. Brucker, *Renaissance Florence: Society, Culture, and Religion* (Goldbach, 1994), *ad indicem*. Lapo the Elder authored a number of influential juridical works, but his most important work with respect to the information it holds about fourteenth-century Florentine elite mentalities is his letter to his son Bernardo; see Lapo Castiglionchio the Elder, *Epistola o sia ragionamento di Messer Lapo da Castiglionchio*, ed. L. Mehus (Bologna, 1753).

3. Palma, "Castiglionchio," 42.

4. See the lengthy excerpts of these works in Luiso; there is a more complete edition, unfortunately unpublished, in E. Rotondi, "Lapo da Castiglionchio e il suo epistolario" (Tesi di laurea, Università di Firenze, Facoltà di magistero, 1970–71), cited in Fubini, 51. Since this thesis, however, is unavailable for photocopying or loan from the Biblioteca della Facoltà di Magistero (even on written request), I shall cite Lapo's letters either from Luiso's excerpts or from the Codex Ottobonianus in the BAV (Ottob. Lat. 1677), henceforth cited as O, with occasional recourse to the Parisinus (MS Paris BN Lat. 11,388), henceforth cited as Par. Lat. 11,388. Another important manuscript source for the letters is MS Como, Biblioteca Communale 4.4.6, for which see *Iter*, ad loc.

5. He may also have been in Bologna at some point in 1427, when a Florentine *catasto* record shows him as being absent from Florence (Fubini, 45).

Toward this end, perhaps the most important person whom Lapo encountered and with whom he studied was Francesco Filelfo.

Born in Tolentino, Francesco Filelfo (1398–1481) was an immensely learned humanist scholar who went to Constantinople for six years in the 1420s to study Greek, in the same fashion as Guarino Veronese and other early humanist pioneers had done. He was a professor from 1429 to 1434 at the Florentine *studium*, where he ran afoul of Niccolò Niccoli and Carlo Marsuppini. Subsequently—or perhaps consequently—he antagonized the Medici (of whom Niccoli and Marsuppini were strong allies) after Cosimo returned from exile to Florence in 1434.[6]

The alienation of Filelfo, Lapo's teacher and friend, from the main source of humanistic patronage in Florence is certainly one of the underlying reasons why Lapo was compelled to seek his fortunes elsewhere. In 1435 Lapo engaged in an interesting but abortive attempt to win Medicean favor, dedicating to Cosimo his translation of Plutarch's *Life of Themistocles*. Given the extensive discourse on exile in this *Life* and the fact that Cosimo himself was newly returned from exile, we can see this as a bold maneuver on Lapo's part, as he finds a way to level the playing field with Cosimo in a manner otherwise unthinkable.[7] In any case this did not result in any subsequent connections between Lapo and

---

6. After his Florentine period came to its end with Cosimo's return, Filelfo moved to Siena. He was there until 1439. Thereafter he went on to become perhaps the single dominant personality in the humanist culture of Milan. Only in 1481 was he reconciled to the Medici, dying in Florence in July of that year. See in general A. Rabil, Jr., "Humanism in Milan," in *Renaissance Humanism: Foundations, Forms, and Legacy*, ed. A. Rabil, Jr., 3 vols. (Philadelphia, 1988), 3:235–63, at 249–52. For Filelfo's life, see C. de' Rosmini, *Vita di Francesco Filelfo da Tolentino*, 3 vols. (Milan, 1808); D. Robin, *Filelfo in Milan, 1451–1477* (Princeton, 1991); eadem, "A Reassessment of the Character of Francesco Filelfo (1398–1481)," *Renaissance Quarterly* 36 (1983): 202–24; G. Gualdo, "Francesco Filelfo e la curia pontificia: Una carriera mancata," *Archivio della Società Romana di Storia Patria* 102 (1979): 189–236. On Milanese culture in the second half of the fifteenth century, see E. Garin "L'età sforzesca dal 1450 al 1500," *Storia di Milano* 7, no. 4 (1955–56): 540–97.

7. See Celenza, "Parallel Lives," for a further elaboration of this argument. Recently Marianne Pade has begun excellent systematic work on Renaissance Plutarch translations. See her "Revisions of Translations, Corrections and Criticisms: Some examples from the Fifteenth-century Latin Translations of Plutarch's "Lives'," in *Etudes classiques IV: Actes du colloque "Méthodologie de la traduction: de l'Antiquité à la Renaissance,"* ed. C.M. Ternes (Luxembourg, 1994), 177–98; and eadem, "The Latin Translations of Plutarch's *Lives* in Fifteenth-century Italy and Their Manuscript Diffusion," in *The Classical Tradition in the Middle Ages and the Renaissance*, ed. C. Leonardi and B.M. Olsen (Spoleto, 1995), 169–83.

the Medici. Later, in 1438, when Lapo was in Ferrara with the papal curia at the council, he would refuse to meet with Cosimo when Cosimo came to town, perhaps because of Cosimo's earlier failure to support him.[8]

In 1435 Lapo went with Filelfo to Siena, where he met with an influential circle of leaders in the humanist and Maecenean community. There he came into contact with Angelo da Recanate, with whom he remained a fast friend. At that time Angelo was the secretary of Cardinal G. Casanova, and in the summer of 1435 Lapo too came into the service of this cardinal, encouraged by Angelo.[9]

In affiliating himself with Cardinal Casanova, Lapo must have hoped to come into the orbit of Eugenius IV, as his letter of self-introduction to the cardinal makes explicit. Humbly presenting himself to Casanova, Lapo mentions that he has been preparing translations to dedicate to the pope. Knowing, however, of his own lowly status, he realizes that he needs a highly placed mediator to intercede for him.[10] During his period of service to Cardinal Casanova, Lapo dedicated to Eugenius IV his translations of Plutarch's *Life of Solon* as well as Lucian's *De fletu* and *De somnio*.[11] In a contemporary letter to the pope, preparing him, as it were, to receive the coming translations, Lapo flatters Eugenius for his

---

8. For the refusal to meet Cosimo, see Lapo's letter to G. Bacci, 14 March 1438 (Rotondi, "Lapo da Castiglionchio," 275; Fubini, 46). The dedicatory preface is edited in Celenza, "Parallel Lives," 148–52; there is a partial translation in J. Hankins, "Cosimo de' Medici as a Patron of Humanistic Literature," in *Cosimo 'il Vecchio' de' Medici, 1389–1464: Essays in Commemoration of the Six Hundredth Anniversary of Cosimo de' Medici's Birth*, ed. F. Ames-Lewis (Oxford, 1992), 69–94, at 87; see also Hankins's discussion loc. cit. In the dedication Lapo writes, "and if I see that this work [i.e., the translation] is approved, I confess that I shall apply myself to more and greater work in your name. Be well" [et me si haec probari abs te percepero, plura ac maiora tuo nomine aggressurum esse profiteor. Vale] (Celenza, "Parallel Lives," 152).

9. For Angelo's encouragement, see Luiso, 212 ("Quare, cum flagitante Angelo tuo vel nostro potius . . ."). Lapo was employed as a letter writer (Fubini, 46–47).

10. "Iampridem mihi proposueram, quibuscumque rebus anniti atque efficere possem, summo Pontifici gratificari; ob eamque causam, cum accepissem illum his nostris studiis admodum delectari, et quaedam ex graecis interpretatus essem, ad eum mittere statueram. Verum ad id mihi dux quidam et princeps opus erat qui pro me hoc onus laboris officiique susciperet, eaque ad summum Pontificem deferret meque sanctitati suae commendaret ac ei omnem statum fortunasque meas et studia declararet. Hunc mihi diu perquirenti tu solus occurristi qui ad id ita idoneus visus es, ut, si ex omnibus unus eligendus sit, neminem profecto habeam qui tecum aut studio aut voluntate aut facultate aut gratia conferendus sit" (Luiso, 211–12).

11. See, in Luiso, letters to Casanova (211–12) and Eugenius IV (213–14). See also Fubini, 47; Fubini corrects Luiso's dating.

well-known generosity[12] and his desire for Christian concord,[13] and having gone through the *prooemium* and *exordium,* he comes to the *petitio* and asks for the pope's support. Lapo cannot offer the pope gold or jewels but rather offers "only" his whole heart and mind and whatever talent for words that he has.[14] Conscious of the value of the wares he has to offer and of his need for patronage, Lapo makes his *petitio* with rhetoric as the quid pro quo.

Lapo's translations of Plutarch's *Life of Pericles* and Josephus's *On the Death of the Maccabees* (a part of *The Jewish Wars*) also belong to this period.[15] Lapo dedicated *Pericles* to Giovanni Vitelleschi, who would become a cardinal in August 1437.[16] The dedication ends with the leitmotiv of Lapo's search for patronage at the curia. Addressing Vitelleschi, he concludes, saying, "think well of me and, by your recommendation, make me as pleasing as possible to the pope. Be well."[17]

When Cardinal Casanova died in March 1436, closing off for Lapo an important channel to the higher echelons of curial patronage, Lapo dedicated his translations of Plutarch's *Life of Theseus* and *Life of Romulus* to Cardinal Prospero Colonna and became part of his household, then in Florence.[18] This channel, too, disappeared for Lapo when Prospero went with the pope to Bologna in April of the same year. Lapo once again found himself in his *patria* without a source of income. A letter from this period to the then papal protonotary Gregorio Correr indicates Lapo's extreme frustration with his intractable housemates in the cardinal's *familia.*[19]

---

12. ". . . nemo adeo inops te adierit, quin auctus et locupletatus discesserit" (Luiso, 213).

13. See O, ff. 190–190v.

14. "Pro hoc [sc., the pope's support] tibi, pater beatissime, non aurum aut gemmas pollicerer, quae nobis nulla sunt et tu minime expetis, sed—quod unum possumus—omnem animum et ingenium, hanc totam, quaecumque est, facultatem meam, hunc denique spiritum, hanc vocem tua ope praesidioque recreatam et confirmatam ad te ornandum et illustrandum libentissime conferemus" (Luiso, 214).

15. See the preface to the *De morte Macabeorum* in Luiso, 291–92.

16. Luiso, 291–92 n. 3. The dedicatee of the *De morte Macabeorum* is uncertain (ibid.).

17. ". . . me diligas et apud summum Pontificem tua commendatione quam gratiosum facias. Vale" (Luiso, 264–65).

18. See the dedication in Luiso, 268–71; Fubini, 47.

19. "Non de Principe haec loquor (est enim nemo melior, nemo probior, et ut vere possum affirmare, nemo humanior nec facilior), sed de illis qui eius domum frequentant, quorum ego, ne quid gravius dicam, inertiam, desidiam, barbaros et agrestes mores non modo nunquam sine stomacho et indignatione perferre, sed ne sine vomitu aspicere quidem potuissem" (letter to Correr, 4 May 1436, in Luiso, 218–20).

Subsequently Lapo hoped to succeed Filelfo at the *studium* of Siena (where the latter had been employed only a short time); but even this hope went unfulfilled, as he relates in a letter to Angelo da Recanate.[20] His distress is apparent, as he speaks of losing his fortune as a result of the bitter misfortunes of Florence, even as he had hoped to win acclaim by means of his constant humanistic labors. Now he must bear his poverty only with the help of others.[21]

He made an unsuccessful try at becoming a part of the court of Alfonse of Aragon, to whom he dedicated his translations of Plutarch's *Life of Fabius Maximus* and Isocrates' *Nicocles* and *Ad Nicoclem*.[22] He even sought patronage—unsuccessfully—from Cardinal Giuliano Cesarini, then in Basel advocating the conciliarist position.[23]

During this difficult period, he sought and received epistolary encouragement from Leonardo Bruni.[24] One of Bruni's letters to Lapo illustrates the manner in which humanists discussed the search for patronage among themselves.[25] Bruni urges Lapo "ad constantiam, perseverantiam, et durationem" and goes on to say that he himself has had experience with the papal curia and has come to know that "whoever perseveres and lasts can have for himself the most certain of hopes of obtaining what he desires" but that "if he lacks perseverance and [his] haste [to leave] is

---

20. See the letter to Angelo da Recanate, 16 June 1436, in Luiso, 223–27, at 226–27.

21. Ibid., 225: "Itaque qui sperabam his meis laboribus vigiliisque mihi ultro honores et praemia delatum iri, idem varie iactatus gravissimis et acerbissimis nostrae civitatis casibus, ne fortunarum quidem mearum statum incolumem retinere potui; sed bonis omnibus amissis aliunde opem et auxilium petere, et alienis copiis meam inopiam substentare coactus sum. . . ." Lapo must be referring to the wealth of his family in general.

22. In a letter of 30 May 1436 to Antonius Panormita (i.e., Antonio Beccadelli) Lapo alludes to the translation of the *Life of Fabius Maximus* that he sent "ad regem." See the letter in Luiso, 222; Fubini, 48. For the Isocrates works, see A. Carlini, "Appunti sulle traduzioni latine di Isocrate di Lapo da Castiglionchio," *Studi classici e orientali* 19–20 (1970–71): 302–9, at 306.

23. See Lapo's letter to Cesarini, 11 September 1436, in Rotondi, "Lapo da Castiglionchio," 12; cit. Fubini, 48.

24. See Lapo's letter to Bruni in Luiso, 234–36. It was written sometime prior to November 1436, according to Luiso; Fubini (48) dates it 23 September.

25. See Bruni's letter of either VI idus mart. 1437 (1436, Florentine style)—according to O, f. 205—or VI kal. mart. 1437—according to MS Ravenna, Bibl. Classense, 182 f. 115v. The letter is edited in Leonardo Bruni, *Epistolarum libri VIII*, ed. L. Mehus, 2 vols. (Florence, 1741), at bk. X, letter 9; here and elsewhere in the Bruni *epistolario*, see the comments *ad loc.* of F. P. Luiso in *Studi su l'epistolario di Leonardo Bruni*, ed. L.G. Rosa, Studi storici, Istituto storico italiano per il medio evo, fascicles 122–24 (Rome, 1980).

untimely, the thing disappears in the middle of its course." Bruni continues:

> do not, therefore, find fault with the beginnings, even if they don't agree exactly enough with your desire; rather, embrace the highest hope, [so that you may attain] such future things as you desire, if you persevere. Let your studies—in which all hope of your status ought to be placed—grow night and day, and do not cease to gain for yourself the friendship and acquaintanceship of older and younger men. For you, this will be surest way of future greatness and worth. Be well.[26]

Finally Lapo seemed on the verge of success when, through the influence of Lodovico Trevisan, a papal *cubicularius* and the bishop of Traù, he received an appointment to teach rhetoric and moral philosophy at the *studium* of Bologna.[27] Elegant speeches given in Bologna in November 1436 as *prolusiones* to his academic employment there belong to this episode.[28] But once again success managed to elude Lapo, as illness prevented him from taking the position. He recounted to Bruni that he acceded to the recommendations of doctors who, on account of his "slenderness of body and weakness," had persuaded him not to continue with his post at the *studium* but to seek rest. He goes on to say that he did this unwillingly, because he knew that vacating his post would hurt his reputation.[29]

Nevertheless, his friend Angelo da Recanate remained a supporter,

---

26. Letter cited in previous note: "Expertus equidem sum omnia, omnia curiae huiuscemodi negotia esse, ut qui perseveret et duret, certissimam sibi spem repromittere possit optato potiundi. Quod si perseverantia desit et immatura sit properatio, in medio cursu res evanescit. Noli ergo principia incusare, etsi non satis tuo desiderio correspondent, sed spem optimam complectere, futura, si perseveras, qualia tu exoptas. Studia vero tua—in quibus omnis spes tui status reposita esse debet—noctu dieque augescant et familiaritates ac notitias maiorum ac minorum hominum tibi conciliare ne cesses. Haec erit tibi via certissima amplitudinis atque dignitatis futurae. Vale." Lapo's response to this letter can be read in Luiso, 242–45.

27. See Lapo's letter to Trevisan, 19 November 1436, in Rotondi, "Lapo da Castiglionchio," 157; Fubini, 48.

28. They are edited in K. Müllner, *Reden*, 129–42.

29. Letter to Bruni, 23 March 1437, in Luiso, 242–45, at 244: ". . . quia medici ob gracilitatem corporis et imbecillitatem mihi eum laborem deponere suadebant, et me ad aliquam remissionem vacationemque conferre, decrevi ab incepto desistere. Itaque invitus feci, quia eam rem mihi dedecori futuram sciebam, nec mediocrem opinionem imperitiae et tarditatis excitaturam esse apud eos qui omnia ad suam libidinem interpretantur. . . ." See also Lapo's letter to Trevisan, 19 November 1436 (cited in n. 27 supra), as well as his letter to Francesco Patrizi, 3 December 1436, in Rotondi, "Lapo da Castiglionchio," 169; cit. Fubini, 48.

and through his efforts Lapo was associated in Bologna with Giacomo Venier, a *clericus camerae* (cleric of the papal chamber). Lapo spent almost the entire year helping to manage Venier's household when the cleric was away in Avignon in the early part of 1437.[30] By this time Lapo had also come to know Lorenzo Valla, whom Lapo describes in a letter to Francesco Patrizi as "a good man and one with whom I am very good friends." Lapo says to Patrizi, "he [Valla] is most attached to me because of our intimate friendship and is highly learned in both Latin and Greek."[31] While Lapo may have been exaggerating the state of his friendship with Valla, there must have been something to his claim, since Valla was kind enough to transport this letter of Lapo to Patrizi.[32]

In December 1437 we find Lapo still in Bologna. During this period, and certainly toward the end of his stay at the house of Venier, Lapo must have been thinking of making English contacts. It was not unknown among humanists in the 1430s that Humphrey, duke of Gloucester, was willing in various ways to patronize Italian humanists.[33] Indeed, in 1437 Leonardo Bruni completed his translation of Aristotle's *Politics* for the duke.[34] Tito Livio Frulovisio (by late 1436 or early 1437) and Antonio Beccaria (by October 1438 at the latest) were actually able to find work in England with the duke,[35] owing largely to the intervention of Piero del Monte.[36]

---

30. Fubini, 48.

31. "Vir bonus et summa mecum amicitia, usu ac familiaritate coniunctissimus, et cum graecis tum latinis litteris adprime eruditus." See G. Castelli, "Nuove lettere di Lapo da Castiglionchio il Giovane" (Tesi di laurea, Università Cattolica Milano, 1966–67), cit. in XX–XXIII; Lorenzo Valla, *Epistole*, ed. O. Besomi and M. Regoliosi (Padua, 1984), 152–53.

32. The letter of Patrizi to Lapo, 22 April (X kal. maias) 1437 (Par. Lat. 11,388, f. 758; cf. Luiso, 247–48), mentions that "Laurentius romanus iampridem una cum tuis litteris mihi reddidit."

33. See A. Sammut, *Unfredo Duca di Gloucester e gli umanisti italiani*, Umanesimo 4 (Padua, 1981); R. Weiss, *Humanism in England during the Fifteenth Century*, 2d ed. (Oxford, 1957), especially chaps. 3 and 4, on Humphrey; K.H. Vickers, *Humphrey Duke of Gloucester* (London, 1907).

34. Weiss, *England*, 46–49. The association of Bruni and Humphrey would not last long and did not bloom into a patron-client relationship. With the translation of the *Politics*, the story came to an end (ibid.).

35. See R. Sabbadini, "Tito Livio Frulovisio: Umanista del sec. XV," *Giornale storico della letteratura italiana* 103 (1934): 55–81; T. Livii de Frulovisiis de Ferraria, *Opera hactenus inedita*, ed. C.W. Previté-Orton (Cambridge, 1932), cited in Sabbadini, op. cit., 56. On Frulovisio's dramas, see W. Ludwig, *Schriften zur neulateinischen Literatur*, ed. L. Braun (Munich, 1989), 70–97. For Beccaria, in addition to Weiss, *England, ad indicem*, see R. Weiss, "Per la biografia di Antonio Beccaria in Inghilterra," *Giornale storico della letteratura italiana* 110 (1937): 344–46.

36. Weiss, "Per la biografia."

In Bologna in 1437 Lapo heard of the duke's generosity, through the praises of the duke and his patronage by Zenone da Castiglione, the bishop of Bayeux since 1432.[37] Sometime during 1437, directly encouraged by Zenone, and perhaps indirectly inspired by Bruni's slight contact with the duke, Lapo sent the duke as samples of his work the *Comparatio inter rem militarem et studia litterarum* together with some translations of Isocrates.[38] Then, in December 1437, still in Bologna, he put the finishing touches on his translation of Plutarch's *Life of Artaxerxes*, which he dedicated to the duke.[39] But no immediate success followed this attempt to win the duke's patronage. It is difficult to say whether Lapo eventually would have had success, since he died about nine months later.

Shortly after his attempts to gain Duke Humphrey's patronage and with the help of Leonardo Bruni, Lapo entered the service of Francesco Condulmer (who would later be the dedicatee of the *De curiae commodis*) and accompanied him to Ferrara and to the church council there, which was just beginning.[40] Still, no important office came Lapo's way. He was dissatisfied, after the council's beginning, to be closed up in the pontifical palace of Ferrara, translating conciliar documents from Greek to Latin and receiving "merces nulla" for his efforts.[41]

It is uncertain how it occurred, but in this period Lapo was placed in the service of his respected friend Cardinal Giordano Orsini, whom he had known since at least September 1436 and whose passing he would lament at the beginning of the *De curiae commodis*.[42] Lapo dedicated his translation of Plutarch's *Life of Publicola* to the cardinal, with praise in classic humanist terms.[43] After a trip with Lapo to the baths of Siena,

37. See Weiss, *England*, 49–50; and see the literature cited there. Zenone was a student of the famous pedagogue Gasparino Barzizza, on whom see R.G.G. Mercer, *The Teaching of Gasparino Barzizza* (London, 1979); G. Martellotti, "Barzizza, Gasparino," *Dizionario biografico degli Italiani* 7 (1965): 34–39.

38. Weiss, *England*, 50–51.

39. See F, at f. 1, also cited in Luiso, 275 n. 3. For more on the translation of of the *Vita Artaxerxis*, see Celenza, "Parallel Lives."

40. For literature on the Council of Ferrara-Florence, see chap. 3 of this study.

41. See the letter to G. Bacci, 12 February 1438, in Rotondi, "Lapo da Castiglionchio," 302 et seq.; Fubini, 48.

42. On Orsini, see E. König, *Kardinal Giordano Orsini †1438: Ein Lebensbild aus der Zeit der großen Konzilien und des Humanismus*, Studien und Darstellungen aus dem Gebiete der Geschichte, vol. 5, pt. 1 (Freiburg im Breisgau, 1906). For a study and critical edition of the cardinal's testament, see C.S. Celenza, "The Will of Cardinal Giordano Orsini (ob. 1438)," *Traditio* 51 (1996): 257–86.

43. See Celenza, "The Will," 264.

Cardinal Orsini died in May 1438,[44] after which Lapo returned to Ferrara and the household of Cardinal Condulmer, to whom he dedicated
his last work.

It was during the summer of that year, in fact, that Lapo wrote the *De
curiae commodis*. As he says (IX.15),

> I, Lapo, finished this at the Council of Ferrara in the Palazzo Maggiore
> on Monday, the seventh day before the calends of September [26
> August], after the third hour of the night, in the year of our Lord 1438.

The last months of Lapo's life are still a mystery. Perhaps he followed in
practice the suggestion of Angelo da Recanate—which he seems to have
been debating in the dialogue—to leave the curia and pursue intellectual
leisure, *otium,* elsewhere. Despite his seeming estrangement from the
Medici, Lapo may have thought he could do this in Florence, since
Filelfo, in a letter of 30 September, had recommended him to Bruni.[45] But
in October—according, at least, to the frontispiece in the autograph
manuscript on which our edition is based—Lapo, aged thirty-three years
old, died in Venice of plague.[46] As if by the echo of Lapo's desire alone,
a half-century after his death Vespasiano da Bisticci, the well-known

---

44. See the preface to the *De curiae commodis*.

45. Filelfo *Epist.* II.44 (entire letter): "Francesco Filelfo sends greetings to
Leonardo of Arezzo. Although I know that all my associates are—even without any
recommendation from me—very well cared for by you, nevertheless let me not neglect
to ask and even to request urgently of you that—if you are well disposed toward me—
you do whatever will be in your power to make our Lapo, a thoroughly learned and
literate man, understand that my recommendation carries great weight with you. Be
well. From Siena, 30 September 1438" [FRANCISCUS PHILELPHUS LEONARDO
ARRETINO S(ALUTEM). Quamquam scio meos omnes familiares, vel nulla mea
commendatione tibi esse commendatissimos, non tamen omittam quin abs te petam
atque contendam ut, si me ames, Lapum nostrum perdoctum et perdisertum virum
quibuscumque rebus poteris ita tractes ut intelligat meam apud te commendationem
plurimum valuisse. Vale. Ex Sena Pridie Kal. Octob. MCCCCXXXVIII].

46. See F, f. iii^v: "Morì nella cit<t>à di Vinegia, anno MCCCCXXXVIII, del mese
d'ot<t>obre d'età d'an<n>i XXXIII di morbo." This is partially cited in Fubini, 50.
Fubini suggests that at that point Lapo "left the curia definitively." See ibid.: "Poco
dopo la stesura del dialogo, secondo le esortazioni quivi attribuite ad A. da Recanati,
il C. lasciò definitivamente la Curia. In settembre era nuovamente a Firenze, dove per
lettera del 30 il Filelfo lo raccomandava a L.Bruni." Fubini cites Filelfo's letter (as in
n. 45 supra), but the letter of recommendation does not mean necessarily that Lapo
gave up hope of ever pursuing a curial career or that he was in Florence for all that
long. Moreover, he died soon after the writing of the dialogue in "Vinegia"—Venice,
not Florence, at least according to the frontispiece in F, which Fubini, too, follows.

fifteenth century biographer and bookseller, believed that Lapo was on the verge of becoming a secretary to Eugenius. But documentation by which we can ascertain the truth of that presumption is lacking.[47]

Although he may have planned to find support for his humanistic labors in Florence, Lapo searched mainly for work in the environment of the papal curia. While the curia, like most other institutions, was in a process of continuous evolution, the 1430s and 1440s were crucial years. Paradoxically, the *curia Romana* was still not permanently at home in Rome and thus must have seemed—as an institution in flux—perfect prey for humanists seeking posts. The problem was that there simply were not all that many opportunities, as Lapo, to his dismay, may have begun to realize.

It has been observed that most humanists, if not already endowed with the traditional accoutrements of social and economic enfranchisement, attempted to avail themselves of those things.[48] In addition, to find *otium* for their literary pursuits, humanists inevitably made concessions to provide for necessities. Secretaries, pedagogues, lawyers, learned courtiers, hired pens of all sorts—these were some of the employment options available. In the papal curia of the 1430s, the positions suited for Lapo would have included those of *scriptor,* abbreviator, and apostolic secretary.

The most realistic position to hope for would have been that of *scriptor,* one of the paths to advancement within the curia. As later thinkers would be, Lapo was fascinated (if somewhat put off) by the relative upward mobility in the curia.[49] The *scriptores litterarum apostolicarum* were located, institutionally, in the chancery, the administrative branch of the curia. On the whole the chancery was the most likely place in the papal curia for humanists to find employment, since the skills required there were the ones they possessed. The chancery was responsible for the

---

47. Vespasiano da Bisticci, ed. Greco (at I, 582) mentions that Lapo "et ebbe da papa Eugenio ch'egli fusse suo segretario, et non so che altro ufficio." Vespasiano goes on: "et era tanto amato in corte et da cardinali et da altri prelati, che, s'egli fussi vivuto, arebbe aquistata qualche degnità magiore in corte di Roma."
48. The four main features were "financial status, public office, . . . marriage, . . . [and] claim to a Florentine family tradition." See L. Martines, *The Social World of the Florentine Humanists, 1390–1460* (Princeton, 1963), 10 and passim.
49. For one such later thinker, see G.F. Commendone, *Discorso sopra la corte di Roma,* ed. C. Mozzarelli (Rome, 1996), cited and discussed in P. Partner, *The Pope's Men: The Papal Civil Service in the Renaissance* (Oxford, 1990), 17–18. I have been unable to locate the edition of D. Rota cited in Partner.

issuance of many different papal bulls, as well as papal briefs, which were a comparatively new way to bypass the longer, more formal process involved in issuing a bull. The brief, especially, offered the humanists a chance to use their rhetorical skill to advantage, since it was a relatively new and thus somewhat malleable form. Within the chancery, the *scriptores* were responsible for copying out chancery-issued documents, so a command of Latin and well-honed calligraphical skills were requisite. In the time of Eugenius IV there were 101 of them.[50] This was occasionally a first stop for humanists in the chancery.[51] Among humanists who at one time held the post of *scriptor* are Leonardo Bruni, Poggio Bracciolini, Cencio de' Rustici, Cristoforo Garatone, and, later, George of Trebizond.[52]

The abbreviators were also located within the chancery. They were responsible for producing short versions from papal bulls that would contain the essential facts once decisions had been made.[53] In Lapo's day the abbreviators functioned as an annex to the *scriptores,* and they were not permanently organized into their own separate college until the pontificate of Sixtus IV.[54] Although later in the century the college of abbreviators would include some humanists,[55] in Lapo's day few humanists held this position.[56]

The post of apostolic secretary would certainly have been the most desirable for a humanist, since it commanded a significant amount of power in its own right, as well as offering direct access to the pope. In general the institution of the secretary was one whose star was on the ascendant in late medieval European governments, and the Roman curia was in step with this trend. The office had evolved in the fourteenth cen-

---

50. Bresslau, 1:304.

51. D'Amico, 29; Bresslau, 1:307–8; B. Schwarz, *Die Organisation kurialer Schreiberkollegien von ihrer Entstehung bis zur Mitte des 15. Jahrhunderts* (Tübingen, 1972), 179.

52. Hoffman, 2:107–12.

53. Usually these were matters relating to a supplication. See D'Amico, 26.

54. Hoffman, 1:121–28, 2:28; D'Amico, 26–28. The *collegium abbreviatorum apostolicorum* was created by Pius II, dissolved by Paul II, and reconstituted by Sixtus IV. For the different divisions of abbreviators and their specific function, see D'Amico, 29.

55. D'Amico, 28.

56. Bruni, Poggio, and Andrea da Firenze at one time held this office. See Hoffman, 2:105–12.

tury, as it became necessary to bypass the sometimes cumbersome chancery procedures for issuing letters.[57]

Aspects of the secretariate were shared between the apostolic chancery (the *cancelleria apostolica*) and the apostolic chamber (the *camera apostolica*).[58] The chamber functioned as the finance department of the curia.[59] A secretary would take his oath of office and receive his stipend from the chamber.[60] But the functions that secretaries fulfilled were much more often connected with those of the chancery, the curia's administrative branch.

Despite the appeal of such an office, Lapo's odds at becoming a secretary would have been long, since with hindsight we can see that the number of humanists who attained posts as secretaries was small, especially for humanists without independent means, as the tendency toward venality in the chancery was growing (even if secretarial venality was not officially instituted until Innocent VIII's 1487 creation of a college of secretaries).[61] In Lapo's lifetime the average number of secretaries was six, and there was also a secretary especially close to the pope—eventually called a *secretarius secretus, domesticus,* or *intimus* or even a secretary *a secretis*—who functioned as a personal secretary to the pope and resided in the papal household. It is generally thought that the first time this office is explicitly mentioned is during the pontificate of Nicholas V (1447–55), when Petrus de Noxeto is spoken of as a "secretarius secre-

---

57. Partner, *Pope's Men*, 42. One sees in the time of John XXII (1316–34) and perhaps even of Clement V (1305–14) that there was in the papal *familia* a *scriptor domini nostri*. In 1333 there are three of them, and in 1341 they are called *secretarii*. See Bresslau, 1:312–13; Hoffman, 1:142.

58. See Partner, *Pope's Men*, 26.

59. The chamber would collect "from spiritual and temporal sources monies due to the Holy See, such as annates and Peter's pence; [direct] the Pope's personal finances; and [govern] the papal states" (D'Amico, 24). Other officers in the chamber included its head, the chamberlain *(cardinal camerarius);* the treasurer general of the Roman church *(thesaurarius generalis Ecclesiae Romanae);* and the *clerici camerae,* seven of which were active members (i.e., *de numero*) along with other supernumerary members with that same title. These all made up the *collegium camerae.* See ibid.

60. Hoffman, 1:143.

61. With the bull *Non debet reprehensibile* of 1487. See Bull. Rom., 5, 332; cit. Bresslau, 1:325. The asking price for the office in 1487 was 2,600 ducats; see Partner, *Pope's Men*, 54. The secretariate and other nonspiritual offices surrounding the curia were important sources of income for those who had them; the fees paid for them, however, functioned as a kind of funded debt for the curia. See D'Amico, 27.

tus"[62]—even if it is recognized that the office existed in fact before this.[63] However, since Lapo speaks of Poggio Bracciolini as *pontificis maximi a secretis* in the *De curiae commodis* (V.5), and since Poggio was kept on by Eugenius as a secretary after having been reinstalled in the office by Martin V in 1423,[64] it seems reasonable to assume that Lapo's 1438 mention of this office is the earliest we have and that Poggio was the domestic secretary of Eugenius IV, at least by 1438.

Another factor limiting the secretariat as a place for humanists to find employment was that it was not simply a post for a learned pen; a secretary was often used for diplomatic or political functions. If one did not command political astuteness and experience in addition to literary sophistication, it would have been difficult indeed to hope for this position.[65] Of the seventy-three secretaries named from the pontificate of Urban VI (1378–89) to that of Eugenius IV (1431–47), only twelve were humanists of note: Leonardo Bruni, Antonio Loschi, Iacopo degli Angeli da Scarperia, Gasparino Barzizza, Poggio Bracciolini, Cencio de' Rustici, Andrea da Firenze, Flavio Biondo, Cristoforo Garatone, Giovanni Aurispa, George of Trebizond, and Enea Silvio Piccolomini.[66] It was really not until the second half of the Quattrocento, when humanism as an educational program became truly infixed in Italian culture, that the apostolic secretariat took on a predominantly humanist flavor.[67]

Moreover, even in the early days of the Quattrocento, rivalry could be fierce for secretarial posts. Vespasiano reports an interesting competition for a position as apostolic secretary between Bruni and Iacopo degli Angeli during the pontificate of Innocent VII (1404–6). Each was pre-

---

62. Hoffman, 2:122.

63. Ibid., 1:152.

64. This is directly after Poggio's return from his three-year stay in England. See E. Walser, *Poggius Florentinus: Leben und Werke* (Leipzig and Berlin, 1914; reprint, Hildesheim, 1974), 84–85. See also ibid., 428, *ineditum* no. 2, where Poggio thanks Cosimo for his help at the curia, which Poggio heard about through Neri di Gino Capponi; it is true that the help is unspecified, but the letter as well as Tommasso da Rieti's report indicate that Cosimo did help Poggio in getting his old position back. See ibid., 85 n. 3. See also Hoffman, 2:110.

65. See Hoffman, 1:144.

66. I use the lists of secretaries in Hoffman, 2:105–22. For a study of the diplomatic missions of one of these secretaries, see L. Pesce, *Cristoforo Garatone trevigiano, nunzio di Eugenio IV* (Rome, 1975).

67. See D'Amico, 29–35. However, it might well be the case that the pontificate of Eugenius IV was a turning point of a sort. Of the twelve secretaries mentioned in text, the last six were appointees of Eugenius. Perhaps Lapo, with his customary astuteness, could sense that something was afoot, although his early death does not allow us to see how he might have negotiated the higher echelons of the curial environment.

sented with the task of writing a letter for the pope on the same topic. The two letters would be judged, and the one who wrote the better letter would be given the position. If we can believe Bruni's own report, his letter won the contest by the acclaim of all who listened, even those who had previously been among Iacopo's supporters.[68]

Although Lapo and others comment on the possibility for upward mobility at the curia, it had only slightly the meritocratic organization one might associate with modern bureaucracies. While there are certainly examples of people who managed to work their way up the ladder in the curia, the vast majority of advancements occurred, as they did in other Italian courts, through networks of kinship and patronage (if one takes the word *kin* in its widest sense, to mean not only blood relations but also protegés of a powerful patron). Advancement was not always linear and did not function in the same way for all curialists. What distinguished the *curia Romana* from other courts, as Peter Partner has shown, was that it offered opportunity of access to the centers of power to "people who would not have had that opportunity in other Italian courts."[69] Lapo, cut off from Medici patronage, was certainly one of those people, so that the curia must have seemed an optimal place to establish new social networks that might at some point lead to support. The wide opportunities for lateral mobility that the larger curial ambient created were just as important as the slimmer opportunities for direct vertical mobility within the Roman curia itself.

In fact, while it may be the case that Lapo had his eye on an office within the administrative structure of the *curia Romana,* the rest of the curial environment is also important, for it offered the most opportunity for humanists in search of work. Of chief importance were the cardinals and their *familiae.* Although their number could vary slightly, the normal

---

68. See Vespasiano da Bisticci, *Le vite,* ed. A. Greco, 2 vols. (Florence, 1970–74), 1:465–66. For Bruni's report, see his letter to Salutati in Bruni, *Epistolarum libri VIII,* I, II, cited by Greco at 465 n. 2: "Hic ego letatus mihi occasionem praestitam cum illo, ut optabam, in comparationem veniendi, rescripsi uti praeceptum fuerat, biduoque post constituto tempore meae illiusque litterae Pontifici, Patribusque recitatae sunt. Quibus lectis, quantum interesse visum sit, nescio, illud tantum scio, fautores illius, qui tam arroganter illum mihi praeferebant, aperte iam confiteri se falsa nimium opinione ductos errasse. Pontifex certe ipse mihi statim gratulatus, reiecto illo, me ad officium dignitatemque recepit." In any case this episode did not prevent Iacopo from being appointed secretary later by Alexander V (1409–10), a pope of the Pisan observance. See Hoffman, 2:108.

69. See P. Partner, "Ufficio, famiglia, stato: Contrasti nella curia Romana," in *Roma capitale (1447–1527),* ed. S. Gensini (Pisa, 1994), 39–50, at 41.

number of cardinals was twenty-four, as stipulated by three of the four concordats between the papacy and various secular powers at the end of the Council of Constance.[70] Since the *familiae* of cardinals were microcosmically akin to the papal *familia,* they offered additional possibilities for patronage to humanists.[71] For one humanist acquaintance of Lapo, Leonardo Dati (1408–72), service as a secretary to Cardinals Giordano Orsini and Pietro Barbo (a nephew of Eugenius IV) led eventually to an appointment as a papal secretary in 1455, in the service of Calixtus III.[72] When the Venetian Barbo was elected pope as Paul II in 1464, Dati moved into the position of domestic secretary.[73] Similarly, Lapo was a protegé of Orsini and subsequently of a papal nephew; had he lived, might his career have followed a similar path? It is impossible to know, but there was one essential difference between the two men: Dati retained strong links to powerful people in Florence, whereas Lapo, the onetime ally of Filelfo, had seemingly lost all such ties irrevocably. In the world of the curia, any and all patronage networks one could utilize were essential. Even in Lapo's short career, estrangement from the Medici probably cost him greatly, since it limited the number of people to whom he could appeal for support.

The best hope for someone aspiring to a curial position at this time was to become attached to a powerful person, preferably of high rank. Lapo's manifold attempts at securing patronage demonstrate that he was obviously aware of this and that like a good fisherman, he had many lines in the water. In his search to find patrons, Lapo dedicated works not only to curialists but to many powerful people outside the Roman curia altogether. It is clear that, in the tradition of Petrarch, Lapo's prime motivation was to find a way to continue his humanistic pursuits.

---

70. See J.A.F. Thomson, *Popes and Princes, 1417–1517: Politics and Polity in the Late Medieval Church* (London, 1980), 65.

71. Cf. D'Amico, 38–60.

72. Lapo must have known Dati, since Francesco Patrizi, in a letter of 19 April 1436 from Siena, asks Lapo to send greetings to Dati. See O, f. 217. On Dati, see F. Flamini, "Leonardo di Piero Dati," *Giornale storico della letteratura italiana* 16 (1890): 1–107; the *Life of Dati* in Bisticci, *Le vite,* 1:299–300; and the literature cited in D'Amico, 254 n. 138.

73. Hoffman, 2:123. In Gaspare da Verona's *De gestis Pauli secundi* (in Muratori, *Rerum italicarum scriptores,* III:XVI [Città di Castello, 1904], 3–64), he is spoken of as "a secretis pontificis maximi Pauli II illum unice amantis et magnifacientis" (23) and as "secretario primo" (51).

Much of Lapo's work consisted of translations from Greek to Latin. For Lapo as for others of his generation, the works of Plutarch, especially the *Lives,* were very important when it came to seeking patronage.[74] Since the *Lives* were short, for a limited effort the translator would have a work suitable to send to a prospective patron. As a translator, Lapo was excellent and fluid, and he has been recognized as such by his own and later generations. He paid attention to Bruni's precepts regarding proper translation, and in addition he gave special attention to verse. In these senses Lapo was very much in step with his generation. However, Lapo's translations are also interesting beyond their technical features.

For Lapo, woven into the enterprise of translation was a web of ideological concerns. He chose his dedicatees carefully, and in offering the works to various patrons, he saw to it that not only his dedicatory prefaces but the translated material itself transmitted messages. Indeed, while the prefaces are often rather ordinary in their mix of sycophancy and moralism, a deeper level can be perceived if one judges the contents of the translated material in light of the perceived characteristics of the dedicatees. Lapo would often match the works he chose to translate to the character of the dedicatees; he even occasionally used the enterprise of translation to address to highly placed people comments that he never could have made in any other manner.

Although Lapo's translations are clearly his most lasting legacy, the other two aspects of his work, his self-collected letters and his prose treatises, also deserve attention. There has been a long-standing historiographical tendency to focus on the translations; for example, when Vespasiano da Bisticci discussed Lapo's work, he never mentioned by name any of Lapo's prose compositions.

> He composed and translated many works, both of Lucian and of Plutarch as well as of others. He was quite well suited to this labor, and because of this, his works, wherever they went, acquired quite a reputation that lasts even until today.[75]

---

74. The arguments in this paragraph and in the following paragraph are more fully developed in Celenza, "Parallel Lives."

75. "Compose et tradusse di molte opere, et di Luciano et di Plutarco et d'altri. Fu atissimo a questo exercicio, et acquistonne assai fama per tutto dove andorono l'opere sua, et ancora oggi dura." See Bisticci, *Le vite,* 1:581–83, at 582. In the last sentence of the *Life of Lapo* Vespasiano indicates that he had intended to give a list of the works Lapo had translated and composed: "L'opere traducte et composte dallui quali

But in addition to the translations, Lapo arranged his letters for publication, in conformity with the custom of the time.[76] All of them offer a window into early Quattrocento humanism and afford us a glimpse into the mechanisms of Renaissance patronage, at least in its literary variety.[77]

The letters are also important as sources for the development of Lapo's thought. Especially noteworthy along these lines is Lapo's lengthy letter to a Simone di Boccaccino Lamberti, which he placed at the head of his *epistolario*.[78] It is an exhortation to Simone, encouraging him in his recent decision to give up a military career in favor of a humanistic one. For the first time Lapo strongly emphasizes a theme that would become persistent throughout his work: the salutary power of the humanities and their character as a refuge against the ills of society.[79] This treatise also reflects and develops in germ many characteristic themes and tendencies in Lapo's thought.

One of these is a familiar, humanistically conditioned enthusiasm for disparaging modernity and making use of the well-worn topos of the golden age. In his arguments to convince Simone that giving up the military life is the right choice, Lapo inveighs against the scandalous practices of contemporary military personnel and compares them unfavorably with virtuous military leaders of both Greek and Roman antiquity. As foreshadowing, almost, of his later criticisms of the curialists, there is also criticism of the "delicacy" of the military leaders under discussion, of the manner in which they "effeminant."[80]

---

arò notitia le metterò qui da piè." But the list does not appear in the authoritative manuscript on which Greco bases his edition. Moreover, in the traditional printed exemplars of *Le vite* this last sentence itself does not appear (see ibid., 583 note b); thus the possibility of transmitting (through Vespasiano, at least) a title list of Lapo's works that would have included the prose works was obviated very early on.

76. Petrarch comes to mind, as does Pierpaolo Vergerio the Elder, on whom see J. McManamon, *Pierpaolo Vergerio the Elder: The Humanist as Orator* (Tempe, 1996), 1. On the question of the ordering of Lapo's *epistolario,* see Luiso, 209–10. Discussing humanist epistolography, Georg Voigt recognized that the letters of Lapo were a "treasure that up until now has remained untouched" (*Die Wiederbelebung des classischen Althertums oder das erste Jahrhundert des Humanismus,* 2 vols. [Berlin, 1960], 2:417–36, at 435).

77. The Renaissance and patronage have been frequently discussed in recent scholarship. For a distillation of the literature and for bibliography, see Robin, *Filelfo in Milan,* 13–17. Among the citations, see the collected studies in F.W. Kent and P. Simons, eds., *Patronage, Art, and Society in Renaissance Italy* (Oxford, 1987).

78. Luiso, 207.

79. Fubini, 46.

80. Par. Lat. 11,388, ff. 6v–9.

In this letter Lapo also includes a catalogue of illustrious contemporaries of his who practice the humanistic arts, which closely resembles the list he will offer later in the *De curiae commodis*.[81] In terms of the evolution of Lapo's prose composition, there is a youthful self-consciousness of the task at hand, which he will later temper but not rid himself of in the *De curiae commodis;* we see him often very aware that he is writing a treatise.[82]

Other letters offer insight into Lapo's view of his social position, which he believed was tenuous at best. In step with his age, when Lapo writes to higher-ups, sycophancy and supplication are the norm. To Pope Eugenius he writes: "For some time now, Pontifex Maximus, great fear and doubt have prevented me from approaching you, even though I desired to do so. After all, when I think in my soul about the splendor and magnitude of your holiness, I am quite put to shame. . . ."[83] To Cardinal Casanova he writes (before Lapo was in his service), "I am quite well aware how impudently and almost insanely I am acting, since I—a humble man and one from almost the lowest place and social order, who has no special excellence or worth—am daring to impose such a burden

---

81. Par. Lat. 11,388, ff. 1v–2: "E quibus, ut preteream reliquos—qui sunt pene innumerabiles—eloquentissimos viros et omni laude doctrine cumulatos, hos tantum commemorasse sat erit qui non modo hanc laudem temporum excesserunt sed pene veteribus illis se adequarunt; //2// Guarinum Veronensem virum exquisita doctrina et summa rerum copia et varietate ornatissimum ac duos illos venetos plurimis maximisque presidiis et adiumentis fortune, virtutis, ingenii, doctrine prestantissimos: Franciscum Barbarum et Leonardum Iustinianum, qui, quasi duo eloquencie rivuli ex Guarini fonte manarunt; tum, e nostris, Nicolaum Nicolum, qui tum precipua morum gravitate ac severitate, tum in perquirendis veterum scriptis ceteris omnibus—meo quidem iuditio—diligentia solertiaque antecellit; ad hos [*MS.* hec] Iohannem Aurispam, Ambrosium abbatem, Carolum Aretinum, ac tria illa lumina latine lingue: Poggium Florentinum, preceptorem meum summum virum Franciscum Philelphum, et horum omnium principem Leonardum Aretinum, qui hec studia sua industria, assiduitate, labore, sua denique eruditione, suisque literis maxime excitarunt, auxerunt, locupletarunt, ornarunt."

82. "Quorsum igitur hec spectat tam longa et tam alte repetita oratio?" (Par. Lat. 11,388, f. 2); "que, si cui longior videbitur oratio, ne quis id mihi adscribat, . . ." (f. 6); "sed eo spectavit oratio mea ut ostenderem . . ." (f. 11); "Sed nimis iam e cursu noster deflexit oratio" (f. 13); etc.

83. Luiso, 213; O, f. 189v: "Iam pridem, Pontifex maxime, sanctitatem tuam adire cupientem non mediocris me diu timor et dubitatio retardavit. Nam cum splendorem et magnitudinem sanctitatae tuae mecum animo reputarem, verebar profecto maxime. . . ."

on you—a man who is so famous and splendid, and who occupies the
highest position after the pope. . . ."[84]

When he writes to friends with whom he sees himself on equal footing,
Lapo does not hesitate to complain about a lack of correspondence and
asks openly for his friends' assistance. To Francesco Patrizi Lapo complains that he has sent letters a number of times with Gaspare, their
mutual friend, but has heard barely a word in return: "For I have often
sent letters to you, but for nine months I haven't had but two letters from
you, and they were small ones at that."[85] To Antonio Tornabuoni (who
would later rise quite high in the papal curia) Lapo complains that he has
had no response, even though Lapo made his own last letter to Antonio
intentionally short to make responding easier.[86] To head off Antonio's
possible objection that he is weighed down by duties, Lapo mentions his
knowledge that Antonio has written long letters to a common friend.[87]
Lapo further admonishes Antonio:

And so, since you can have no excuse left, you had better take care that
your letters get to me as quickly and rapidly as possible, so that with
them you can purge yourself of this crime and satisfy my desire, or else
get ready to be cursed! What else can I do other than inveigh against you
as I might against a man who is idle, neglectful, proud, disrespectful,
and a hater of friendship? Or I could just be forever silent with you.
Now it is up to you that neither of the two options happens.[88]

---

84. O, f. 192 (cf. Luiso, 211): "Non me fugit quam impudenter ac prope dementer
agam, cum ego, homo humilis ex infimo pene loco atque ordine, qui nec praestantia
aliqua aut dignitate valeam, tibi viro clarissimo ornatissimoque et summo post
pontificem maximum gradu collocato, tantum oneris imponere ausim. . . ."

85. O, f. 217. Parenthetically, we might add that Lapo dedicated his translation of
Xenophon's *Praefectus equitum* to Gaspar; on this, see D. Marsh, "Xenophon," in
Catalogus Translationum et Commentariorum, 7, ed. V. Brown (Washington, DC,
1992), 75–196, at 140–42.

86. O, f. 178: ". . . et ad te perbrevem epistolam scripsi, quo facilior tibi responsio
videretur. Atqui ad eam tu ad hunc diem nihil respondisti."

87. O, f. 178v: "Occupationes vero quae tantae esse possunt ut te a tam honesto,
tam facili, tam officioso munere abducere debeant, cum praesertim scribas aliis amicis? Nam Giglofortes noster tuas saepissime et quidem longissimas epistolas legit, ut
non ab occupato homine, sed ab ocioso et loquaci et negociorum inopia laboranti pro-
fectae appareant!"

88. O, f. 179: "Quare cum nulla tibi iam reliqua excusatio esse possit, tu operam
dato ut tuae ad me quam crebro et quam celeriter litterae perferantur, quibus et te hoc
crimine purges et meo desiderio satisfacias, aut conviciis et maledictis responsurum te
parato. Quid enim aliud facere possum quam ut vel in te veluti in hominem inertem,
desidiosum, superbum, contumeliosum, contemptoremque amiciciae inveham, aut perpetuo tecum silentio utar. Quorum utrunque ne eveniat, tuae iam partis erat providere."

In his fear that his friends are forgetting him, Lapo goes somewhat beyond friendly banter.

Lapo's prose work the *Comparatio inter rem militarem et studia litterarum* is, as Riccardo Fubini notes, no mere "humanist commonplace,"[89] coming instead out of a late medieval literary tradition that has as its centerpiece a conflict between a representative of *militia* and a representative of *jurisprudentia*.[90] Here the place of the representative of *jurisprudentia* is taken by a representative of the *humanae litterae*. According to Fubini, Lapo here follows Bruni, who in a letter had placed the *humanae litterae* ahead of *jurisprudentia*. In addition, the work is one of the first of the fifteenth century, along with Alberti's *De commodis litterarum atque incommodis,* to argue for the social, as well as intellectual, prestige of the learned person in society.[91] In this respect it is consistent with Lapo's early long letter to Simone di Boccaccino Lamberti.

Lapo also authored two orations held at the beginning of the academic year in November 1436 at the *studium* of Bologna, where Lapo was to teach rhetoric and moral philosophy.[92] Both are characterized by optimism and a rekindled faith in the power of learning to produce intellectual, moral, and financial advantage. In the first Lapo emphasizes what becomes a repeated topos in his prose: the papal curia as a place of upward mobility. Yet even here, in 1436, we observe seeds, perhaps, of something that Lapo would emphasize much more starkly two years later. Simply put, the upward mobility of the curia, as Lapo must have learned even by 1436, was bound up inevitably with its disadvantages.

> . . . we see in the Roman curia itself—which I would have no doubt in calling a theater of all races and nations—in the Roman curia itself, I say, we see that men bereft of learning are on so much more disadvantageous footing than the educated and learned; the result is that holy orders are conferred on almost no other basis than the basis of learning, or reputation for learning. I could enumerate here quite a few men who were born into a poor social class and were endowed with the scantiest wealth and abilities and who, [nonetheless,] owing only

89. Pace Luiso; see Fubini, 46.
90. Present in manuscript in MS Cambridge, Cambridge University Library, LI.I.7, ff. 49–66v; MS Florence, Bibl. Riccardiana 149, ff. 64–84; MS Paris, BN Lat. 1616, ff. 58–73. The first two locations are noted in L. Bertalot, *Initia humanistica latina,* Vol. 2, pt. 1, ed. U. Jaitner-Hahner (Tübingen, 1990), 275–76, no. 5071. For the third, see the siglum P in chap. 5 infra.
91. Fubini, 46.
92. Edited in Müllner, *Reden,* 129–42.

to the supports and distinctions of learning, gradually gained [control over] the greatest and most abundant polities; some even became popes.[93]

There is upward mobility in the curia, to be sure, at which Lapo never ceases to wonder. Yet he also demonstrates a degree of distaste for those who were "born into a poor social class," were endowed with scant means, and nonetheless managed to climb their way to the top of the curial hierarchy.[94]

One more word might be said about Lapo's thought and his own concept of upward mobility. He had an abiding faith in the essential goodness not only of the *studia humanitatis* but also of other branches of study. In his view, study betters the scholar not only in a moral and sapiential sense but also monetarily. Both in the 1436 oration at the *studium* of Bologna and in the *De curiae commodis,* we see the papal curia invoked as a place of upward mobility. Yet in both of these works, as in other works as well, it is as if Lapo feels an irresistible pull to mention the distasteful side of upward mobility. This might be, for instance, that the people who are therewith engaged are naturally "endowed with the scantiest wealth and abilities" or are, like the cooks in the curia (VII.30), "men covered with grease and grime in the middle of the kitchen, embroiled in the smoke and stench." Of the latter, Lapo points out that "out of nowhere, you see them move back to their homeland, raised not only to the priesthood but even to the highest degrees of honor." What could this negative depiction of upward mobility represent for Lapo?

At the beginning of the fifteenth century, in the wake of Lapo the Elder's misfortunes, the family of the Castiglionchio found itself a representative of the growing class of the financially debased aristocracy. Yet, paradoxically, it was exactly upward mobility that Lapo, throughout his

---

93. Müllner, *Reden,* 133: "... videmus in ipsa Romana Curia, quam ego omnium gentium et nationum theatrum appellare non dubitem, in ipsa inquam Romana Curia videmus tanto iniquiore loco esse homines eruditionis expertes quam doctos atque eruditos, ut nulla fere re alia quam doctrina aut opinione doctrinae sacri ordines demandentur. possem hic enumerare plurimos, qui malo genere nati, quam tenuissimis opibus ac facultatibus praediti, praesidiis tantum ornamentisque doctrinae maximos principatus atque amplissimos gradatim consecuti sunt, nonnulli etiam in pontifices maximos evaserunt."
94. In this oration Lapo goes on to praise extensively the *artes liberales* and the many benefits of learning. The second oration, the very short *De laudibus philosophiae,* stresses the advantages of philosophy as an incitement to virtue and as a protection against the ills of society.

whole life, was compelled to seek through the humanities and failed to achieve. Perhaps Lapo's repeated failures represent in some way a cause of his negative valuations and distaste; and perhaps the negative valuations and distaste represent a sort of disdain of self and of the position in which he had, through *fortuna inconstans,* been placed in society. Maybe it is no wonder that he acquired a reputation, with Vespasiano, as "melancholic, and of a nature that rarely laughed."[95]

Finally, there is the *De curiae commodis* itself, a work that Lapo wrote in the summer of 1438, completing it only a few months before his death. Here I shall offer only the shortest of overviews, since I address certain aspects of the dialogue in more detail in chapters 2 and 3. Lapo begins with a dedicatory preface to Cardinal Francesco Condulmer, a churchman who came from the family that had produced Pope Gregory XII and Eugenius IV, the reigning pope.[96] After opening comments about the greatness of the Roman curia, which compares favorably with any of the great empires of history, Lapo sets the stage. On returning from the baths of Siena to the curia (which was then in Ferrara for the council), Lapo stopped at the house of his friend Angelo da Recanate.

During their meal, Angelo consoled Lapo, who was grieving over the death of his friend and patron Cardinal Giordano Orsini. After the meal and after Lapo had been consoled, the conversation took a different turn, and the two found themselves talking about "the fall, the want, of the Roman church, which is surrounded by the most serious of troubles and difficulties and is being despoiled by its own princes. . . ." (I.10). Later, Lapo decided to re-create the conversation in dialogue form and dedicate it to Francesco, whose great reputation is well known.

As the dialogue proper begins, Angelo laments the way fortune has treated Lapo, and he encourages Lapo to leave the corrupt curia, so that he can pursue his studies in an environment of intellectual leisure, of true *otium* (II.1–5). Lapo is surprised at this and opines that, since patronage in his *patria,* Florence, is not in these times readily available to him, one cannot imagine a place better suited to living well than the curia (II.11). Angelo challenges Lapo to prove this (II.14); Lapo makes an unsuccessful attempt to avoid the discussion and then suggests that they engage in

---

95. ". . . maninconico, di natura che rade volte rideva, . . ." (Bisticci, *Le vite,* 1:582).

96. See chap. 3.

a Socratic discussion, in which, Lapo is sure, he will convince Angelo of the curia's worthiness. (II.18–19).

The dialogue is structured as a series of examinations of the benefits— the *commoda*—of the Roman curia. As such, it divides into a number of different sections. In the first, the curia is presented as a good place because it is a concentrated seat of religion. In the treatise's next section, the curia is presented as a good place because one can, through experience, acquire virtue there (IV).[97]

We are then treated to what amounts to a cataloguing of reputable humanists who managed to flourish at the curia: Poggio Bracciolini, Flavio Biondo, Giovanni Aurispa, Andrea da Firenze, and Leon Battista Alberti, among others (V).[98] Their achievements, it is argued, show that one can attain great glory with the curia as a home: Athens could not give this much glory to Alexander, nor Olympia to Themistocles; after all, theirs were praises only of one country, while the internationalism of the curia allows the laudable figure to hear praises sung by many different nationalities (V.13). This section also intends to show by the examples of the named humanists that scholarly leisure, *otium*, can indeed be pursued with the curia as a home. The curia is viewed as a grand theater where all acts are seen by all people, where nothing notable can be done without having it viewed by all (V.14).[99] To its denizens of the time, the curia appeared to be a very public place where all acts were on display.

There follows a section analyzing the earning potential at the curia (V). And in the dialogue's next section, the interlocutors enumerate the ways in which one can delight the senses at the curia (VII). They discuss auditory, visual, gustatory, and sexual pleasures. Each of these discussions of pleasure is attended by interesting, often highly revelatory side observations. The final major section of the dialogue encompasses arguments for and against the possession of great wealth on the part of the pope and other, lower-ranked curialists (VIII). Wealth is defended, mainly by stressing the position that it enables one to practice the virtues of *magnanimitas* and *liberalitas* (VIII.17–18). There is also an interesting

---

97. On the intricacies of these passages, see chap. 2.

98. *Honoris causa* he mentions two who were at that point lacking at the curia: Filelfo, his esteemed teacher and friend, and Bruni.

99. Garin's edition ends with this passage (at 208–10). Approximately two years prior to completing the *De curiae commodis,* Lapo had described the curia with similar language in his *prolusio* at Bologna. Cf. Lapo's "Oratio Bononiae habita in suo legendi initio . . ." in Müllner, *Reden,* 129–39, at 133: "Romana Curia, quam ego omnium gentium et nationum theatrum appellare non dubitem . . ." and see pages 21–22 in this chapter. Lapo has taken the terminology from Cicero (*In Verr.* V.35 and *Brutus* VI).

argument made regarding Christ's poverty and its place in considering curial wealth. But some of the arguments offered in the "defense" of wealth and curial luxury really, in an implicit fashion, function as expositions of vice.[100]

Historiography

Lapo's dialogue has often been noticed, in his own century and beyond. The dialogue was known to the mid-Quattrocento Benedictine monk, Girolamo Aliotti. At the end of December 1454 Aliotti sent a copy of the text to Domenico Capranica, and in May 1470 Aliotti sent a copy to Francesco Castiglione, calling it a *praeclarum opusculum.*[101] Later, enlightenment era Florentine aristocrats also became interested in Lapo and even made plans to have his work printed, but the plans never came to fruition. Lorenzo Mehus and Etienne Baluce (Stephanus Balutius) were both interested in Lapo.[102] Baluce was especially engaged, calling Lapo a *scriptor non contemnendus;* he made a short catalogue of Lapo's works in his possession, which is preserved in manuscript.[103] Also preserved in manuscript are certain letters from Baluce, then in Paris, to Magliabecchi, in which Baluce expresses his desire to see Lapo's work printed.[104] In the English world, the *De curiae commodis* was known to the Oxford don Humphrey Hody, who, in his work *On Famous Greeks,*

---

100. On these latter sections, see chap. 3.

101. See Hieronymus Aliottus, *Epistolae et opuscula,* ed. G.M. Scarmatius (Arezzo, 1769), I.346 (i.e., bk. IV, no. 49) and 553 et seq. (i.e., bk. VI, no. 59), cited in R. Scholz, "Eine humanistische Schilderung der Kurie aus dem Jahre 1438, herausgegeben aus einer vatikanischen Handschrift," *Quellen und Forschungen aus italienischen Archiven und Bibliotheken* 16 (1914): 109–10 n. 2, 113 n. 1. In his letter to Capranica, Aliotti called the work a text "in defensionem Romanae Curiae plures iam annos editum adversus nonnullos mordaces latratores." In his letter to Francesco Castiglione he sends to "Francesco Castiglionensi, Lapi, gentilis tui, praeclarum opusculum, Dialogum scilicet de commodis Curiae Romanae, qui nuper in manus venit." Since he does not speak in any more detail about the work in these letters, it is difficult to determine whether Aliotti in fact saw the work as a straightforward defense of the curia or was aware of its more satirical aspects and simply chose, wisely, not to emphasize these in his letters.

102. See L. Mehus, *Historia litteraria florentina* (Florence, 1769; reprint, with an introduction by E. Kessler, Munich, 1968), 141–42 and *ad indicem.*

103. MS Florence, BN Magl. IX.50. I have examined this manuscript in person. It is a rebound miscellany containing a number of different items; no. 14 (ff. 51–53) is the "Catalogus operum Lapi Castelliunculi quae penes me sunt." It is anonymous but identified as of Baluce in Mehus, *Historia,* 142.

104. These are in MS Florence, BN Magl. VIII.262, also noted in Mehus, *Historia,* 142. The letters are of 1730 and 1731.

printed from the dialogue a short passage that described the coming of the Byzantines to the Council of Ferrara.[105]

Modern scholarly discourse on Lapo began, unsurprisingly, with scholars writing in German in the late nineteenth century. In his famous study *Die Wiederbelebung des classischen Althertums,* Georg Voigt called Lapo's self-collected letters an "untouched treasure" of the early Renaissance.[106] Although he also took notice of the *De curiae commodis,* correctly noting that it had never been printed, he did not describe the work, calling it simply a treatise "in defense of the Roman curia against its enemies."[107]

In 1902 the Italian scholar Arnaldo della Torre commented on Lapo's dialogue in his monumental *Storia dell' accademia platonica di Firenze,*[108] where he sought to describe the literary influence on Florence of the presence of the papal curia there during the pontificate of Eugenius IV. He made very brief use of Lapo's work, citing from the autograph (F in this study), to help describe and illustrate his conviction that the curia functioned as an "alma mater studiorum." Again, the critical or ironic aspects of the dialogue were ignored.[109]

Richard Scholz was the first to study the *De curiae commodis* in depth. In two different articles, Scholz presented first an interpretation of the dialogue and then a Latin edition.[110] While he recognized the dialogue's

---

105. Humphrey Hody, *De graecis illustribus,* ed. S. Jebb (London, 1742), at 30–31 (in his *Life of Chrysoloras,* to show the diverse customs of the Greeks) and 136 (in his *Life of Bessarion,* to illustrate the esteem in which the Greeks' level of learning was held). Hody lived from 1659 to 1706. This forms the only exception to the fact that Lapo's dialogue work was never printed in the early modern period. Hody does not specify his source other than calling it a manuscript (30: "ex Lapi Castelliunculi tractatu MS"; 136: "in dialogo MS De curiae [*Romanae*] commodis").

106. Voigt makes the mistake, also made by Vespasiano, of asserting that Lapo was a curial secretary; see *Die Wiederbelebung,* 2:36–37, 52, 175, 257, 435. As Luiso notes (205), Voigt's attention was called to Lapo by the work of A. Wilmanns, who pointed out that MS Vat. Ottob. 1677 contains Lapo's *epistolario;* see *Göttingische gelehrte Anzeigen* 47 (1879): 1489–1504, at 1491.

107. Voigt, *Die Wiederbelebung,* 2:36–37: "Er hat hier kurz zuvor [i.e., in Ferrara at the council shortly before his death] eine Schrift in dialogischer Form zur Vertheidigung der römischen Curie gegen ihre Feinde verfasst, die gern gelesen aber bisher nicht gedruckt worden ist." To show that the treatise was "gern gelesen" Voigt cites the letters of Aliotti mentioned in n. 100 supra.

108. A. Della Torre, *Storia dell' accademia platonica di Firenze* (Florence, 1902; reprint, Turin, 1968).

109. Ibid., 246–48.

110. For the interpretation, see R. Scholz "Eine ungedruckte Schilderung der Kurie aus dem Jahre 1438," *Archiv für Kulturgeschichte* 10 (1912): 399–413; for the edition, see his "Eine humanistische."

importance and saw fit to present it to the scholarly public, he based both
of his studies on only one manuscript copy of the text, thanks to which
his edition is often lacking.[111] In his interpretation Scholz emphasized the
defense of wealth in the treatise and discussed the manner in which this
was consistent with certain aspects of emerging humanist culture,[112] a
point Hans Baron would later emphasize forcefully. However, as we
shall see, this issue is not without its complications in the dialogue. The
defense of wealth in the treatise does not go completely untempered by
protest and is not nearly as simple and unequivocal as Scholz made it out
to be.[113]

More recent historians who have touched on the dialogue include
George Holmes,[114] John D'Amico,[115] Hans Baron,[116] Riccardo Fubini,
and Peter Partner. The latter two offer especially interesting insights into
the dialogue. Fubini points out the negative aspects of the papal curia
that Lapo presents in the *De curiae commodis*.[117] He also emphasizes

---

111. See chap. 5 infra.

112. Scholz, "Eine ungedruckte," 410.

113. See ibid., 407, where Scholz discusses what he sees as "eine Verteidigung der
kurialen Praxis." See also Scholz, "Eine humanistische," 114–15: "Im Ganzen ist der
Traktat ernst gemeint, als wirkliche Verteidigung der Kurie und des kurialen Lebens.
. . . Was Lapo interessiert, sind allein die Freuden des Weltlebens im Sinne der Renaissance: dieses Renaissance-Ideal findet er in Ferrara an der Kurie. . . ."

114. George Holmes, *The Florentine Enlightenment, 1400–1450* (Oxford, 1969),
83.

115. D'Amico, 118. For D'Amico, the importance of Lapo's dialogue lay in its
stress on the unifying force of the Latin language in the curia, a point that Lorenzo
Valla would later develop widely and powerfully in his *Oratio in principio sui studii*
of 1455. For Valla's treatise, see the edition in Lorenzo Valla, *Opera omnia*, ed.
J. Vahlen (Basel, 1540, reprint with additions, Turin, 1962).

116. Baron's analysis focused on the text as evidence for a feature that he saw as
part and parcel of early Quattrocento Florentine humanism: the positive rehabilita-
tion of the value of private wealth. However, Baron seems to stress the passages of the
dialogue that defend the curial accumulation of wealth and he does not take much
notice of its countertendencies. See his *In Search of Florentine Civic Humanism:
Essays on the Transition from Medieval to Modern Thought*, 2 vols. (Princeton,
1988). Baron had discussed the treatise much earlier in his article "Franciscan Poverty
and Civic Wealth as Factors in the Rise of Humanistic Thought," *Speculum* 13
(1938): 1–37; chaps. 7–9 in his 1988 collection represent an amplified and revised version of his 1938 article. For his discussion of Lapo, see *In Search of Florentine Civic
Humanism*, 2:244–46. As far as text-critical matters go, Baron used the autograph
manuscript but judged that the autograph "differs from Scholz's version at unimportant points only" (2:245 n. 16). This judgment was correct for the sections of the dialogue that Baron examined but would be difficult to maintain if applied to the whole
treatise.

117. See Fubini.

Lapo's literary methodology, which Fubini terms a "pro and contra style" of argumentation. He argues that whenever a thesis is expounded in the dialogue, the most pessimistic point of view is set forth first. Then the dialogue offers a counterposition that does not contradict the first position but tempers it, by sticking more closely to reality.[118] Because of this, it is difficult to come up with a consistent interpretation of the dialogue, as Fubini recognizes.[119]

Peter Partner's interpretation of the dialogue stresses its ambiguities.[120] He emphasizes the notion that its critical tendencies show, along with certain treatises of Valla and Poggio, that there was a certain latitude of opinion possible at the papal court. In addition Partner (114–15) lays stress on the importance of considering the environment in which this treatise on the curia was written: "Eugenius IV had been chased out of Rome, was threatened outside Italy by the council of Basle, inside by a host of enemies, and was seeking reconciliation with the Greek church to support his threatened prestige."

I shall argue that at least one of the things motivating Lapo as he composed the treatise was the desire to present himself as a skillful papal propagandist. The relative instability of the curial environment in which Lapo was working must have made this seem all the more necessary. Before I can move on to the ambient of the papal court, a question sug-

---

118. Fubini, 49: "Nel corso del dialogo il C. sviluppa un tipo di argomentazione già altre volte adottato, vale a dire il procedimento retorico del pro e contro, dove all'esposizione della tesi, che rispecchia il punto di vista più pessimistico, fa seguito una confutazione che, senza negarlo, lo contempera con uno sforzo di maggiore e più spregiudicata aderenza alla realtà."

119. Fubini, 50: "It remains difficult to establish if, with his little work, Lapo da Castiglionchio had really aimed to flatter the dedicatee, offering a sort of model for a new curial apologetic, or if he had intended—given the all too transparent polemic and casual open-mindedness of opinions—to launch a sort of challenge to the world of the curia from which he saw himself rejected, almost as a recapitulation of an unfortunate career" In a recent article focusing on Bruni's *Dialogi ad Petrum Histrum,* Fubini emphasizes the anti-institutional potentiality inherent in humanistic works like Lapo's, which are often suffused with irony. This often allowed humanists to say things in opposition to traditional cultural institutions that they could not have done using then-traditional modes of discourse. See R. Fubini, "All'uscita dalla Scolastica medievale: Salutati, Bruni, e i 'Dialogi ad Petrum Histrum,'" *Archivio storico italiano* 150 (1992): 1065–99. The argument I shall develop regarding the dialogue is influenced by Fubini's insightful and penetrating position but does not follow it directly, since I believe that, alongside the obvious irony, Lapo presents a sincere admiration for the curia's potential. See infra.

120. See Partner, *Pope's Men,* 114–18.

gests itself. Despite the dialogue's many and brilliant ambiguities, can Lapo have been staking out any consistent positions? In chapter 2, after sketching out a literary context for Lapo's work, I attempt to offer an answer.

CHAPTER 2

The Literary Environment: Genealogies

Lapo's work on the *curia Romana* fits into a number of literary streams. Closest to home for him would have been the literature of humanism with which he would have been familiar, such as Petrarch's *Liber sine nomine*, which presents a polemic against the papacy at Avignon.[1] Although Petrarch does not fault the institution of the papacy, one hears there an angry voice calling for reform. Moreover, although Petrarch unceasingly complains about the city of Avignon, when he looks deeply at the situation, he realizes that not the city itself but rather its inhabitants deserve blame. Similar to what Lapo would later write concerning the evil men at the curia who were undermining what was basically a good institution, Petrarch writes (92), "Confess that it is not so much the city they inhabit that is evil, as they themselves who are vile and deceitful."

Petrarch's own negative feelings about the curia of his day were clearly bound up with a kind of protonationalism for which he was so admired by modern Italian nationalists; he ended the *Sine nomine* with a call to the then emperor Charles IV to free the papacy from the Babylon of Avignon and restore it to its proper place in Rome. While Lapo's treatise is free of this sort of nationalist sentiment, it is reasonable to suppose that he knew and was inspired by Petrarch's work. Petrarch was the archetype of the disenfranchised intellectual who heroically sought to continue with his humanistic work despite the hardships of repeated dislocation. Lapo probably saw in Petrarch a kindred spirit and perhaps even felt a deeper sense of kinship, since Lapo's uncle, Lapo the Elder, was among the cor-

---

1. See Francesco Petrarca, *Petrarcas 'Buch ohne Namen' und die päpstliche Kurie: Ein Beitrag zur Geistesgeschichte der Frührenaissance*, ed. P. Piur (Halle an der Saale, 1925). I cite from the translation of N.P. Zacour, *Petrarch's Book without a Name: A Translation of the "Liber sine nomine"* (Toronto, 1973).

respondents in the *Sine nomine* and was a friend and admirer of Petrarch.[2]

While there do not seem to be any direct quotations of the *Sine nomine* in the *De curiae commodis,* Lapo often echoes Petrarch. The most notable similarities occur during the angry speeches in the dialogue, bewailing the excesses of the curia. Petrarch makes use often in the *Sine nomine* of a type of topos in which the world seems upside down. For example, he writes (59),

> it is shocking to see pious solitude replaced with shameful comings and goings and swarming troupes of the most debased hangers-on, to see rich feasts in place of sober fasts, rude and revolting slothfulness for sacred pilgrimages—and instead of the naked feet of the apostles, to gaze upon the prancing snow-white mounts of thieves, bedecked with gold, covered with gold, champing on gold bits, soon to be shod with gold shoes if the Lord does not curtail this debased excess.

Lapo often echoes this type of angry argument in his treatise. In addition, as Lapo would later do, Petrarch took care in his *De otio religioso* to discuss wealth, suggesting that "in our own age . . . gold and silver are cultivated with as much reverence as Christ himself is not, and often the live God is despised out of admiration for inanimate metals."[3] However, Lapo turns this usage of the topos of the golden age on its head in his defense of wealth in the *De curiae commodis,* when he suggests that precisely because pomp is so respected in modern times, curialists should be possessed of ample wealth (VIII).

The *De curiae commodis* represents part of the rich tradition of Italian

---

2. Letter V of the *Sine nomine* is part of a larger letter that Petrarch wrote to Lapo the Elder (Petrarch, *Le Familiari,* ed. V. Rossi, 4 vols. [Florence, 1933–42], XII.8). He later judged the opening too harsh and thus excerpted it, leaving it in its present form in the *Sine nomine.* Lapo the Elder is the addressee of *Fam.* VII.16 and XVIII.12, in addition to the letter mentioned. He is also alluded to twice in the Petrarchan *epistolario* (according to the index in *Le Familiari,* ed. Rossi, vol. 4), once in a letter to Bocaccio (XI.6.10) as one of "our three compatriots" ("ad hec et ad tres compatriotas nostros, optimos illos quidem ac probatissimos amicos . . . salvere iubeas ore tuo meis vocibus"). The other mention is in a letter to Francesco Nelli (XVIII.11.1–3), where Petrarch discusses Lapo the Elder's decision to pursue legal studies in Bologna.

3. For the treatise, see Francesco Petrarca, *Il 'De otio religioso' di Francesco Petrarca,* ed. G. Rotondi and G. Martellotti (Vatican City, 1958). The quoted passage is cited and translated in C.M. Trinkaus, *"In Our Image and Likeness": Humanity and Divinity in Italian Humanist Thought,* 2 vols. (London, 1970), 2:656–57.

Renaissance Neo-Latin dialogues. David Marsh has established a loose typology of the Quattrocento dialogue.[4] Focusing on five figures—Bruni, Alberti, Poggio, Valla, and Pontano—Marsh argues that the main inspiration for most humanist dialogue writers was the Ciceronian dialogue, in which different (usually philosophical) positions were set forth and discussed by a number of interlocutors. The Ciceronian dialogue would often end with a lack of resolution as to which of the positions was best.

One Ciceronian dialogue that Lapo certainly would have known was Poggio Bracciolini's *De avaritia,* a piece that deals out some fairly heavy-handed anticlerical criticism, an example of which follows:

> Then Cencio laughingly said: "When Antonio said 'all men,' he meant it to be understood also about priests. For a long time now this is an evil that is in them and is proper to their characters. For from the very beginning of our religion, it seems to me, this plague began to grow in them. First of all Judas of the disciples, once he accepted the coins, betrayed the Savior; from him onward, this gluttony for gold has spread into the rest of them and has lasted to our era. It dwells in them to such an extent that it is rare to find a priest free from greed."[5]

In addition, in Poggio's dialogue preachers are criticized for lacking the very qualities that they preach, clerics are spoken of as often studying only for the sake of monetary gain, and monks are criticized for being burdens to the state. Moreover, as Lapo later will do (VII.18) and as Petrarch had done in his *Sine nomine,* Poggio uses the Tantalus myth when speaking of the clergy. For Poggio, the clergy are tormented by a lust for gold, even though they live in abundance and can lack nothing;

---

4. See D. Marsh, *The Quattrocento Dialogue: Classical Tradition and Humanist Innovation* (Cambridge, Mass., 1980).

5. "Tum subridens Cincius: Atqui, inquit, cum omnes Antonius dixit, de sacerdotibus voluit intellegi, quibus iam dudum hoc est commune malum et moribus consuetum. Ab ipso enim, ut mihi videtur, exordio religionis nostrae coepit haec pestis vigere in illis. Iudas primum ex discipulis Salvatorem prodidit, acceptis nummis, et ab eo in reliquos ingluvies auri manavit perseveravitque ad nostram aetatem, adeoque in eis insedit, ut rarum sit reperire sacerdotem cupiditatis expertem." See Poggio's *De avaritia* in Poggio Bracciolini, *Opera omnia* (Basel, 1538; reprint, with a preface by R. Fubini, Turin, 1964), 1–31, at 22. It is interesting that Poggio, unlike Lapo, sets the origins of clerical greed in apostolic times. On the date of the *De avaritia,* see Walser, *Poggius Florentinus,* 126; for literature on Poggio, see the collected studies in Poggio Bracciolini, *Poggio Bracciolini, 1380–1980: Nel VI centenario della nascita,* Istituto Nazionale di Studi sul Rinascimento, Studi e Testi VIII (Florence, 1982).

yet, like Tantalus's desire for food, their lust for gold can never be fully satisfied. Beyond the anticlerical tendencies of the work, Poggio has his interlocutor Andrea discuss virtue in technical terms, as will Lapo's interlocutors. For Poggio's Andrea, the real blame to be laid on the head of the miser is that he does not practice temperance, which is the mean between the two extremes of prodigality and parsimony.

Marsh also outlines three other ancient traditions that were followed in the Italian Renaissance: the Socratic dialogue, the symposiac dialogue (as in the work of Xenophon or Plato's *Symposium*), and the Lucianic comic dialogue. In reading Lapo and in placing him in the tradition of the Quattrocento dialogue, we should keep the Socratic form in the forefront. Authors of Quattrocento "Socratic" dialogues changed the morphology of the Socratic dialogue as it had been realized in the works of Plato. Whereas Plato had removed his own presence from the dramatic equation, a number of fifteenth-century authors appeared as interlocutors in and even introduced their works. Despite the differences, however, the Quattrocento "Socratic" dialogues share in the same spirit as the dialogues of Plato, even if they do not possess the same level of technical philosophical depth.[6]

Marsh mentions three "Socratic" dialogues from the first half of the Quattrocento, Alberti's *Pontifex* (1437), Valla's *De libero arbitrio* (1439), and Valla's *De professione religiosorum* (1442).[7] An explicit assertion on the part of Lapo's interlocutor Angelo alerts us that Lapo's dialogue is part of this tradition (II.19): "You wish to handle me in the manner of Socrates." Given that it was written in 1438, Lapo's dialogue must be seen as an essential part in the development of this Socratic trend that began in the late 1430s.

Alberti addresses the question of wealth and the church in his *Pontifex*.[8] In one section an interlocutor speaks as follows:

Even if, perhaps, those things that I called vices before—that is, pleasure, ambition, and desire—are occasionally on view in high priests, unless you think we should do otherwise, let us single out that vice that, almost to a one, all of them admit is rather detrimental to themselves, inasmuch as at the beginning of our discussion you had spoken

6. Marsh, *Quattrocento Dialogue*, 6.
7. Ibid.
8. Edited in Leon Battista Alberti, *Opera inedita et pauca separatim impressa*, ed. G. Mancini (Florence, 1890), 67–121.

of their sumptuousness and ostentation, [from which] we easily understood how incredibly dedicated to wealth they are.[9]

Alberti thus points out for particular condemnation the vices associated with ostentation.

Lapo must also have known Alberti's *Intercenales*.[10] Intended to be read *inter cenas et pocula,* the short pieces that comprise this work were brief, often satirical comments on various aspects of life, written in a sometimes ponderous Latin, and collected by Alberti into eleven books sometime after the year 1437. Sometimes they were written in dialogue form, sometimes not. In a number of places Lapo echoes the sentiments and often the prose itself of certain of these works. In terms of actual language, Lapo owes most, perhaps, to the *intercenale* "Poverty," a very short dialogue between Peniplusius and Paleterus.[11] When one hears one of the interlocutors advising the other that he is "in the public eye no less than other prominent men" and that his "character and behavior are closely scrutinized,"[12] one thinks of Lapo's argument that the public position of the highly situated curialists prevents them from doing wrong out of concern for their reputation (VIII.9). The interlocutors of "Poverty" also discuss the utility of wealth.

> Consider what the public must think when they behold a prominent man's family clothed with insufficient decency, his horses neglected, and the master himself attired with insufficient dignity—in short, the entire house less sumptuous and elegant than it was in previous generations and than public customs and standards require.[13]

---

9. Ibid., 92: "Tametsi fortassis illa in pontificibus, quae dixi vitia, voluptas, ambitio et cupiditas perspicua interdum sunt, ni aliter agendum censeas, id unum excipiamus quod illi sibi deterius putant, quive ad unum usque ferme omnes, quantum a principio dixeras de illorum apparatu et pompis, facile quam deditissimi sint intelligimus."

10. There is still no complete critical edition of the *Intercenales,* but some are collected and translated in Leon Battista Alberti, *Dinner Pieces,* trans. D. Marsh, Medieval and Renaissance Texts and Studies, 45 (Binghamton, New York, 1987), and there is an excellent bibliography in the notes there. The two main printed sources for the Latin texts are in Alberti, *Opera inedita,* and E. Garin, "Leon Battista Alberti: Alcune intercenali inedite," *Rinascimento,* 2d ser., 4 (1964): 125–258, reprinted as *Intercenali inedite,* ed. E. Garin (Florence, 1965). For other bibliography and notes on the manuscript situation, see Marsh's introduction and notes in *Dinner Pieces.* I cite from the translations of Marsh.

11. Alberti, *Dinner Pieces,* 46–50.

12. Ibid., 46.

13. Ibid., 47.

Lapo uses just such reasoning to argue that curialists should be attended by much pomp and circumstance (VIII.48–49). In describing poverty, Alberti also suggests:

> a reputation of wealth enhances our dignity and esteem, and . . . we must completely shun the very name of poverty. For hand in hand with an indigent condition, there goes a reputation for instability, impudence, audacity, crimes and vices which are condemned by everyone's suspicions and rumors.[14]

Lapo's interlocutors argue that wealth is to be preferred to poverty since the crimes committed by the poor are baser than those committed by the wealthy (VIII.20–22), a position that bears indubitable similarities to Alberti's stance here in favor of wealth.

Other affinities between the *De curiae commodis* and the *Intercenales* reflect the concern, occasional discomfort, and sometimes outright bitterness in the humanist community concerning the proximity of wealth and religion. In "The Coin," Alberti offers a fable in which, after much suspenseful waiting at the oracle of Apollo, ancient priests came to the realization that money was their "sovereign and supreme god" and wound up swearing to this notion. Alberti goes on to say that "priests value this oath so highly that, even to the present day, no priest has incurred even the slightest suspicion of perjury in this regard."[15] Along the same lines, in the short fable "Pluto" (in which Pluto is identified with Ploutos, god of wealth) we are told that Hercules "could not patiently tolerate in the society of the gods one whom, during his travels across the earth, he had only seen as a close friend of the most slothful and indolent men."[16]

Finally, certain parallels to Lapo's dialogue are evident in a work not part of the *Intercenales*, Alberti's famous Tuscan dialogue, the *Libri della famiglia*.[17] In book 4 Alberti has the interlocutor Piero suggest that "excessive greed for money" is "the most common and most notorious vice of all priests" (262 Watkins trans., 280 Grayson ed.). We hear from the interlocutor Ricciardo that "virtue ought to be dressed in those

---

14. Ibid.

15. Ibid., 50–51.

16. Ibid., 52.

17. Here I cite from the translation of R. N. Watkins (*The Family in Renaissance Florence: A Translation of . . . "I libri della famiglia"* [Columbia, S.C., 1969]) but give also the reference to the Grayson edition of the Italian text for each passage (from vol. 1 of Leon Batista Alberti, *Opere volgari,* ed. C. Grayson, 3 vols. [Bari, 1960]).

seemly ornaments which it is hard to acquire without affluence" (250 Watkins trans., 267–68 Grayson ed.).

One landmark work in the tradition of humanist polemic against clerical wealth was Valla's *De professione religiosorum,* written a few years after Lapo's dialogue, in 1442. In a number of places Valla's concerns resonate with Lapo's work. The usual protestation against wealth held by the religious is present: "The church, therefore, also has treasures, but it is not the possession or use of these treasures that is criticized but rather their tight hold and abuse of them."[18] Valla also mentions the sexual immorality of many religious, a topic that is not absent from Lapo's work. Valla laments:

> Oh, would that bishops and priests "were deacons of one wife for each man" and not—pardon me—lovers of one prostitute. No one will be able to become angry with me, unless he is someone who doesn't wish to look into his own conscience. Many are good, but—and it pains me to say it—more are bad.[19]

Given their acquaintanceship, it is probable that Valla knew Lapo's dialogue, but in any case these sorts of ideas were clearly in the air in the humanist community.[20]

Another contemporary with whom Lapo has affinities is Enea Silvio Piccolomini, who became Pope Pius II in 1458. The specific point of connection comes in an epistolary treatise that Piccolomini composed in 1444, six years after the final redaction of the *De curiae commodis.* The treatise is entitled *De curialium miseriis* (On the miseries of courtiers)[21] and there are

---

18. Lorenzo Valla, *De professione religiosorum,* ed. M. Cortesi (Padua, 1986), X.22: "Habet ergo et Ecclesia thesauros, nec eorum possessio aut usus, sed tenacitas atque abusus reprehenditur. Quod de Ecclesia, idem de privatis singulisque dicendum est, maxime pro qualitate persone."

19. Ibid., XI.7–8: "Utinam, utinam episcopi, presbyteri, 'diacones essent unius uxoris viri' et non potius (venia sit dicto) non unius scorti amatores. (8) Nemo mihi irasci poterit, nisi qui sibi conscius de se noluerit confiteri. Multi sunt boni, sed, quod dolore cogente loquor, plures mali."

20. As many have realized. See Trinkaus, *"In Our Image and Likeness";* S. Camporeale, *Lorenzo Valla, umanesimo e teologia* (Florence, 1972); idem, "Lorenzo Valla tra medioevo e rinascimento, Encomium Sanctae Thomae," *Memorie Domenicane,* n.s., 7 (1976): 3–190.

21. I cite from Aeneas Silvius, *De curialium miseriis epistola,* ed. W.P. Mustard (Baltimore and London, 1928); this also edited in R. Wolkan, *Der Briefwechsel des Eneas Silvius Piccolomini,* I, 453–87 (Vienna, 1909). There is a good discussion on this treatise's debt to Lucian in K. Sidwell, "Il *De curialium miseriis* di Enea Silvio Piccolomini e il *De mercede conductis,*" in *Pio II e la cultura del suo tempo,* ed. L.R.S. Tarugi (Milan, 1991) 329–41. On Lucian in the Renaissance see D. Marsh, *Lucian and the Latins: Humor and Humanism in the Early Renaissance* (Ann Arbor, 1998); see esp. 35–36 for Lapo's translations of Lucian.

a number of fruitful points of comparison between the two works. Both the differences and the similarities are instructive. First, there is the obvious difference in form. Piccolomini's work is an epideictic treatise rather than a dialogue. This allows him less in the way of the deliberate ambiguity with which Lapo's work is suffused. Moreover, Piccolomini's work differs in that it concerns life at a secular court, rather than at the papal court. So if he reports the presence of excessive luxury, sexual vices, and greed at the court, it is not quite as radical and risky as Lapo's description of those things at the *curia Romana*.[22] Finally, it differs throughout in that Piccolomini uses more scriptural and religious imagery than does Lapo.

The similarities are numerous and allow one to suppose that Piccolomini may have seen Lapo's work. Both authors are concerned that their patrons not think that any of the enumerated vices pertain to them.[23] The structure of Piccolomini's treatise is not dissimilar to Lapo's and in some places overlaps directly. Its purpose, Piccolomini says, is to dissuade its dedicatee, Johann von Eich, from beoming a courtier. Piccolomini finds that men will serve princes with five ends in view: honor, reputation in the world, power, wealth, or pleasure. In his work he intends to show that none of these ends is easily attainable by the courtier.[24] The general theme throughout, in fact, is that the vicissitudes of court life prevent the courtier's attainment of these things, and that the outward veneer of court life conceals a none too appealing reality.

As to honors, they are given at court only to the wealthy and powerful.[25] If it is objected that some have risen from relative poverty and obscurity to preferred positions, we find that they have pleased the king because they match him in vice.[26] Reputation gained at court is without

---

22. Along these same lines, there is more direct moralizing quotation of scripture in Piccolomini's treatise.

23. Cf. Lapo, *De curiae commodis,* Introduction, 5–12 and Piccolomini, 6. There Piccolomini praises Frederick III, his patron, and Frederick's court, giving a list of ancient, medieval, and modern rulers who were good; he goes on: "quibus, si vel pietatem vel mansuetudinem vel pacis amorem vel iusticiae zelum vel religionis affectum requiris, Fredericum nostrum nulla in re minorem invenies; tantum abest meis ut sibi scriptis velim detractum, ut eius laudes illustrare et versibus, quoad possim, et oratione soluta decreverim. Nec me nunc eius curia detineret, nisi sua me bonitas allexisset."

24. Piccolomini, 5.

25. Ibid., 7. "Dantur honores in curiis non secundum mores atque virtutes, sed ut quisque ditior est atque potentior, eo magis honoratur."

26. Ibid., 8. "Audio quod obiicis. Fuerunt nonnulli, dicis, obscuro nati loco atque inopes quondam, qui nunc omnibus sunt praelati; sic enim principes voluerunt. Sed quos, oro, sic praelatis ais? Nempe quos suis moribus conformes invenerunt. Quibus moribus? Avaritiae, libidini, crapulae, crudelitati. Sic est sane. . . . Nemo acceptus est, nemoque ex parvo statu praefertur aliis, nisi magno aliquo facinore sese principi conciliaverit."

foundation, since the people offering praise are like actors and jokers. Real praise is that which is offered by those who are themselves praise-worthy.[27] True power is impossible to achieve; princely power is so sub-ject to constant envy and conspiracies that the prince is always on the lookout for enemies. So, "often, someone who pleased the prince yester-day, displeases him today."[28] Wealth cannot really be acquired at court, or at least not without great cost, for whoever gains great wealth sacrifices his liberty; he must laugh when the king laughs, cry when the king cries, praise whomever the king praises, and condemn whomever the king condemns.[29]

Finally, Piccolomini arrives at pleasures. He admits frankly that all people like pleasures ("nec quisquam est qui voluptati non obsequatur") but suggests that whoever goes to a court to find them will be deceived.[30] As Lapo had, Piccolomini discusses the pleasures affiliated with various senses. The pleasures of sight—grand processions and pomp—are there in court life, to be sure. But since the courtier is often a participant in these events, he cannot really enjoy them.[31] Piccolomini's discussion of the "pleasures" of hearing can be interestingly compared with Lapo's dis-cussion of the same pleasure. For Lapo, the "pleasure" of hearing was that in the papal court one heard much news from all over as well as things which were useful for one's advancement in court life. As Lapo wrote (VII, 15):

> From this one acquires not only pleasure but also the greatest utility, since the life and character of all is thus placed before your eyes. No one can escape you when the whole curia is like this. And so, if you

---

27. Ibid., 9: "Praetereo histriones atque ioculatores et totius vulgi laudes, quas vir prudens pro nihilo reputabit; quid nulla est vera laus, nisi a viris proveniar laudatis." This should be compared with Cicero's letter to Cato (*Fam.* XV. 6.1) and Lapo's use of same at *De curiae commodis,* VI. 16.

28. Ibid., 10: "Saepe qui heri placuit hodie displicet." He goes on, using language which evokes Lapo's description of the papal court as a place where all eyes are on one; to Lapo's *De curiae commodis,* V.14, compare the following passage: "Si quis potens est, mille circa se oculos habet et totidem linguas ad ruinam eius aspirantes, et unus hinc allius illinc praemit."

29. Piccolomini, 12: "Sunt qui se posse putant divitias cumulare principibus servientes, at hi ut divitias comparent, libertatem vendunt, nec tamen divitias asse-quuntur. . . . oportet . . . ridere et flere cum rege, laudare quem laudat, vituperare quem vituperat."

30. Ibid., 14.

31. Ibid., 15.

ever need a favor from these people, the result is that, almost like a
learned doctor, you have your medications ready and prepared.

Piccolomini pays less attention to the low-level gossip that circulates at
court and focuses rather on other matters. One might think, he argues,
that at court one will hear "news from the whole world, the wisest of
men speaking, the deeds of great men, and the songs and sounds of musicians." But on all these accounts one is disappointed.[32] One does hear
much news, but it is almost all bad, as one is told of captured cities, the
death of great men, kidnappings, and other such catastrophes.[33] When
learned philosophers and orators come, they cannot speak freely as they
might in republics, so they bide their words carefully.[34] There are those
of course who tell the histories of great and ancient men, but they do so
in a lying, twisted way, preferring the inane fables of authors like Marsilio of Padua and Vincent of Beauvais to the great works of ancients like
Livy, Sallust, and Plutarch.[35] Finally, when it comes to music, the singers
have the same flaw attributed to singers by Horace: when their friends
ask them to sing, they refuse; unasked, they never desist.[36]

---

32. Ibid., 16. "At in auditu, dices, magna est curialium delectatio, dum novitates
totius orbis, dum viros sapientissimos loquentes, dum gesta virorum magnorum, dum
cantus sonosque audiunt musicorum. Credo et hoc plaerosque decipere."

33. Ibid. ". . . cum plura illic displicentia quam grata audiantur, cum nunc civitates
captae, viri praestantes occisi, spolia facta, rapinae commissaee, victores mali, victi
boni saepius referantur."

34. Ibid. "Now if learned orators and philosophers sometimes come to courts and
give speeches before princes, it is not as pleasing to hear them there, since they have to
speak more carefully there than they do in schools, where they are free and speak
truthfully and not only with the aim of pleasing [their audience]. This is why at Athens
(when it was a free city) and at Rome (when the consuls governed the republic) literary studies were at their highest point." ["Quod si nonnunquam oratores atque
philosophi diserti curias adeunt, orationesque coram principes habent, non tam dulce
est eos illic audire, ubi cum metu magis loquuntur quam in scholis, ubi sint liberi et ad
veritatem, non ad complacentiam, fantur. Hinc est quod Athenis, dum libera civitas
fuit, et Romae, dum consules rem publicam gubernabant, litterarum studia maxime
floruerunt."]

35. Ibid. "Sunt qui veterum narrant historias, sed mendose atque perverse; claris
auctoribus non creditur, sed fabellis inanibus fides adhibetur. Plus Guidoni de
Columna, qui bellum Troianum magis poetice quam hystorice scripsit, vel Marsilio de
Padua, qui translationes imperii quae nunquam fuerunt ponit, vel Vincentio Monacho
quam Livio, Salustio, Iustino, Quinto Curtio, Plutarcho aut Suetonio, praestantissimis
auctores, creditur."

36. Ibid. "'Omnibus hoc vitium est cantoribus,' inquit Horatius, 'inter amicos ut
nunquam inducant animum cantare rogati, iniussi nunquam desistant." Piccolomini
quotes Horace, *Sat.*, I,3,1–3.

Piccolomini's discussions of the "pleasures of Venus" are less explicit than Lapo's and contain none of the homoerotic subtexts which Lapo employed. Piccolomini argues that while there are many beautiful women at court, the individual courtier will have many rivals for each and will be hard pressed to find a woman satisfied with only one man.[37] If one is lucky enough to find a woman who is *fida*, it will be impossible to satisfy her and the king at the same time, since both are "insolent lords and want the whole man for him- or herself."[38] As to the senses of smell and taste, here too the courtier's privileged position is a myth tempered by a stark reality: the king gets all the good food and wine and the very odors of the food destined for the kingly plate makes one into a latter day Tantalus, condemned to physical proximity to unenjoyable pleasures.[39]

When Piccolomini's discussion of the senses comes to a close, he goes on at length about other disadvantages of court life: traveling with military campaigns is difficult and dangerous (35); the need to travel takes away the courtier's personal liberty (36); the relatives of the highly placed are given privileged positions (39); again, Tantalus-like, the courtier's apparent *otium* is not what it seems—because there is always so much clamor and noise, he really never has time to read the ancients and engage in humanistic study (41); real friendship is impossible, since even those who seem virtuous conceal ulterior motives (44); and, whatever your position at court, from the lowliest cook to the highest placed chancellor, there will always be someone who complains about the way you do your job (45).

Much of Piccolomini's imagery, argumentation, and sometimes actual verbiage, is similar to Lapo's. But there is an essential difference, beyond the formal ones noted above, between the social places of the two men and the perspectives from which they write. One comparison will suffice: of Lapo's arguments regarding the pleasures of sound and sight and Pic-

---

37. Piccolomini, 17.

38. Ibid., 17: ". . . quia uterque insolens dominus est, et qui hominem totum vult sibi." Piccolomini goes on to argue there that if the courtier comes to court already married, he cannot hope to keep her uncorrupted at court because of the manifold temptations to sin.

39. Ibid., 18–27. Lapo had employed the image of Tantalus at *De curiae commodis*, VII.18. Just to give one example of the types of food Piccolomini laments, he writes (22) "Cheese rarely comes to you and if it does, it is alive, full of worms, with holes everywhere, squalid-looking, and harder than stone." ["Caseus raro ad te venit, aut, si venit, vivus est, plenus vermibus, undique perforatus, situ squalidus, saxo durior."]

colomini's. Lapo's wonder at the papal court shines forth when he praises the pomp and beauty of all the great visiting figures and the spectacular grandiosity of curial ceremony.[40] As we have seen, however, Piccolomini regards this as an empty pleasure, since the courtier, as a participant, cannot take great enjoyment in these sorts of things. The difference between the two men and its reflection of their respective social positions could not be more apparent: Lapo, liminal, the quintessential outsider, dazzled by court ceremonial; Piccolomini, the weary insider, far enough within the court environment to make distinctions between the external veneer and the internal reality. Piccolomini's discussion comes from one who is fully established in a powerful position in the ambient of court life. Even their different perceptions of the sorts of news one hears at court reflects this. Lapo views news about the private lives of courtiers as a means of personal advancement, to be used as a learned doctor might use a medicine. Piccolomini, on the other hand, is accustomed to hearing news of truly high import—of the sacking of subject cities, of kidnappings, of evil conquerors and good men slain, news, in other words, of the sort to which Lapo might not have been privy and, even if he had, would have been utterly powerless to do anything about.

Lapo's work had humanistic literary ancestors and contemporaries in a number of different senses. The style of discourse used in the dialogue, termed by Fubini a "pro and contra style," is similar to arguments *in utramque partem,* recommended as a form of training by Cicero, in whose footsteps Quattrocento humanists happily followed. Cicero wrote:

> For concerning virtue, duty, concerning the fair and the good, concerning dignity, utility, honor, dishonor, reward, punishment, and similar things, we too should possess the power and the facility to speak on both sides of a question.[41]

Naturally, training one's mind to be able to think on both sides of question—that is, *in utramque partem*—does not mean that humanists did not have opinions or were insincere, molding themselves only to the exi-

---

40. Cf. *De curiae commodis,* VII.2–11.

41. Cic. *De or.* III.107: "De virtute enim, de officio, de aequo et bono, de dignitate, utilitate, honore, ignominia, praemio, poena similibusque de rebus in utramque partem dicendi etiam nos et vim et artem habere debemus." Cf. *De or.,* I.263, III.80; *Or.* 46: "Haec igitur quaestio a propriis personis et temporibus ad universi generis

gencies of the moment.[42] One must simply make distinctions when it comes to the final purposes for which this type of rhetoric was used.

Paul Oskar Kristeller argues that the humanists were representatives of an intellectual movement that went hand in hand with a curricular shift stressing the *studia humanitatis* of grammar, rhetoric, history, poetry, and moral philosophy; that with a passion for resurrecting antiquity, they engaged in a stylistic revival of Latin culture; that the movement is thus an important phase in the history of the rhetorical tradition.[43] This is true. It is the most empirically inclusive view of the humanist movement; it gives a synchronic picture of the movement and is essentially irrefutable.

But have all the possibilities for analysis and examination been exhausted? One can also look diachronically at the movement, for instance, and suggest that within it were trends in which some but not all humanists partook.[44] We can judge these trends as important and worthy of analysis in themselves, even if they are not representative of the movement as a whole. One must thus be on one's guard not to conflate the trend or specific thinkers under consideration with humanism in its entirety.[45]

Bearing that in mind, I suggest that Lapo's use and variation of *in utramque partem* argumentation is part of one such trend. One can describe this trend as "rhetoric as a way of thought," in which one leans more on inference and enthymematic reasoning than on *apodeixis* and syllogisms.[46] As is the case with the subtextual subtleties behind his

---

orationem traducta appellatur θέσις. In hac Aristoteles adulescentes non ad philosophorum morem tenuiter disserendi, sed ad copiam rhetorum, in utramque partem, ut ornatius et uberius dici posset, exercuit; idemque locos—sic enim appellat—quasi argumentorum notas tradidit unde omnis in utramque partem traheretur oratio."

42. This is essentially the opinion of J. Seigel, in his *Rhetoric and Philosophy in Renaissance Humanism: The Union of Eloquence and Wisdom, Petrarch to Valla* (Princeton, 1968).

43. See P.O. Kristeller, *Renaissance Thought and Its Sources* (New York, 1979).

44. For a diachronic examination of the evolution of the term *studia humanitatis* in humanist thought, see B.J. Kohl, "The Changing Concept of the *Studia Humanitatis* in the Early Renaissance," *Renaissance Studies* 6 (1992): 185–209.

45. As occasionally happened in the case of Hans Baron's "civic humanism" thesis.

46. Cf. R.G. Witt, "Medieval Italian Culture and the Origins of Humanism as a Stylistic Ideal," in *Renaissance Humanism: Foundations, Forms, and Legacy,* ed. A. Rabil, Jr., 3 vols. (Philadelphia, 1988), 1:31–32.

translations,[47] Lapo is able to use this type of rhetorical approach to his advantage. It is not the case that Lapo and other humanists employing this style of thought are necessarily criticizing the reigning cultural, educational, or political establishment, although they may often choose to do so. In the case of the *De curiae commodis,* whenever one of the many harsh criticisms of the curia is proffered by one of the two interlocutors, it is almost always tempered by a counterargument. Yet the counterposition is itself posed in a manner that leaves the original criticism hanging in the air, imbued with resonance. This style of thought enables Lapo to pose some harsh criticisms of contemporary religious life, even if the dialogue is not always and everywhere critical.

Seen in this light, Lapo's dialogue may also be considered as taking part to a certain extent in the literary tradition of irony, wherein the opposite of what is explicitly stated is intended.[48] It may be less than pure coincidence that a thirteenth-century ironic dialogue ostensibly praising the Roman curia, the *Liber de statu Curie Romane,* was copied in a *de luxe* edition sometime during the papacy of Eugenius IV (1431–47).[49] Whether this work was known to Lapo is unclear, but it does show, at the very least, that literary irony was seen (as early as the late thirteenth century) as a reasonably secure means by which one could launch criticisms of curial morality. Lapo articulates his positions in a more sophisticated fashion than does the author of the *Liber,* and he certainly did not intend the *De curiae commodis* as a simple piece of polemic tout court. But in its general aspect, like the *Liber,* it is a work that purports to set forth the advantages of the curia and many times does anything but that.[50] An example might make this clearer.

---

47. See Celenza, "Parallel Lives."

48. See D. Knox, *Ironia: Medieval and Renaissance Ideas on Irony,* Columbia Studies in the Classical Tradition 16 (Leiden, New York, 1989).

49. See the edition of the dialogue and the discussion of its *fortuna* in H. Grauert, *Magister Heinrich der Poet in Würzburg und die römische Kurie,* Abhandlungen der Königlichen Bayerischen Akademie der Wissenschaften, Philosophisch-philologische und historische Klasse 27 (Munich, 1912); see also P. Lehmann, "Zur *Disputatio Ganfredi et Aprilis de statu curiae Romanae,*" *Historische Vierteljahrschrift* 17 (1916): 86–94. Both are cited in Knox, *Ironia,* 17–18.

50. For another, nonhumanistic critique of the curia that was not at all written in the ironic mode, see the 1405 work of the Polish cleric Matthew of Krakow, *De praxi Romanae curiae,* which also circulated under the title *De squaloribus curiae Romanae.* See the edition of Władysław Seńko (Breslau, 1969).

The dialogue is structured as a series of examinations of the "benefits" of the Roman curia. The first examination presents the curia as a good place because it is a concentrated seat of religion. The summum bonum is most desirable, and this highest good, this most desirable thing, is God; both the summum bonum and God must exist, because people have an inborn desire for them (III.1–5). Means that lead us to the highest good are themselves goods and are more so the closer they bring us to the highest good. Religion is the best of these means, and the most concentrated place of religion is the curia.

So one of the curia's "benefits" is that it is a concentrated seat of religious practice. When pressed for proofs of this assertion by Angelo, Lapo responds (III.16): "For where else might you find such a great number of priests?" Angelo argues that the high number of priests is unsurprising, given the curia's importance as a religious center, and he goes on to aver that this is no proof that the curia's priests are good. Lapo's ultimate response is noteworthy and worth quoting in extenso (III.18–21).

This at least I would not hesitate to affirm: first, in a small number [of men], there are few good men, even if they were all good; but in a great multitude there can exist very many most upright men. In fact—as far as I can follow it with human ability—I am convinced and I judge that a multitude of priests who are not the worst is more pleasing to God than a paucity of priests who are not the best. [This is so] since we learn from the old traditions of sacred scripture that God always wanted to be worshiped by the multitude. Certainly, if I make a conjecture about us human beings, worship and veneration are usually pleasing, whoever carries them out. This is also most wisely established by our divine laws: that every sacrifice, even if it is made by the most corrupt of priests, provided that the ritual is done correctly, is a sacrifice that is true, integral, absolute, intact, and inviolate and is to be deemed as accepted in the eyes of God. . . . For this reason we cannot doubt that a multitude of worshipers—in which it is necessary both that there are many good men and that sacrifices, worship, and ceremonies are celebrated and renewed amid the greatest concourse—is most beloved in the eyes of immortal God himself, in whose honor these things happen.

What is happening here? Angelo convincingly refutes the notion that where there are many priests, there is an abundance of holiness. The response Lapo offers to this refutation is as follows: in a small group of all good men, one still finds only a small number of good men, because the group is numerically small; but in a large group, even if the ratio of good men to the whole is less than in the small group, one still finds, in terms of pure numbers, more good men. This weak, enthymematic counterargument stresses quantity rather than quality and by implication asserts that there are in fact quite a few bad *sacerdotes* in the curia.

This passage is important not only in itself but also because it shows Lapo's method: all the arguments given in the treatise, in fact, are a mélange of argument and counterargument; the original position here, that the curia is a concentrated seat of religion, is severely tempered by the "many priests" argument. Here and elsewhere in the dialogue, no position is allowed to go completely unchallenged—no position, that is, but that advanced on the virtues.

Prudence and the Virtues

The general point of the discussion on the virtues is clear: since many different peoples and customs can be observed there, the curia provides useful experience of the world. Experience is the basis for acquiring virtue, especially prudence; therefore the curia is a good place to be if one wishes to acquire virtue. To understand this position on the virtues, it is necessary to fill out the background a bit. As always, antiquity is important, and in this case two authors jump to the forefront: Aristotle and Cicero.

A key event in Florentine intellectual history was Leonardo Bruni's translation and popularization of Aristotle's *Nicomachean Ethics*. Far from a manual of conduct or a work that postulated proscriptive rules, the *Nicomachean Ethics* was a creative work of doctrinally flexible, inductive, observational anthropology. Aristotle was less concerned overall with either recommending specific courses of action to human beings or, like his teacher, Plato, describing how people ought to act. Instead Aristotle was interested in determining what people did, how they did it, and what common rules human beings seemed to share when they approached what we would now call ethical problems. No better

match could have been found for the concerns of Florentine humanists than the *Ethics,* and no better person for introducing it than Bruni.

In dedicating to Cosimo de' Medici his translation of Plutarch's *Life of Themistocles,* Lapo spoke of Bruni as "the prince of eloquence of this age, the beautification and ornament of the Latin language."[51] Lapo's sentiment certainly reflected contemporary *opinio communis.* The translations and manuscript diffusion as well as the printing histories of Bruni's many influential works demonstrate the respect in which he was held by contemporaries and his enduring influence.[52] Bruni's translation of Aristotle's *Nicomachean Ethics,* completed in the years 1416 to 1417, was no exception.[53] This is an episode in the history of the reception of Aristotle that itself has its own, well-studied history.

In his polemic *On His Own Ignorance and That of Many Others,* Petrarch misunderstood Cicero and Quintilian and complained that barbarous translations had ruined the natural eloquence of Aristotle, who had been "pleasant, abundantly eloquent, and admirable in his language."[54] Cicero, in his *Academica,* and Quintilian, in his *Institutio,* had of course been referring to Aristotle's dialogues—his exoteric works— which are now almost exclusively lost to us.[55] But the memory of this

---

51. ". . . princeps eloquentiae huius aetatis, decus et ornamentum latinae linguae." See the edition of the text in Celenza, "Parallel Lives," app. 1, sec. 26.

52. See J. Hankins, "The Man and His Reputation," 42–46 in the general introduction (3–50) in Leonardo Bruni, *The Humanism of Leonardo Bruni,* ed. G. Griffiths, J. Hankins, and D. Thompson (Binghamton, N.Y., 1987), at 45–46; and see the literature cited there.

53. See E. Garin, "Le traduzioni umanistiche di Aristotele nel secolo XV," *Atti dell'Accademia fiorentina di scienze morali "La Colombaria"* 16 (1951): 55–104: on Bruni, see especially 62–68; for the date of the translation, see 62. See also B. Copen-haver, "Translation, Terminology, and Style," in *CHRP,* 77–110.

54. See Petrarch, *Le traité "De sui ipsius et multorum ignorantia,"* ed. L.M. Capelli (Paris, 1906), 67 et seq.

55. Cicero (*Acad.* II.38.119) speaks of the "flumen aureum orationis" of Aristotle. Quintilian (*Inst.* X.1.83), in a judgment of the philosophers ("from whom Tullius confesses he drew most of his eloquence" [ex quibus plurimum se traxisse eloquentiae M. Tullius confitetur] (X.1.81), says: "What of Aristotle? I doubt whether I judge any-one more outstanding when it comes to knowledge of things, abundance of writings, power and sweetness of speech, precision of inventions, or variety of works" [Quid Aristotelen? Quem dubito scientia rerum an scriptorum copia an eloquendi vi ac suavitate an inventionum acumine an varietate operum clariorem putem]. On Aristo-tle's exoteric works in general, see E. Berti, *La filosofia del primo Aristotele* (Padua, 1962). See also O. Gigon, "Prolegomena to an edition of the *Eudemus,"* in *Aristotle and Plato in the Mid-fourth Century,* ed. I. Düring and G.E.L. Owen (Göteborg, 1960), 19–33; I. Düring, *Aristotle's "Protrepticus": An Attempt at Reconstruction* (Göteborg, 1961); A.-H. Chroust, "*Eudemus* or *On the Soul:* A Lost Dialogue of Aris-totle on the Immortality of the Soul," *Mnemosyne,* 4th ser., 19 (1966): 17–30.

humanistic mistake, itself stimulated by a polemic against scholastic philosophy, remained strong. Even stronger was the humanist desire that had given rise to the mistake: the desire, that is, to appropriate ancient culture in not only its Latin but also its Greek manifestations and to do so in a Latin that was adequate to the humanists' new, largely Ciceronian ideals of eloquence, if not always *adaequata* in the philosophical sense of the term.

When it came to this desire Bruni was no exception among humanists.[56] In the case of the *Nicomachean Ethics,* the translation that he had read in school was the one that had become the standard full translation of the work since the 1250s, that of Robert Grosseteste, the thirteenth-century bishop of Lincoln.[57] Without naming Grosseteste, Bruni strongly criticized this received translation, saying that the *Nicomachean Ethics* "seemed to have been made more barbarian than Latin."[58] He also complained about the many incorporations into Latin of Greek terminology, transliterations that in Bruni's view were unnecessary.[59]

Despite these criticisms it is probable that Bruni had Grosseteste's version of the *Nicomachean Ethics* in front of him as he worked. His method of translation had more to do with sprucing up Grosseteste's Latin and giving the language more *ornatus* than it did with freshly translating from the Greek in a philosophically informed manner. In a debate with Bruni, Alonso Garcia da Cartagena, himself admittedly Greekless,

---

56. Quotations from Bruni are taken from Leonardo Bruni, *Humanistisch-philosophische Schriften,* ed. H. Baron (Berlin, 1928; reprographischer Nachdruck, Stuttgart, 1969). The citations have been compared with the suggested modifications in L. Bertalot, "Forschungen über Leonardo Bruni Aretino," in *Studien zum italienischen und deutschen Humanismus,* ed. P.O. Kristeller, 2 vols. (Rome, 1975), 2:375–420. James Hankins has provided English translations and helpful discussions of many of Bruni's works that dealt with the *Nicomachean Ethics:* see Bruni, *The Humanism of Leonardo Bruni,* sec. 4, "The New Language" (197–234), especially Hankins's discussion of the ethics controversy (201–8); sec. 6, "The New Philosophy" (255–99).

57. Cf. the passage Bruni quotes in his *Praefatio quaedam ad evidentiam novae translationis Ethicorum Aristotelis,* in Bruni, *Humanistisch-philosophische Schriften,* 76–81, at 78 (which is *Eth. Nic.* II.7.1108a23–26; *praemissio* is the first word in the Baron edition), to Grosseteste's translation of the same in R.A. Gauthier, ed., *Aristoteles Latinus,* XXVI 1–3, fasciculus tertius, *Ethica Nicomachea: Translatio Roberti Grosseteste Lincolnensis sive 'Liber Ethicorum' A. Recensio Pura* (Leiden, Brussels, 1972), at 174, line 23, to 175, line 1, as well as in *B. Recensio recognita* (Leiden, Brussels, 1973), at 406, lines 28–31.

58. "Aristotelis *Ethicorum* libros facere Latinos nuper institui, non quia prius traducti non essent, sed quia sic traducti erant, ut barbari magis quam Latini effecti viderentur" (Bruni, *Humanistisch-philosophische Schriften,* 76).

59. Bruni, *Humanistische-philosophische Schriften,* 78–79.

defended the worth of the older translations and even the practice of incorporating Greek words into the Latin language.[60] Later, Agnolo Manetti would report that his father, Giannozzo, had decided to retranslate the *Nicomachean Ethics* because he thought Bruni's version was too free.[61] And at the end of the fifteenth century, Battista de' Giudici would question whether Bruni had had the philosophical erudition to have taken on such a job.[62]

The debate shows that Bruni's translation, historical and philosophical discussion, and consequent popularization of various works of Aristotle all had a powerful effect on the moral philosophical discussions of the fifteenth century. More specifically, owing to Bruni's stimulus and the great respect in which he was held, discussion of Aristotle's *Nicomachean Ethics* (as well as of individual issues contained in that work) was especially alive for many years after Bruni's translation.[63] If one were a humanist, then, one way to achieve a connection with one's audience would have been to use terminology from the *Nicomachean Ethics,* which at that point would have been fashionably familiar to the reading public. Lapo certainly does this in the *De curiae commodis;* that he believed he could include a fairly detailed discussion of the virtues in a treatise ostensibly about the *curia Romana* is an index of just how familiar the *Ethics* had become.

Lapo's discussion of prudence and the virtues also reveals the close relation of the *De curiae commodis* to the philosophical works of Cicero.[64] Cicero permeates the dialogue, but his influence is more

---

60. See A. Birkenmajer, "Der Streit des Alonso von Cartagena mit Leonardo Bruni Aretino," *Beiträge zur Geschichte der Philosophie des Mittelalters* 20, no. 5 (1922): 129–210, cited in Garin, "Le traduzioni," 64 n. 1. See also Hankins's discussion of the ethics controversy, cited in n. 36 supra.

61. Agnolo's edition of his father's translations appears in MS Florence, BN Magl. VIII, 1439, f. 23, and MS Vatican City, Urb. Lat. 223, f. 1; both manuscripts are cited in Garin, "Le traduzioni," 72 n.1.

62. See M. Grabmann, "Eine ungedruckte Verteidigungsschrift von Wilhelms von Moerbekes Übersetzung der Nicomacheischen Ethik gegenüber dem Humanisten Leonardo Bruni," in *Mittelalterliches Geistesleben,* 1:440–48 (Munich, 1926), cited in Garin, "Le traduzioni," 64 n. 1.

63. See, e.g., Bruni's 1441 letter responding to Lauro Quirini in Luiso, *Studi,* letter IX:3. The letter is translated in Bruni, *The Humanism of Leonardo Bruni,* 293–99 (see also the discussion of Hankins in ibid., 264–67).

64. On Cicero's philosophical works, see A.E. Douglas, "Cicero the Philosopher," in *Cicero,* ed. T.A. Dorey (London, 1964), 135–70; P. Boyance, "Les méthodes de l'histoire littéraire: Cicéron et son oeuvre philosophique," *Revue des études latines* 14 (1936): 288–309; P. Poncelet, *Cicéron traducteur de Platon* (Paris, 1957); P.A. Sullivan, "The Plan of Cicero's Philosophical Corpus" (Ph.D. diss., Boston University, 1951).

strongly felt in the discussion of prudence than anywhere else, both in terms of content and in terms of expository style. Perhaps the most salient stylistic characteristic of Cicero's philosophical works is that he consciously and intentionally avoided dogmatism—indeed, he despised it.[65] The works have therefore sometimes been blamed for vagueness or lack of purpose, other times praised for their open-mindedness.[66] Cicero was content to transmit opinions accurately to his contemporaries, and his approach to philosophy was conditioned by his rhetorical concerns.[67] His style of exposition in the philosophical works is thus sensitive to the demands of his audience, that is, to the demands of the elite readers and listeners of the second half of the first century B.C. The audience was adapted not to apodictic exposition but rather to *ornatus,* which was itself conditioned in Cicero's own (somewhat revolutionary) view by *probitas* and *prudentia.*[68]

Florentine Renaissance thinkers followed this Ciceronian lead. Part of their self-imposed task was to express themselves as Cicero had himself and to express the moral philosophical ideas that they discussed as Cicero had (if not always with the exact same language).[69] As a whole— and there are exceptions—when the humanists approached any topic or area of study in which detailed, syllogistic, technical exposition had been the rule, they transformed the discourse, deeming it necessary that the ideas under discussion be transmitted in a manner that they considered eloquent. This was the case with theology, for example; one scholar has

---

65. See, e.g., the attack on the Pythagorean "ipse dixit" in *Nat. D.* I.10–11.

66. On Cicero's vagueness, cf. Michel de Montaigne: "I want arguments which drive home their first attack right into the strongest point of doubt: Cicero's hover about the pot and languish. Thay are all right for the classroom, the pulpit or the Bar where we are free to doze off and find ourselves a quarter of an hour later still with time to pick up the thread of the argument" (from "On Books," in *The Complete Essays,* trans. M.A. Screech (New York, 1987), 464).

67. On the philosophical background to Cicero's rhetorical works, see A. Michel, *Rhétorique et philosophie chez Ciceron: Essai sur les fondements philosophique de l'art de persuader* (Paris, 1960), especially 112–37, 537–85, 642–45.

68. See Douglas, "Cicero the Philosopher," 154.

69. The attempt to employ only language or expressions used by Cicero is known as Ciceronianism. On this interesting, multifaceted ideological movement, see R. Sabbadini, *Storia del ciceronianismo e di altre questioni letterarie nell'età della Rinascenza* (Turin, 1886). See also J. D' Amico, "Humanism in Rome," in *Renaissance Humanism: Foundations, Forms, and Legacies,* ed. A. Rabil, Jr., 3 vols. (Philadelphia, 1988), 1:264–95, at 280–83; and see the literature cited there. Cf. D'Amico's description on 280–81: "Ciceronianism was an attempt on several levels by many humanists to locate in time the perfect expression of the Latin language, and in so doing to recapture and recreate the cultural ideals that undergirded ancient civilization."

characterized the humanist contribution to theology as a *theologia rhetorica.*[70]

This meant that humanists usually did not approach areas of thought like metaphysics and logic, where detailed, technical, apodictic discussion was not only the norm but also necessary. This antiapodictic tendency in humanist method is articulated by Lapo himself, in the person of the interlocutor Angelo (III.15).

> Now make all this clearer to me, but not like the mathematicians usually do, who argue from "what has been said above" and "conceded thus far" and then demonstrate what has been propounded. Instead do it in your customary manner, with many arguments and theories— so that necessity compels me to concede your arguments and I am persuaded both by the abundance of the oration as well as by its rhetorical sweetness.

As discussed earlier, Lapo's treatise is clearly not a Ciceronian dialogue on the model of, say, the *Tusculans.* The *De curiae commodis* resembles much more closely the Socratic type of dialogue, identified by Marsh as one of the minor strands in the Quattrocento dialogue tradition. Yet this trend against *apodeixis*—against traditional philosophical demonstration—was the crux of the change that Renaissance humanism wrought in Western patterns of thought, if it wrought any at all. Their successful revival of ancient rhetoric was the humanists' most original and lasting contribution not just to the history of rhetoric but to the history of Western thought taken as a whole.

Certainly, however, this was not without its consequences, and oftentimes, when humanists did approach philosophical problems of all different sorts, their style of communication failed them and left them unable to make philosophically satisfactory contributions to the problem under consideration.[71] But this humanist method of thinking and expressing—this "rhetorical way of thought"—was suited to incorporat-

---

70. See Trinkaus, *"In Our Image and Likeness."* See also J. D'Amico, "Humanism and Pre-Reformation Theology," in *Renaissance Humanism: Foundations, Forms, and Legacy,* ed. A. Rabil, Jr., 3 vols. (Philadelphia, 1988), 3:349–79.

71. Bruni's translation of Aristotle's *t'agathon* as *summum bonum* comes to mind. On this cf. Hankins in Bruni *The Humanism of Leonardo Bruni,* 201–8 and the literature cited in the notes.

ing elements of moral philosophy. If this humanist way of thought considered very generally bears indubitable similarities to Cicero in a stylistic expository sense, the following analysis of the interlocutors' discussion of prudence in the *De curiae commodis* will make Lapo's debt to Cicero explicit.

The discussion begins, typically enough, with a backhanded presentation of the topic. Having just mentioned Aristotle's *Nicomachean Ethics* VI.8, on the importance of *empeiria*, Lapo (IV.8–9) introduces Homer's *Odyssey* into the discussion and, in typical humanist fashion, uses literature to read philosophy, Homer to read Aristotle.

> *L:* Well then, I think that Aristotle read the poem of Homer and that he imitated him. When Homer wanted to portray the prudent man in the person of Ulysses, he wrote as follows: "Having been cast onto various shores, he came to know the cities and customs of many peoples";[72] that is, Homer denoted the same things [mentioned earlier] by the length of wandering and variety of places and men.

Then comes the important point.

> I never thought that for the sake of pursuing this most precious thing [i.e., this virtue], anyone—like Ulysses—had to seek out Calyps, Circes, the Phaeacians, the Laestrygones, the Sirens, the Cyclops, and Hades. After all, what he gained by long wandering and with extreme danger to his life—well, the Roman curia will offer you all of it in abundance.

The curia helps one acquire prudence because of the variety of experience one can gain there.

Implicitly, however, Lapo is suggesting that not all of those experiences are of the most savory sort. Ulysses' experience with the Cyclops might have provided him with some useful *empeiria*, but it certainly was not enjoyable or even salutary to do it. Indeed, a number of his comrades died during that episode. Virtue is used as a prima facie persuasive tool in the *De curiae commodis,* but it is no accident that the virtue Lapo chose as his focus was prudence, whose basis was experience that could often

---

72. See Hom. *Od.* I.3–4.

be harsh. Given the Ciceronian coloration of the work, the presence of Ulysses is also no accident. In Cicero's works Ulysses is often mentioned in connection with wisdom and prudence.[73]

The interlocutor Lapo points out (IV.9–10) that, because so many important matters pass before the eyes of the pope, the resident of the curia must inevitably see, hear, learn, and do many things. Eventually, as long as one is not completely dim-witted and negligent, one emerges with much valuable experience of life. Angelo agrees (IV.11–12), commenting that there are indeed some amazing teachers at the curia.

Then he asks (IV.12): "But what about the rest of the virtues? In the curia isn't there any practice of them, any training in them, any function for them?" This initiates the only properly philosophical discussion in the dialogue. Lapo begins his answer to Angelo's query by suggesting that the virtues are all inextricably bound to one another (IV.13–14).

> *L:* Of course. After all, it is difficult for someone to be prudent without at the same time being just, brave, and temperate. Really, who would dare to call the prudent man unjust, or ignorant and cowardly,

---

73. Cf. Cic. *Tusc.* I.98, where Ulysses is used as an example of one who possesses prudence ("temptarem etiam summi regis, qui maximas copias duxit ad Troiam, et Ulixi Sisyphique prudentiam"), and V.7, where Ulysses is designated as wise ("[sapientia] quae divinarum humanarumque rerum, tum initiorum causarumque cuiusque rei cognitione hoc pulcherrimum nomen apud antiquos adsequebatur. Itaque et illos septem, qui a Graecis σοφοὶ, sapientes a nostris et habebantur et nominabantur, et multis ante saeculis Lycurgum, cuius temporibus Homerus etiam fuisse ante hanc urbem conditam traditur, et iam heroicis aetatibus Ulixem et Nestorem accepimus et fuisse et habitos esse sapientes"). Cf. II.49, where Cicero cites an instance of Ulysses having the ability to withstand great pain, owing to his great experience; then Cicero says: "the prudent poet knew that the habit of withstanding pain was a teacher that was not to be criticized" [intelligit poeta prudens ferendi doloris consuetudinem esse non contemnandam magistram]. At *Fin.* V.49, Cicero argues that Homer's meaning was that the Siren's songs were so appealing because they promised knowledge; Ulysses went to them because he was desirous of knowledge: "<ut> mihi quidem Homerus huius modi quiddam vidisse videatur in iis, quae de Sirenum cantibus finxerit. Neque enim vocum suavitate videntur aut novitate quadam et varietate cantandi revocare eos solitae, qui praetervehebantur, sed quia multa se scire profitebantur, ut homines ad earum saxa discendi cupiditate adhaerescerent. Ita enim invitant Ulixem . . . [Cicero quotes Homer]. Vidit Homerus probari fabulam non posse, si cantiunculis tantus irretitus vir teneretur; scientiam pollicentur, quam non erat mirum sapientiae cupido patria esse cariorem"—the last thought translates, "it was no wonder that knowledge was more dear than one's homeland, to the man who was desirous of wisdom." This context must have been in the front of Lapo's mind—directly hereafter (*Fin.* V.50) Cicero goes on to name famous thinkers who have traveled much to gain wisdom; Lapo will do the same a bit later in the *De curiae commodis.*

or intemperate? All of these vices seem to be characteristic of the highest folly and insanity.

Besides, all of the virtues, even though they flow from one source and one point of origin and are contained among themselves, singularly bonded in relationship, nonetheless are distinguished one from another in their duties. Thus whoever does those things that are characteristic of prudence is said to be prudent; whoever does those things that are characteristic of bravery is said to be brave; whoever does those things that are characteristic of temperance is said to be temperate. If all of these things are gathered together in one man, then we call that man good. And so it is necessary that someone who possesses prudence or any other virtue possess all the virtues. Whoever is lacking one lacks them all.

Lapo points out that virtue is something that is actualized by repeated praxis (terminology that would have been fashionably familiar to his audience, given the prominence in the humanist community of Bruni's comparatively recent translation of the *Nicomachean Ethics*). He further argues that the virtues are connected with one another, and he adopts an extreme position, the Stoic *locus communis:* "whoever is lacking one lacks them all."[74]

Next Lapo reveals the orientation of this opinion (IV.15).

Because of this it seems that the Stoics were not being rash to have thought that the man who is lacking anything toward the attainment of the highest virtue is polluted by all vices.

Lapo's orientation here regarding the virtues is Stoic, of the kind that Cicero had his interlocutors discuss in the *De finibus.* Although Cicero himself occasionally leaned toward this virtue-venerating position, in the final analysis Cicero remained undecided, owing to the seeming impracticality of the life of the Stoic sage, with its *apathia* and its extreme moral

---

74. Perhaps from Peter Lombard, perhaps from Jerome? Cf. Lapo with Peter Lombard, who himself quotes Jerome. Lapo: "Itaque necesse est qui prudentiam sive quanvis aliam virtutem habeat, eum virtutes omnes habere; cui una desit, deesse omnes." Peter Lombard *Sententiae* III.36: "Solet etiam quaeri utrum virtutes ita sint sibi conjunctae ut separatim non possint possideri ab aliquo, sed qui unam habet, omnes habeat. De hoc etiam Hieronymus ait: 'Omnes virtutes sibi haerent, ut qui una caruerit, omnibus careat. Qui ergo unam habet, omnes habet.'"

philosophical positions.[75] Although Lapo goes on to examine other aspects of the question of virtue, this position is key and is the only major position in the entire dialogue that remains unassaulted by counterargument. It is especially important if one wishes to arrive at a consistent interpretation for a dialogue that seems inevitably to prevaricate. Why is this so?

Lapo's position on the virtues can be extrapolated: for a good person, there are no excuses and no ways out; to be a good person, one must possess all the virtues. The very next sentence (IV.16) is extremely important: "But Aristotle and others argue more precisely about virtue." In the Latin, the sentence reads, "Sed Aristoteles et alii de virtute accuratius disputant." On first sight, one might be tempted to translate this as "But Aristotle and others argue more accurately about virtue." One would then construe Lapo to be dismissing the extreme Stoic view and moving on to a preferable point of view, in the same way that Cicero seemed to reject the extreme Stoic view as unreasonable. But a further look at the passage shows that this is not the case.

> But Aristotle and others argue more precisely about virtue. They set forth that there are two genera of virtue. One of these turns on the investigation and cognition of truth, the other on action. They call the first genus "intellectual virtues" and the second "moral virtues." Cicero followed them in the first book of the *De officiis*. He says that there are two genera of duties. One of these pertains to the end of goods, and the Greeks called it κατόρθωμα [katorthōma]; we can call it "complete duty." The other comprises the principles of common life, and they called it "middle duty."

---

75. Cf. Cic. *Fin.* V.77–78 (77: "nam illud vehementer repugnat, eundem beatum esse et multis malis oppressum") and especially 95: "Haec igitur est nostra ratio, quae tibi videtur inconstans, cum propter virtutis caelestem quandam et divinam tantamque praestantiam, ut, ubi virtus sit resque magnae <et> summe laudabiles virtute gestae, ibi esse miseria et aerumna non possit, tamen labor possit, possit molestia, non dubitem dicere omnes sapientes esse semper beatos, sed tamen fieri posse, ut sut alius alio beatior." Cf. Cic. *Off.* III.11: "nam, sive honestum solum bonum est, ut Stoicis placet, sive, quod honestum est, id ita summum bonum est, quemadmodum Peripateticis vestris videtur, ut omnia ex altera parte collocata vix minimi momenti instar habeant, dubitandum non est, quin numquam possit utilitas cum honestate contendere. Itaque accepimus Socratem exsecrari solitum eos, qui primum haec natura cohaerentia opinione distraxissent. Cui quidem ita sunt Stoici assensi, ut et, quicquid honestum esset, id utile esse censerent, nec utile quicquam, quod non honestum." Also see Cic. *Tusc.* V.39 et seq., especially 47–48.

Instead of presenting a less extreme point of view about the virtues, Lapo simply addresses a different aspect of the question and sets forth a discussion of the types of virtue. The distinction of the different types of virtue that Cicero mentioned in the *De officiis* and to which Lapo alludes here was rooted in the traditional Pythagorean-Platonic division of the soul into a rational and nonrational part, of which Cicero was well aware.[76] Aristotle had followed this division in the *Nicomachean Ethics*, dividing the virtues into intellectual and moral virtues on precisely that basis (even if in *De anima* he did present a different psychological scheme, dividing the soul into five faculties).[77] But Lapo adopts the Stoic position regarding the connection of the virtues. This is revealed by what is next articulated (IV.17).

[17] Certain ancient philosophers judge that these two genera are contained under the single name of wisdom, and they say that all these virtues are collected together and, hanging together among themselves, constitute wisdom. They mean that whoever is completely composed of these virtues is wise and is called wise. Indeed, they define wisdom as the very knowledge of divine and human things, from which we can gather that they thought that virtue was very much one thing and that whoever has obtained it is wise and good, whereas whoever is lacking even a part of virtue is neither wise nor good.

If it is true that "whoever is lacking even a part of virtue is neither wise nor good," then Lapo's criticisms of the curia in the rest of the dialogue must be taken somewhat more seriously than they have been hitherto. As

---

76. Cf. Cic. *Tusc.* IV.10: "Because we like to call the things that the Greeks call *pathe* 'disturbances' rather than 'sicknesses,' in explaining them [the *pathe*], for my part, I follow that old distribution first of all of Pythagoras but then of Plato. They divide the soul into two parts: they say that the one part partakes of reason and that the other is unknowing of reason. In the part that partakes of reason they place tranquillity, that is, a placid and peaceful constancy; in the other part they place the turbulent movements of both anger and desire, which are contrary and inimical to reason" [Quoniam, quae Graeci πάθη vocant, nobis perturbationes appellari magis placet quam morbos, in his explicandis veterem illam equidem Pythagorae primum, dein Platonis descriptionem sequar, qui animum in duas partes dividunt: alteram rationis participem faciunt, alteram expertem; in participe rationis ponunt tranquillitatem, id est placidam quietamque constantiam, in illa altera motus turbidos cum irae tum cupiditatis, contrarios inimicosque rationi].

77. This discrepancy on Aristotle's part was cause for reflection on the part of certain later Renaissance philosophers, such as Crisostomo Javelli and Pier Vettori. See J. Kraye, "Moral Philosophy," in *CHRP*, 303–86, at 333–34.

we have seen, the attempted refutations of the criticisms are always made in such a way that the original opinion retains a certain resonance. Even after the defense of wealth much later in the dialogue, Lapo will be unable to resist concluding the discussion without having an interlocutor point out the vice present in the curia. But the Stoic position he here articulates regarding the virtues—whoever has one has them all—is an all-or-nothing affair. If one extends the notion from the personal, which is its focus in Stoic moral philosophy, to the corporate—that is, in this case, the curia—one could draw some interesting conclusions about the curia as a whole. To use more modern language and to mix metaphors, if even a shadow of doubt remains, all bets are off. And much more than a shadow of doubt remains in the rest of the dialogue about the vice present in the curia.

Throughout the treatise, Lapo's expository method reveals the following, fairly consistent message. On the one hand, given the particular historical circumstances in which it finds itself situated, the curia is a place of almost unbounded positive potential on many different fronts. On the other hand, if the greater part of the curialists who dwell there do not engage in some serious soul-searching, the curia is doomed to remain in its largely corrupt state and has no hope of traveling the difficult, straight road that will lead it from potentiality to actuality.[78] To put it simply, the curia is in essence a good thing, but the practice of corrupt individuals there has led it to fall far short of the desirable ideal.

---

78. David Quint's work on Bruni's *Dialogi* shows the manner in which a literary work can develop internally consistent tendencies even in the context of the often seemingly contradictory *modus loquendi* that arguing *in utramque partem* represents. See Quint's "Humanism and Modernity: A Reconsideration of Bruni's *Dialogues*," *Renaissance Quarterly* 38 (1985): 423–45.

CHAPTER 3

Politics and Persuasion, Bureaucracy and Behavior

A good portion of what is behind the writing of the *De curiae commodis* has to do with Lapo's attempt at self-advertisement and his longing to show that he could be a real curialist with a high position, instead of the liminal, curial outsider that he probably believed himself to be. Lapo the propagandist for the contemporary Council of Ferrara-Florence, Lapo the protester against curial vice, Lapo the insider who knows his way around the curia, and Lapo the practical man who realizes that wealth is necessary in the curial ambient—all of these facets are present in the dialogue.

The piece was written in the summer of 1438, at a time when the institution of the papacy was undergoing a crisis and when there was a great deal of uncertainty as to who held supreme power in the church.[1] On 3 March 1431, after the death of the Colonna Pope Martin V, Gabriele Condulmer, his collaborator, was elected pope as Eugenius IV. As we have seen from the cursory overview of Lapo's life, Eugenius was most probably the person whose patronage Lapo ultimately sought during the last two years of his life, when he was following the curia. It is thus no surprise that he dedicated the dialogue to Francesco Condulmer, given that Lapo was in Francesco's service at the time, and given Francesco's political power and prominence. Not only a nephew of Pope Eugenius, from 1432 to 1440 Francesco was also his chamberlain *(camerarius),* which meant that he was the head of the papal chamber, the curia's

---

1. See J.W. Stieber, *Pope Eugenius IV, The Council of Basel, and the Secular and Ecclesiastical Authorities in the Empire: The Conflict over Supreme Authority and Power in the Church* (Leiden, 1978); J. Gill, *The Council of Florence* (Cambridge, 1959); idem, *Personalities of the Council of Florence* (Oxford, 1964); K.A. Fink, "Eugene IV and the Council of Basel-Ferrara-Florence," in *Handbook of Church History,* ed. H. Jedin (New York, 1970), 4:473–87 (the *Handbook* originally appeared in German [Freiburg-im-Breisgau, 1968]); Hofmann.

financial bureau. And from 1437 until his death in 1453 he was also the *vicecancellarius sacre romane ecclesie* (vice-chancellor of the holy Roman church), which meant that he stood at the head of another major branch of the curia, the apostolic chancery, or *cancelleria apostolica*.[2] In a discussion of the curial bureaucracy (VI.6–7), Lapo shows that he was quite aware of the power that accrued to Francesco's positions. As he begins to develop the dialogue's general praise of wealth, Lapo has a chance here not only to flatter his dedicatee with a quick and accurate resumé of his power but also subtly to oblige him by reminding him of just how much money he has. This reminder would have been all the more pressing if the reader had in mind the dialogue's opening, where Angelo set forth the shortages of money and patronage that Lapo was suffering.

The name of the dedicatee, Condulmer, leads one inevitably to a consideration of church politics. From a political point of view, as with the other aspects of the dialogue, the outward expository aim of the piece is *au courant*. In fact the content of the dialogue indicates clearly Lapo's awareness of the contemporary political struggles in the church. In a time of self-definition for the ever evolving papacy, one of the main points of contention was the extent of power held by church councils.

With the decree *Haec sancta,* the fifth session of the Council of Constance had in April 1415 declared that church councils possess the highest power in Christendom in three crucial areas: heresy, reform, and settling schisms.[3] According to this decree, all Christians, even the pope, were subordinate to the power and decisions of church councils in these matters. The decree *Frequens,* made by the same Council of Constance two years later (in its thirty-ninth session), stipulated that church councils meet on a frequent and regular basis.[4] The Council of Basel com-

---

2. See D'Amico, 24–26; Hofmann, 2:69 (for *vicecancellarius*), 87 (for *camerarius*); N. del Re, *La curia Romana: Lineamenti storico-giuridici,* 3d ed. (Rome, 1970), 295–309 (for the development of the *camera*), 277–91 (for the development of the *vicecancellarius*). From the time of John XXII (r. 1316–34), the office of *vicecancellarius* supplanted the duties of the *cancellarius*. Francesco was also well connected in Venetian humanist circles; see M.L. King, *Venetian Humanism in an Age of Patrician Dominance* (Princeton, 1986), *ad indicem.*

3. I have relied heavily in this section on the account presented in Stieber, *Pope Eugenius IV,* 10–57.

4. This was the reason, e.g., why the abortive, poorly attended Council of Pavia-Siena met in 1423–24. On the Council of Constance, see the study of P. H. Stump, *The Reforms of the Council of Constance,* Studies in the History of Christian Thought 53 (Leiden, New York, and Cologne, 1994); see also W. Brandmüller, *Das Konzil von Konstanz, 1414–1418,* 2 vols. (Paderborn and Munich, 1991–97).

menced in July 1431 on the order of Pope Martin V. He himself had died in February of that year, and in his last days he had appointed as his legate Cardinal Giuliano Cesarini, who assumed the presidency of the council as it began.[5] At the outset the council's leaders publicly renewed certain provisions from Constance, among them aspects of *Frequens.* Then, in its second public session, in February 1432, the council renewed parts of *Haec sancta,* including the important section where conciliar supremacy was announced. According to that section, the council "had power directly from Christ," and "to this power, everyone, of whatever status and worth, even if of papal status and worth, is held to be obedient in those matters that pertain to the faith, to the extirpation of the said schism, and to the general reform of the Church of God, in its head as well as in its members." Whoever contumaciously disobeyed any proclamation of a legitimately convoked general council was to be punished.[6] This heated concern even led the Council of Basel eventually (and, ultimately, inefficaciously) to depose Eugenius IV from his office in June 1439.[7]

The issue was obviously very alive in its day, and Lapo was no doubt sensitive to it. Toward the beginning of the *De curiae commodis,* his

---

5. On Cesarini, see Gill, *Personalities,* 95–103; Stieber, *Pope Eugenius IV, ad indicem.*

6. Latin text cited in Stieber, *Pope Eugenius IV,* 405–6: "Et primo declarat, quod ipsa Synodus in Spiritu sancto legitime congregata, generale concilium faciens, et ecclesiam militantem repraesentans, potestatem a Christo immediate habet, cui quilibet cuiuscumque status vel dignitatis, etiam si papalis exsistat, obedire tenetur in his quae pertinent ad fidem et exstirpationem dicti schismatis et ad generalem reformationem ecclesiae Dei in capite et in membris.

Item, declarat, quicumque cuiuscumque conditionis, status, vel dignitatis, etiam si papalis exsistat, qui mandatis, statutis seu ordinationibus, aut praeceptis huius sacrae synodi et cuiuscumque alterius concilii generalis legitime congregati, super praemissis, seu ad ea pertinentibus, factis, vel faciendis, obedire contumaciter contempserit, nisi resipuerit, condignae poenitentiae subiiciatur, et debite puniatur, etiam ad alia iuris subsidia, si opus fuerit, recurrendo."

7. This is not to oversimplify. Enea Silvio Piccolomini, e.g., was himself a conciliarist during the Council of Basel and participated in that council—well before his accession to the papacy as Pius II. He defended the election of Prince Amadeo of Savoy as (anti-) Pope Felix V, who at the time of his election not only was a layman but also had a family, including children. He wrote, "So what is wrong with a Roman pontiff having powerful sons, who are able to come to their father's aid against tyrants?" See Enea Silvio Piccolomini, *De gestis concilii Basiliensis commentariorum libri duo,* ed. D. Hay and W.K. Smith (Oxford, 1967), 248, quoted and translated in P. Prodi, *The Papal Prince, One Body and Two Souls: The Papal Monarchy in Early Modern Europe,* trans. S. Haskins (Cambridge, 1987), at 13–14; see the entire study of Prodi for an invaluable discussion of the subtleties of the evolution of the papal monarchy.

interlocutors argued that the curia was a good place because it was a concentrated seat of religious activity. Within the argument, the interlocutor Lapo describes the curial hierarchy in a very general fashion. Lapo's position concerning the conciliarism controversy seems very clear (III.22–23): "there is the pope, who takes the place of God: after him we have no greater. He has been given power not by human counsel but divinely. . . ." The pun on the word *consilium*, "counsel" (so close to *concilium*, "council") is not at all subtle and works as well in English as it does in Latin.[8]

To flesh out Lapo's awareness of political circumstances, a brief pause with Cardinal Cesarini will be helpful. In 1431 Cesarini had assumed the leading role in the Council of Basel, and in the ensuing years he and Eugenius increasingly came to find themselves on opposite sides of the conciliarism issue. They would only be reconciled in 1438, at the start of the Council of Ferrara-Florence. It is interesting that Lapo had appealed to Cesarini for patronage in 1436, two years before the writing of the *De curiae commodis*.[9] So Lapo's first, vague appeal to Cesarini back in 1436 was made at a time when the cardinal was still at loggerheads with Eugenius IV. Yet two years later, with the beginning of the Council of Ferrara and the arrival of the Greeks, Cesarini had reconciled himself to the papacy.[10] Indeed, at that council he would be one of the most important actors in the Latin cast of characters.

After the council was successfully underway in the summer of 1438 and Cesarini was obviously, actively working for papal interests, Lapo chose to dedicate to Cesarini his translation of Plutarch's *Life of Aratus*,[11] a work he claimed to have completed in October 1437.[12] If Lapo's own dating in the autograph manuscript can be trusted, he waited almost

---

8. Indeed both of these words can denote gatherings or assemblies of people. The word *consilium*, i.e., "counsel," however, has an important secondary meaning of "advice," or "wisdom." The word *concilium*, "council," was used to refer to church councils.

9. According to the dating of Rotondi: see Lapo's letter to Cesarini, 11 September 1436, in Rotondi, "Lapo da Castiglionchio," 12; Fubini, 48.

10. The first, principal Greek delegation arrived in Ferrara on 4 March 1438; see Gill, *Personalities*, 4.

11. On 15 July 1438, precisely; see F, f. 18 (Luiso [275 n. 3] erroneously reports f. 19).

12. This dating is possible according to Lapo's Greek *explicit* formula at F, f. 46 (edited in Luiso, 276 n. 2, and in chap. 5 infra), where the translation itself ends.

a year to choose a dedicatee.[13] His choice to appeal to Cesarini two years earlier had been unwise (given the opposition that existed at that time between Cesarini and the papacy) and probably reflected the desperation whose borderline Lapo was always on the verge of crossing. But his favorite virtue, prudence, must have guided him in 1438 in choosing Cesarini as his dedicatee, with the security of knowing that everybody was then on the same side. Yet again, however, things are not as clear as they seem: both the material of the translation—the choice of the life of Aratus, who was known, among other things, as a hater of tyranny—and certain parts of the dedication show that Lapo may very well have been trying to appeal to what he thought were continuing conciliarist sympathies on Cesarini's part.[14]

As the conciliarist controversy raged unabated, Lapo was writing the *De curiae commodis*, with the Council of Ferrara-Florence of 1438–39 already underway.[15] The council's main purpose was to end the long-standing division between the Eastern and Western churches. The Greeks had arrived in Ferrara in early March 1438, at which time Lapo was employed by Francesco Condulmer to help in translating Greek docu-

---

13. Lapo alludes to an unspecified period of deliberation in choosing a dedicatee in his preface to the translation; see my edition of this preface in Celenza, "Parallel Lives," app. 2, sec. 1: "After I had translated into Latin Plutarch's account of the peacetime affairs and military deeds of the most famous leader Aratus the Sicyonian, I determined—in line with my customary practice—to send it to some prince. For quite a while I was in doubt and was wondering to which prince I would like most of all to dedicate this little lamplight work of mine. But both in terms of understanding, prudence, greatness, integrity, and constancy and in terms of the deeds of war and military glory, nobody really occurred to me whose life seemed to agree with the life of Aratus" [Cum Arati Sicyonii clarissimi ducis res domi militiaeque gestas ex Plutarcho latine interpretatus essem, easque ad aliquem principem—pro mea consuetudine—mittere statuissem. Dubitanti mihi diu ac deliberanti cuinam nostrorum principum potissimum dedicarem has lucubratiunculas meas, nullus sane occurebat cui consilio prudentia cum magnitudine, integritate, constantia, tum bellicis rebus et gloria militari Arati vita convenire videretur]. Lapo goes on to say that Aratus appeared to him in a dream; after conversing with Aratus in the dream and later considering the dream encounter (as well as some choice words from a sermon of Ambrogio Traversari), Lapo decided on Cesarini as a dedicatee (for the mention of the preaching he heard "ab eruditissimo ac religiosissimo viro Ambrosio amicissimo tuo," see ibid., sec. 32). Lapo received the Greek codex in which the *Vita Arati* was contained from Ambrogio Traversari; see Mehus, *Historia*, 8.

14. See Celenza, "Parallel Lives," 134–38.

15. See Gill, *The Council*; and see the criticisms regarding the issue of representation in Stieber, *Pope Eugenius IV*, 42 with n. 61. See also Gill, *Personalities*; Fink, "Eugene IV."

ments. Despite Lapo's dissatisfaction with his own position,[16] Lapo makes ample mention of the council in the dialogue.

Throughout, he presents a best-case scenario, reflecting the somewhat propagandistic hopefulness by which the council must have been attended in its early phases. Lapo praises the fame of the curia under the direction of Eugenius and waxes enthusiastic about the council's historic importance, stressing that it will bring together East and West (III.26–27). He describes the council (III.27) as a "coming together of men that is so great, so variegated, so famous, so engendered by God, and such a great and admirable unanimity that the likes of it has never been heard of or read about before." With this and other similarly rhapsodic descriptions, Lapo exercises his propagandistic talent to show what a good papal secretary he could be if only he were given the opportunity. The same tendency is evident later on, with the defense of wealth.

The council also later offers the opportunity for humor, as the interlocutors present a droll description of the Easterners' appearances (VII.6–7). In the description, Lapo uses literature—Plutarch and Virgil—that would have been familiar to his intended audience, and he creates descriptions that are both readable and perceptive. It is significant that this segment on the appearance of the Easterners is one of only two sections that anyone saw fit to print before the twentieth century.[17]

Lapo's realistic descriptions are especially forceful whenever he approaches matters that we would today consider psychological. These behavioral analyses are always closely bound with considerations about the effects of the curial environment on its inhabitants. While any analysis of the dialogue must take into account the overt intention of the work—that is, to praise the curia—along with this there is always a dynamic occurring between praise and blame, as if Lapo cannot let an advantage of the curia be expounded without also, almost in the same breath, flipping the coin.

In his discussion of the curial bureaucracy, we get a taste of Lapo's sharp insight into human motivation. A merit of this discussion is the manner in which Lapo documents the influence of the close-knit world of the curial bureaucracy on the behavior of its actors. One comes to universal conclusions after hearing the presentation of specific cases. In one

16. See chap. 1, p. 9 supra.
17. The other section, which Humfrey Hody (1659–1706) included in his monograph on illustrious Greeks, was Lapo's praise of Greek learning (V.4). See Hody, *De graecis illustribus*, at 30 and 136.

such case (VI.1–2) the preteritic tone could easily exemplify the spirit and literary methodology of the whole dialogue.

> I am deeply concerned indeed by an attack that I have often heard made by many: that in the Roman curia influence, bribery, and corruption provide easier access in attaining office and rank than do learning, uprightness, and purity. Really, you have to look not at what is done there but rather at what was intended. [2] After all, our honored elders wanted these things [office and rank] to be not incitement to vice but rather ornaments of virtue. If sometimes fortunes are handed over to the unworthy or to those who are not so worthy as they might be, the whole business has to be ascribed to the age and the men, not to the vice of the curia.

Perhaps for the sake of achieving a measure of verisimilitude (and along the way maintaining adequate persuasive force), Lapo frankly acknowledges curial corruption. Lapo is not alone in the fifteenth century in offering criticism of the papal curia. In fact in the decades following his death, the number of treatises condemning various aspects of the curia, especially its extravagance, multiplied.[18] In any case, Lapo argues, it is possible to gain great wealth at the curia (VI.2). Lapo praises the curia based on the potential it holds for upward mobility. But, as elsewhere in the dialogue, there is at the same time distaste for the people who are actu-

---

18. See J. Monfasani, "The Fraticelli and Clerical Wealth in Quattrocento Rome," in *Renaissance Society and Culture: Essays in Honor of Eugene Rice, Jr.,* ed. J. Monfasani and R. Musto (New York, 1991), 177–95 (in Monfasani, *Language and Learning* as #XIV) at 178 passim. For background on early modern anticlericalism see P.A. Dykema and H. A. Oberman, *Anticlericalism in Late Medieval and Early Modern Europe*, Studies in Medieval and Reformation Thought 51 (Leiden, New York, and Cologne, 1993), especially the study of Gordon Griffiths, "Leonardo Bruni and the 1431 Florentine Complaint against Indulgence-Hawkers: A Case Study in Anticlericalism," 133–43, and the letter of Bruni, 138: "Tacemus vero referre que sit vita, qui mores istorum qui hec profitentur, que prandia, que sumptuositas, que voluptates. Monstro quippe videri potest persimile hoc qui salutem animabus aliorum se profitentur afferre, ita vivere ut nichil unquam de salute propria cogitasse videantur." See also in that volume the important study of Silvana Seidel Menchi, "Characteristics of Italian Anticlericalism," 271–81, who describes "the most distinctive characteristic of Italian anticlericalism in the early modern era" as stark recognition of "the disjunction between words and actions, the contradiction between conscience and comportment." See also R. Fubini, *Umanesimo e secolarizzazione: Da Petrarca a Valla* (Rome, 1990), especially 303–38 for an edition and discussion of Poggio's 1417 oration to the council of Constance, in which Poggio protests against clerical vice.

ally being upwardly mobile and making use of the "benefit" under discussion. Lapo realizes that his "speech" might seem "malicious" if he were to recount the humble origins from which some of the curial higher-ups have sprung (VI.3).

Lapo mentions various curial offices as honorable and suggests that it takes learning and diligence to belong to these groups. The interlocutor Angelo responds in a passage that is revelatory and permeated with Lapo's intense scrutiny of people's motivations (VI.4–5). Angelo reveals that it is "characteristic of men of cunning, skillful, crafty, and tricky— as well as knavish—intelligence to know the natures of those whom they desire especially to win over. They perceive the deepest recesses of their spirits and minds; all of their intentions; their plans, longings, and desires." Having thought about these things, the ambitious will "apply what amount to stratagems in order to capture them by storm, to be in their company, to flatter them; they try to take some of them in by feigned friendship, others by personal appearance, others by pandering, and still others with presents."

Perhaps once again we see a mirror of Lapo's melancholic state of mind. How unpalatable it seems to be compelled to investigate so carefully all of the habits, friends, and associations of one's possible patrons. Yet this is exactly what the real-life Lapo must have been doing. It is accepted as a frank matter of fact that those persons seeking patronage must be solicitous of "those whom they desire especially to win over," and in his own life Lapo had certainly made attempts in this direction. But at the time he wrote the dialogue he had achieved no success with which he had allowed himself to be satisfied, and thus in writing the psychology of curial seekers, Lapo writes also his own. The profound but implicit disturbance, the dissatisfaction with seeking patronage, is balanced at the same time by a fatalistic resignation to its necessity, showing that the mechanisms of Italian Renaissance patronage constituted an object of learned discussion in the fifteenth century as well as in the twentieth.

To delve more deeply into the question of the attainment of wealth at the curia, Lapo has his interlocutors engage in a discussion of the curial bureaucracy. In the course of the exposition, he mentions various offices and emphasizes the great wealth and power that is available to the holders of the offices. The protonotaries, the chamberlain, the vice-chancellor, the *referendarii*, the *cubicularii*, the keepers of the apostolic treasury—all these and more are mentioned (VI.6–8). Along with its function

as an expository aid to the presentation of curial wealth, this passage serves as a prime witness to the state of development that the curial bureaucracy had attained in the year 1438.

The interlocutors go on to suggest that the money the curia takes in as well as its ability to do so is common knowledge. In a passage whose irony cannot go unnoticed, Angelo concludes the discussion by suggesting that many curialists actually lack ambition for wealth but are indeed very desirous of "the allies and followers of wealth: pleasure and delight" (VI.11). In answering Angelo, Lapo makes the transition to the interlocutors' discussion of the next "advantage" of the curia, that it offers sensory pleasures (VII.1).

They begin by addressing the visual pleasures that the curia has to offer, in a discussion whose centerpiece is the description of the Easterners then present for the Council of Ferrara-Florence (VII.2–11). The transition from visual to auditory pleasures is made, accompanied by Lapo's typical *modus procedendi*. He has provided a brief sketch of the curial bureaucracy; now he tells how it really works. In this instance, as always, he starts with praise, this time for the abundance of news one can hear at the curia (VII.12). Then he begins to narrow things down by introducing the curia's many wild gossipers, who tell of things that might be untrue but that "nevertheless give pleasure for a little while, under the guise of truth" (VII.13). Then the distasteful truth is revealed about curial praxis, as we learn that, during all this gossip, "dinner parties, tavern life, pandering, bribes, thefts, adultery, sexual degradation, and shameful acts are publicly revealed" (VII.14). Finally, Lapo once again offers an unvarnished, fatalistic half-acceptance of the necessity of engaging in these distasteful practices. At least implicitly, he chalks it up to the "advantage" of the curia already discussed, that is, the ability to acquire virtue (in this case wisdom) through experience (VII.15–16). One gains "utility" by having heard the gossip about others at the curia (VII.15).

> ... if you ever need a favor from these people, the result is that, almost like a learned doctor, you have your medications ready and prepared. You can apply them as if to some kind of illness, so that, if you know how to use your medications correctly, you are never turned away by anyone. I do not know if there can be any place better or more desirable than the curia for one who wishes to live opportunely among men.

Concessions to seemingly regrettable circumstances are expressed throughout the dialogue, but nowhere perhaps more baldly than here. Nothing of the curial denizens' habits lies hidden in their home. One turns this to one's advantage by using the knowledge one gains from probing into one's colleagues' affairs and applying it to one's own benefit. It is perhaps not the best thing to be considered crude and scheming, the argument goes on, but it is far worse to be considered a fool.

The advantages that relate to auditory pleasure are, as with the virtues, tied to volume. The more one hears, the better—the more "pleasurable"—it is, because one gains the experience necessary to succeed, win patrons, and acquire what one wants and needs. There is a parallel to this utilitarian *mentalité* in book 4 of Leon Batista Alberti's *Libri della famiglia*. There the interlocutor Piero avers to his fellows (252 Watkins trans., 270 Grayson ed.):

> I shall tell you, therefore, first, of what means I made use in order to become an intimate and follower of Gian Galeazzo, the duke of Milan; then I shall tell you how I went about winning the good will of Ladislas, King of Naples; finally I shall recount to you what sort of conduct enabled me to preserve the favor and good will of Pope Giovanni. I think, too, that you will be pleased to learn of my various and different devices, my cautious and seldom used means, which have rarely been described. These are most useful ways to deal with men in civic life; therefore listen well to me. In order to arrive at the friendship of the duke, I saw that it would be necessary to make use of one of his old friends and present intimates. . . .

As Piero goes on in his account and expands on his dealings with these men, the parallels to Lapo's *De curiae commodis* VII.13–17 are obvious. There is a focus on a utilitarian morality and a kind of pride in the use of cleverness when dealing with others. It is accepted that in group situations, one must sometimes use a subtle web of obligation, deceit, and skillful rhetoric to achieve one's objectives.[19]

Two pleasures remain, gustatory and sexual. First, the sense of taste is praised as an innate part of us that does not wane with age (VII.19–20). It motivates all other desires, including sexual desire; it is "the mother

---

19. Grafton (*Commerce*, 75) argues that "Alberti's characters analyze human relationships as a game of manipulation, which one plays to connect and endear oneself to the powerful."

and maker of the rest" (VII.20). Lapo quotes from the well-known line of Terence "Venus freezes without Ceres and Liber,"[20] perhaps thinking of Cicero, who had himself explained the Terentian passage in the *De natura deorum* and argued that "Ceres" stood for grain, "Liber" for wine.[21] The curia is presented as a real paradise of gustatory pleasure, as the interlocutors set forth the variety and abundance of foods of all different kinds as well as the many banquets and other opportunities available to the curial gourmet (VII.21–36). Angelo (VII.22–24) mentions examples of curial excess, of "refined men, as well as those who live luxuriously and delicately," who "squander their fortunes pointlessly [on] what pleases them at the moment," making "their lewd desire the limit to their expenditures." Their desires are all-consuming, and thus they seek out the best chefs as well as emissaries to procure these things for them. In addition they "zealously seek out beautiful servant boys to serve the meals, as well as catamites and men whose hair is done a little too finely."

Angelo has expounded yet another of the dialogue's condemnations of excessive curial luxury, this time with a sneaking criticism of "delicacy." The curialists he criticizes are dandies, concerned only to sample the finest foods prepared in the most exotic manner. They wish to be served by beautiful servant boys, the flush of whose cheeks has not yet been marred by beard.[22] Although he cites the custom of Alexander of Macedon (perhaps from Plutarch's *Life of Theseus*), who would order his soldiers to shave so that the enemy could not get a hold on them, it is clear that Lapo considers the "delicate" cardinals to be akin to *erastai* and the boys to be their *eromenoi*.[23]

Parenthetically, another implicit criticism of curial pederasty is perhaps to be noted when the interlocutors discuss education in the curia. Angelo mentions (IV.11) "young men who have advanced recently into

---

20. Ter. *Eun.* 732.

21. Cic. *Nat. D.* II.60–61.

22. This notion was itself an ancient literary topos. Cf. K.J. Dover, *Greek Homosexuality*, 2d ed. (Cambridge, Mass., 1989), 86.

23. Whether we should take this as representative of reality is a difficult question. Lapo's criticism of "delicacy" was also leveled in much the same sort of way and with very similar language at morally corrupt practitioners of the military arts. See Lapo's epistolary treatise to Simone Lamberti, discussed in chap. 1 (for the criticism, see, e.g., Par. Lat. 11,388, ff. 6v–9). So perhaps this was just a stock criticism. However, it has recently been shown convincingly by Michael Rocke that homosexual contact between men and adolescent boys was, at least in the Florentine context, very prevalent. See M. Rocke, *Forbidden Friendships: Homosexuality and Male Culture in Renaissance Florence* (Oxford, 1996).

the curia and, while they had great natural ability, have come on teachers who were so skilled and diligent that in a few months they emerged as
men, so that I think that not even Tiresias or Caeneus changed their form
so swiftly or in such a great degree." Certain curialists, it is suggested
(IV.12), are "endowed with a certain unaccustomed, marvelous, and
unheard-of teaching system, one well suited for training very young
men." Angelo adds, "I am impeded by scruple from revealing its name,
as if it were the famous Eleusinian mysteries."[24]

Tiresias and Caeneus were ancient mythological figures who were
reported to have changed genders completely. Angelo does say that
owing to their teachers' skill and "unheard-of" teaching systems, the
"young men" emerged as "men." But the fact that this change is mentioned along with Tiresias and Caeneus, coupled with Angelo's "scruple" at mentioning this secret teaching system, leads one to suspect that
Lapo was launching another attack on the sexual conduct of certain
curialists.

To return to the banquets, for Lapo there is always a right way to do
things and a wrong way. Banquets are no exception. Lapo outlines the
results of the conduct of "those who, in the midst of the greatest wealth
and luxury, live in such a way that they would come by nothing at all
in a dishonorable fashion," who are sparing with themselves, and who
"do and think nothing weak or shameful" (VII.25–26). They have into
their homes only the most worthy of domestic and foreign guests
(VII.27).

Yet Lapo still cannot allow himself to leave off here with praise alone,
even of the virtuous curial banqueters. Concerning the banquets, the
interlocutor Lapo comments (VII.28):

> fear deters me from saying with what pomp, variety, and abundance
> they are carried out, lest I seem to reprove the extravagance of these
> affairs or seem myself to take excessive pleasure in this kind of thing.

Once again curial vice is uncovered through a preterition, a "passing
over" of the extravagance of the banquets. But the undertone is that such
excess is being practiced at the curia that it might seem unbelievable to

---

24. Renée Neu Watkins has noticed this passage in her "Mythology as Code: Lapo
da Castiglionchio's View of Homosexuality and Materialism at the Curia," *Journal of
the History of Ideas* 53 (1992): 138–44.

one who was not there.[25] Angelo responds, unsurprised, that he has witnessed this sort of extravagance, and in his answer he opens another interesting window into the practice of everyday life at the curia, offering also a sense of what curialists talked about from day to day (VII.29).

In addition, in mentioning the "cooks, sausage makers, and gourmet food makers," Angelo echoes the language of Terence, again from the Roman comedian's *Eunuch*,[26] but it is no surprise that it is mediated by Cicero's *De officiis*, in the same way that Lapo's earlier quotation of Terence was mediated by Cicero's *De natura deorum*. At the end of the first book of the *De officiis*, Cicero had quoted Terence in a section whose intention it was to discuss worthy and unworthy ways of coming by money.[27] Cicero argued that the trades that deal with people's pleasures are the worst of all, and he quoted Terence to single out the trades that deal with food.[28] Lapo's description of the cooks brings to the fore an already noticed tendency toward distaste for those who must work to raise themselves up in society, and this time, as we have seen, he is supported by Cicero, his favorite authority. Lapo contrasts the situation of the cooks, "covered with grease and grime in the middle of the kitchen,

---

25. This sort of curial excess was especially criticized later on in the century, so much so that certain curialists, such as Jean Jouffrouy, Niccolò Palmieri, and Fernando da Cordova, either took it on themselves or were asked by curial higher-ups (though, notably, not by popes) to provide defenses of curial life. Cf. the discussion infra and Monfasani, "Fraticelli"; "A Theologian at the Roman Curia in the Mid-Quattrocento: A Bio-Bibliographical Study of Niccolò Palmieri, O.S.A.," *Analecta Augustiniana* 54 (1991): 321–81; 55 (1992): 5–98 (printed separately with continuous pagination, from which I cite); *Fernando of Cordova: A Biographical and Intellectual Profile*, Transactions of the American Philosophical Society 82, no. 6 (Philadelphia, 1992).

26. Ter. *Eun.* 257.

27. As one might expect, the question as to what was a worthy way and what was an unworthy way to earn money was especially interesting to a number of the leaders in the Florentine humanist movement. In a treatise written contemporaneously to the writing of the *De curiae commodis*, Matteo Palmieri, e.g., made use of this section of the *De officiis*, quoting Cicero practically verbatim. See Matteo Palmieri, *Della vita civile*, ed. F. Battaglia (Bologna, 1944), 157, cited in Martines, *Social World*, 31 with n. 48. On the question of wealth in the world of Florentine humanism, see Martines, op. cit., 18–39.

28. Cicero *Off.* I.150: "Least of all to be approved are those trades that serve the pleasures: 'fishmongers, butchers, cooks, sausage makers, fishermen,' as Terence says. You can add to that, if you like, ointment sellers, dancers, and the whole gambling business" [minimeque artes eae probandae, quae ministrae sunt voluptatum: 'cetarii, lanii, coqui, fartores, piscatores,' ut ait Terentius. Adde huc, si placet, unguentarios, saltatores totumque ludum talarium].

embroiled in the smoke and stench," with the station they can acquire: "Then, out of nowhere, you see them move back to their homeland, raised not only to the priesthood but even to the highest degrees of honor" (VII.30). The discussion concerning the cooks thus also reveals an interesting sociohistorical detail. The curia as a seat of patronage could not only in various ways endow its denizens with wealth. It could also confer prestige and, by extension, power, completing in its possibilities—to put the cart five centuries before the horse—the Weberian triad of power, prestige, and wealth. These foreign would-be priests used the possibility open to those living in the curia to their full advantage, entering and working as lowly cooks, leaving as priests.

After the interlocutors stress the internationalism of the curial gustatory scene, they go on to examine "the matters related to Venus" (VII.36). As the discussion begins, the sarcasm is only very barely disguised when it is suggested that at the curia "the pleasures of Venus are certainly most apparent" and that "the curialists indulge in them no less than in the others" (VII.37). Lapo continues:

> What good is it to have fired up your sexual appetite if there is nothing with which you can release your sexual desire, where you can put out the fire that has been ignited? And so, prudent and diligent men have energetically provided for this sort of thing, so that nothing toward the end of filling the cup of pleasure to the full would be lacking in the curia.

Obviously the concept of diligence has its negative side, ethically considered. Earlier the interlocutor Angelo detailed the manner in which career-minded curialists behave, knowing everything about their colleagues and applying this knowledge as if it were a medicine. Based on their behavior, and even though it was obviously distasteful, they were described at the end of that monologue as "diligent" (VI.5). Here it seems that Lapo even wishes to mock the concept of "prudence," to which so much attention had been devoted in the earlier discussion of the curia's sapiential advantages. Now the "prudent" man who is seeking sexual experiences could not find a better place than the curia. As the discussion advances to a fairly detailed exposition of the behavior of the prostitutes who frequent the curia, with their "milk white little lapdogs, whom—people say—they use to lick up filth about your loins" (VII.39), it becomes clear that image

and reality at the papal curia are two different things and that the institution is far from the community of virtue it should be.[29]

Christianity and the Defense of Wealth

When Angelo asks Lapo how it is justifiable that the popes and priests in
the curia possess so much wealth, Lapo responds that only the foolish
"disapprove of the luxury and opulence of the popes of this age, as they
term it, and . . . earnestly long for the ancient fathers' purity of life"
(VIII.1). This longing for a return to paleo-Christian morality and behavior is an opinion that had indeed been held by thinkers or groups of
thinkers as diverse as the Waldensians, the Franciscans in all their vari-
eties, and Lapo's contemporary and acquaintance Lorenzo Valla.[30] The
interlocutor Lapo's goal is to win Angelo away from this opinion.

Lapo must have considered this part of the argument important, as he
placed it at the end of the dialogue and devoted quite a bit of time to it.
The Socratic method of the earlier part of the work is brought back into
more prominent use for this section. The first, obvious query that Lapo
puts to Angelo is whether he thinks "that only the poor are respectable,
chaste, and religious and that all of the wealthy are rogues, corrupt, disgraceful, and nefarious" (VIII.3). Angelo sees the point but still believes
there are great temptations in wealth toward luring one away from a holy
life (VIII.4).

Lapo's first response is to offer a strained apologia for the curialists.
He argues that high curial officials have a difficult time of it, owing to the

---

29. On medieval and Renaissance prostitution, see R.C. Trexler, "La prostitution
florentine au XVe siècle: Patronage et clientèles," *Annales* 6 (1981): 983–1015; M.H.
Rosenthal, *The Honest Courtesan: Veronica Franco, Citizen and Writer in Sixteenth-
Century Venice* (Chicago, 1992); J. Rossiaud, *Medieval Prostitution*, trans. L.G.
Cochrane (Oxford and New York, 1988); L.L. Otis, *Prostitution in Medieval Society:
The History of an Urban Institution in Languedoc* (Chicago and London, 1985);
B. Schuster, *Die freien Frauen: Dirnen und Frauenhaüser im 15. und 16. Jahrhundert*
(Frankfurt and New York, 1995); G. Masson, *Courtesans of the Italian Renaissance*
(London, 1975); L. Lawner, *Lives of the Courtesans: Portraits of the Renaissance*
(New York, 1987).

30. See G. Leff, *Heresy in the Later Middle Ages,* 2 vols. (Manchester and New
York, 1967); M.D. Lambert, *Medieval Heresy: Popular Movements from Bogomil to
Hus* (London, 1977); idem, *Franciscan Poverty: The Doctrine of the Absolute Poverty
of Christ and the Apostles in the Franciscan Order, 1210–1323* (London, 1961). For
these tendencies in the thought of Valla, see Camporeale, *Lorenzo Valla, umanesimo
e teologia;* "Lorenzo Valla tra medioevo e rinascimento."

fact that their lives are hidden from all—"barely anybody cares" what they do. On top of that, he adds, they often find themselves in situations where, for diplomatic reasons, they must conform to the shameful habits of their colleagues, so that they do not seem inhuman (VIII.5–6). But in the same monologue the interlocutor Lapo manages to assert that the high curialists have an easy time of it. This is both because they are secluded from the view of all and because the obligation of their office compels them, if only for the sake of reputation, to behave virtuously (VIII.6–9)—an argument that is similar to that of Valla's *De professione religiosorum*. Moreover, they are protected from sinning not only because of the dignity of their office but also because they lack energy, owing to their dissolute lifestyles. The argument is intended outwardly to exonerate the curialists from the charge that they can be corrupted by wealth, but in a backhanded, enthymematic fashion, it points out viceful conduct. The curialists against whom Lapo here takes aim are so lazy that they do not even desire pleasure. This is why, it is argued, "men of this sort either end their life in a short time or come down with leprosy, gout, dropsy, and other incurable diseases" (VIII.14).

Angelo is willing to agree that wealth is not dangerous for high priests with the lifestyles mentioned. He does, however, think it is dangerous for others. In responding to this assertion, Lapo leads the interlocutors into a discussion in which they will employ a number of the classic Florentine Renaissance topoi in defense of wealth, topoi that have their roots in the Aristotelian tradition (including its Thomistic variety). But there is also quite a bit that makes Lapo's argument in defense of wealth unique.

First, in an exposition designed to show the dangers of poverty, we see the manner in which the interlocutor Lapo once again fatalistically accepts humankind's propensity to sin. Wealth is better than poverty because the sins of the wealthy are not as serious as those of the poor (VIII.20). The sins of the wealthy include "gourmandizing, sleep, idleness, and extravagance" and "ostentation, debauchery, and power," which lead to "payoffs and bribes"; but poverty leads to "thefts, plundering, and robbery" and to "treachery, betrayals, slaughter, and destruction" (VIII.21). It is assumed that whatever the economic status, sins will be committed.

Lapo will admit, certainly, that poverty has been beneficial for many and that many have gained a great reputation owing to it (VIII.23), but it is clear already that he accepts the utility of wealth. Employing traditional Aristotelian (and Thomistic) arguments then current in Florence,

he argues that certain virtues, like liberality, simply cannot be practiced without wealth. As such, wealth actually helps priests fulfill their charitable duties, such as providing poor girls with dowries[31] and building for the glory of god, and it helps cover the priests' diplomatic expenses, which, given the dangerous times, even include soldiers for use as bodyguards (VIII.27–28).

Lapo thus accepts and endorses many of the traditional positions in defense of wealth, mounting arguments equivalent in their reasoning, argumentation, and tenor (if not exactly equal in content) to those of contemporaries like Bruni and Matteo Palmieri. Still, Angelo will not relent completely, and in Lapo's concern to employ to its fullest potential the genre of rhetorical argumentation known as sorites—in which an overpowering "heap" of arguments is employed to persuade—he perseveres and offers an elegant concern for religious scruples balanced with a practical, historically situated acceptance of a world that circumstance has altered.

The interlocutor Lapo brings up the wealthy ancient Hebrew priests and uses them to support his notion that priests should be allowed to accumulate wealth (VIII.31). Angelo in turn objects that examples from the Hebrew tradition are not really valid and that Lapo had better turn his attention to the laws of Christ when it comes to poverty, since when Christ was born all the laws of the Hebrews were automatically repealed (VIII.34). This opens the door to Lapo's more original contribution to the Florentine Renaissance defense of wealth. If present-day priests are to engage in the *imitatio Christi* in all respects, should we not also ask them "to perform miracles, heal the sick, and raise the dead," also "to be bound to a post, beaten with whips, crowned with thorns, and hung on a cross, and to descend into hell and fly out thence with the ancient fathers into heaven" (VIII.35)? Angelo replies simply that the priests are men whereas Christ was God; thus one could not require them to do the various things Christ had done. Lapo goes on to wonder why it is, then, that priests are required to be poor, if these other things are not asked of them. Historical circumstances change. Along with this, so does morality (VIII.38): "Do not, therefore, examine present times on the basis of former ones. Those times required one set of morals, these another."

Lapo then discusses the reasons why Christ had to adopt the stance of poverty. Because of the wealthy environment in which he was situated,

---

31. On dowries in Florentine Renaissance life, see Martines, *Social World, ad indicem.*

Christ had to do something new to make the religion he was propounding appealing by making a radical break with traditional patterns of life (VIII.39). To establish the new religion, Christ could not use "force or fear" or "power" or even "reasoned arguments" to persuade his ancient audience away from their religion; Christ had to do something novel, so that people would be "so affected that no uncertainty or mistrust remained in their minds" (VIII.40). Had he done this with wealth, people would not have trusted in the new religion (VIII.41). In Lapo's presentation Christ becomes a skilled rhetorician, exactly conscious of the manner of life, thought, and speech necessary to persuade his reticent audience. Born a pauper, he was so wise that he could refute the learned Hebrews, leaving them "mute and stunned in their astonishment" (VIII.42). Lapo's eloquent argument continues with the ring of sincere religious belief and is remarkably free of his usual double-meaning preterition (VIII.42–43).

> Shortly thereafter, he [i.e., Christ] gave his attention to spreading the new law, to educating men, to purifying them with the holy bath of baptism, and to forgiving the converted. He raised the dead and expelled incurable illnesses. With his voice alone he freed men disturbed by abominable spirits. [Because of all these things,] what else could they suspect, unless it was this (which was really true): that he was a divine man, or rather God, born of God, filled with the divine spirit and sent down from heaven for the benefit and liberation of the human race. . . .

The interlocutor Lapo goes on to suggest that the foundations of the religion of Christ have now been laid and that all ambiguities have been removed from Christianity.[32] Lapo views Christianity as a religion natural and inborn in humankind. He argues that because of its success and greatness, "it should be adorned with riches and honored with wealth, so that it brings souls to itself not only by its power but also by deeply affecting the eyes with its magnificence and brilliance" (VIII.46).

---

32. This is somewhat disingenuous, especially given the debates regarding the *filioque* question then raging at the council as Lapo was writing. For the *filioque*, see Gill, *Personalities*, 1–14, 254–63. Directly thereafter in the dialogue (VIII.45), however, this statement is qualified in such a way that the *filioque* issue does not become a problem: "For about Christ everybody means the same; they say the same thing: that he is the truest and only son of God and the only God."

Lapo has yet to explain, really, why this is so. When he does so in a Lucretianizing passage (VIII.46–47), his reasoning is crystalline and almost makes him a Machiavelli *ante litteram*. He suggests that "one should draw back a bit from that ancient severity and energy of Christ and add something new." The very nature of humankind is asserted to be such that it grows tired of tradition, even if it is old and valuable. Implicitly, therefore, Lapo goes beyond one of the traditional arguments that had been used against wealth: that since some of the greatest heroes of the Roman Republic had been poor, poverty was to be praised over and above wealth.[33] Without naming the argument, Lapo accounts for it implicitly and offers an answer: "This is the state of all things: that the greatest things, born from humble beginnings, augment themselves and in growing reach their apex."

According to Lapo, the custom of the present day is that wealth and opulence are respected to such an extent that a curialist would not be taken seriously if he were to conduct his life in poverty. Lapo even goes so far as to flirt with idolatry and praise the ancients because they made their images of gods out of gold, since they wisely "saw that the beauty of gold itself would impel the minds of men even more toward divine worship and religion" (VIII.49). In response to one more objection from Angelo, Lapo returns to traditional arguments, suggesting that Christ was really preaching not against wealth but against avarice and that wealthy curialists should practice the virtue of liberality (VIII.52–56).[34]

Finally, Angelo confesses that he has been beaten and says that he is now ready to submit happily to Lapo's opinion. But the author Lapo could not resist one final salvo against the arrogance and vanity he perceived among the curialists. What did it feel like to be snubbed at the curia? How did it happen? In a coda to the argument, which is in its positioning generally representative of Lapo's style of discourse, Angelo vents his rage against arrogant and haughty curialists who are quick to take and slow to repay, who make one wait all day at their door and then give

---

33. See Baron, *In Search of Florentine Civic Humanism*, 1:210–11 and chap. 8, sec. 3, passim.

34. The Florentine chancellor Benedetto Accolti would later make an argument defending curial magnificence; cf. R. Black, *Benedetto Accolti and the Florentine Renaissance* (Cambridge, 1985), 208. The notion that laws of governance and of wisdom change with the times is also present a bit later in the century in the work of two of Ficino's scholastic mentors, Niccolò Tignosi and Lorenzo Pisano; see A. Field, *The Origins of the Florentine Platonic Academy* (Princeton, 1988), 143–44 (for Tignosi) and 166–67 (for Pisano).

one a brief and unsatisfactory hearing (IX.1–3). Angelo has been persuaded, he will admit, of the necessity of wealth for the curialists and even that the curia offers considerable advantages. But the inclusion of this passage in the work testifies to its nature as a kind of manifesto for a generation of itinerant intellectuals.

If the stars of the humanist movement found their places as chancellors, secretaries to princes, and papal secretaries, what about the rest of the qualified practitioners who were then interested in plying this new, literary trade? How did they go about it? Lapo was a highly qualified humanist translator, even at the young age of thirty-three, when this treatise was written. In reading the just cited burst of anger, one gets a glimpse into what it must have felt like—in the eyes of someone who was well qualified and knew it—to have to go, almost literally, banging on the doors of possible patrons to win support for one's humanistic efforts, and this in a society where there really was no fixed place for many able practitioners of this new and growing literary movement.

Certainly, it is necessary to consider the issue of patronage in evaluating Lapo's defense of wealth. Lapo, in defending the wealth of the curialists, is defending his own interests as well; and the outburst at the end of the *De curiae commodis* displays his frustration with the mechanisms of patronage, a frustration that simply could not be kept silent.[35] Keeping that in mind, it is also interesting to see where Lapo's argument in defense of wealth fits in the medieval and Renaissance tradition touching on this theme. First and foremost one recognizes that Lapo's presentation of the utility and necessity of curial wealth could have functioned as a powerful arrow in the quiver of arguments that were amassed and used to justify the development of the evolving papal monarchy.[36] The fact that it was not so utilized is probably due to its being embedded in a treatise that contained so many bits of negative information about the curia. But other questions suggest themselves. How original was Lapo's contribution? Where should it be set in the literary tradition discussing curial wealth?

Lapo's defense of wealth belongs to two different literary subgenres of

---

35. R. Weissman has argued that among those involved in Mediterranean patronage both in antiquity and the Renaissance, sometimes dissenting voices were to be heard and objections to the morality of the processes of patronage were made. See his "Taking Patronage Seriously: Mediterranean Values and Renaissance Society," in *Patronage, Art, and Society in Renaissance Italy,* ed. F.W. Kent and P. Simons (Oxford, 1987), 25–46.

36. On the papal monarchy, see Prodi, *Papal Prince;* Thomson, *Popes and Princes.*

the Renaissance defense of wealth. On the one hand, Lapo was a Florentine and was an admirer of Leonardo Bruni. He must have been affected by the thought of his immediate contemporaries who used Aristotle and the Aristotelian tradition to defend the acquisition of wealth; Bruni, Palmieri, Alberti, and others come to mind.[37] In a despotic environment, Pier Candido Decembrio, whom Lapo knew and corresponded with,[38] also discussed the utility of wealth.[39] On the other hand, Lapo's positions also have a place in the tradition of arguments about the wealth and extravagance possessed by members of the Roman curia.

In fact the argument historicizing Christ's poverty bears a similarity to arguments that Roman curialists would use later on in the century, in the 1460s, against the branch of the Franciscan order then known as the Fraticelli *de opinione*.[40] These sectarians desired conformity to the early-fourteenth-century bulls of Pope John XXII taking away the Franciscan order's claim to propertylessness. They even went so far as to follow Michael of Cesena, the Franciscan rebel against Pope John XXII. With Cesena they maintained that this pope and all of his subsequent followers were heretics.[41]

In the papal Rome of the second half of the Quattrocento, the Fraticelli *de opinione* were already marginalized. But the curialists Jean Jouffroy, Niccolò Palmieri, and Fernando of Cordova were nonetheless impelled to write treatises in defense of curial wealth.[42] This was owed to

---

37. For Bruni, see Baron, *In Search of Florentine Civic Humanism,* passim; for Matteo Palmieri, see especially ibid., 234–35. Matteo Palmieri was writing his *Vita civile* contemporaneously to Lapo's most active professional years, the late 1430s; see G. Belloni, "Intorno alla datazione della *Vita civile* di M. Palmieri," *Studi e problemi di critica testuale* 16 (1978), cited in Baron, op. cit., 139–40 n. 13. On the problem of wealth, see also R.A. Goldthwaite, *Wealth and the Demand for Art in Italy, 1300–1600* (Baltimore and London, 1993), especially 204–12; J. Onians, "Alberti and ΦΙΛΑΡΕΤΗ: A Study in Their Sources," *Journal of the Warburg and Courtauld Institutes* 34 (1971): 96–114; A. D. Fraser-Jenkins, "Cosimo de' Medici's Patronage of Architecture and the Theory of Magnificence," *Journal of the Warburg and Courtauld Institutes* 33 (1970): 162–70.

38. See Lapo's two letters to Pier Candido in Luiso, 255–59.

39. Pier Candido Decembrio discussed the utility of wealth in his *De vitae ignorantia*, ed. E. Ditt, *Memorie del R. Istituto lombardo di scienze e lettere* 24 (1931), cited in Baron, *In Search of Florentine Civic Humanism,* 1:241.

40. See Monfasani, "Fraticelli."

41. See ibid., 180–84; and see the literature cited there.

42. See ibid.; Monfasani, "Theologian"; idem, *Fernando.* For Jouffroy, see M. Miglio, "Vidi thiaram Pauli papae secundi," *Bullettino dell' Istituto Storico Italiano per il Medio Evo* 81 (1969): 273–96, reprinted in M. Miglio, *Storiografia pontificia del Quattrocento* (Bologna, 1975), 119–53, 245–49.

the memory and the sting of the earlier attacks of the Fraticelli on curial wealth, their trial in 1466, and three works attacking curial wealth that had not hitherto seen the light.[43] It will not be necessary here to go into extensive detail about the treatises of these curialists. It is sufficient instead to note some of their salient features that can help shed light on Lapo's earlier position.[44]

First, these treatises of the 1460s were all directed against specific targets.[45] Because of this and because their authors belonged more to a scholastic than to a humanistic tradition, the style that their writers employed was akin to scholastic, *quaestio*-style argumentation. Jouffroy and Fernando both mounted extensive point-by-point defenses of the right of curialists to live in a well-appointed fashion.[46] Palmieri's self-collected corpus of treatises on evangelical poverty also has a scholastic flavor.[47]

As Lapo had done, Jouffroy stressed that times had changed from the time of Christ.[48] Palmieri went so far as to refashion a traditional idea— possibly from an earlier confrere—concerning the ages of the world. Palmieri modified the Christian era into three distinct stages, or *status*.[49]

---

43. Jouffroy acted on his own initiative; Palmieri and Cordova were commissioned. See Monfasani, "Fraticelli," 178–79 *et passim*.

44. For a wider context for the debates surrounding curial wealth, vice, and virtue in the second half of the Quattrocento, see the fundamental study of J.W. O'Malley, *Praise and Blame in Renaissance Rome: Rhetoric, Doctrine, and Reform in the Sacred Orators of the Papal Court, c. 1450–1521,* Duke Monographs in Medieval and Renaissance Studies 3 (Durham, N.C., 1979). Chaps. 5 and 6 of that work contain a wealth of valuable information and argument on this theme.

45. Monfasani, "Fraticelli," 185.

46. See Monfasani, *Fernando,* 83–88, for an edition of the preface to Fernando's *Adversus Hereticos;* see especially 86–88, for Fernando's statement of the ten *tractatus* contained in the treatise. For Jouffroy, see Miglio, "Vidi."

47. For information about the texts that comprised this corpus, see Monfasani, "Theologian," 75–76 (= Bibl. 1–8).

48. Monfasani, "Fraticelli," 187 with n. 52. Jouffroy also developed an elaborate defense of the papal use of gems and other precious things, stressing both their stupefying and their talismanic value: see ibid.; Miglio, *Storiografia,* 139–45.

49. Monfasani ("Theologian," 42) suggests that Palmieri was possibly dependent, in his *De statu ecclesie,* on the Augustinian theologian Jordan of Saxony (ob. 1327). For Jordan's treatise, see Jordanus de Saxonia, O.S.A, *Liber Vitasfratrum,* 3:2, ed. R. Arbesmann and W. Hümpfner (New York, 1943), cited in Monfasani, op. cit., 42 n. 136. See also F.A. Mathes, "The Poverty Movement and the Augustinian Hermits," *Analecta Augustiniana* 31 (1968): 5–154; 32 (1969): 5–116, cited in Monfasani, loc. cit. As Monfasani notes, Palmieri may have picked up the idea for the stages of ecclesiastical history from Jordan, his earlier confrere; in no way, however, does he share Jordan's "desire to justify the evangelical poverty of the Augustinian order" (op. cit.,

In the first stage of the Christian period, Palmieri argued, Christ had been compelled to use poverty as a means of persuasion, as an aid in his quest to evangelize. Undeniably, this argument is similar to Lapo's earlier position, although Palmieri does not seem to cite Lapo verbatim.[50] It is not unreasonable to suppose that Lapo's treatise was known in the curial ambient of the 1460s. It was written among curialists, and, as we have seen, the Benedictine monk Girolamo Aliotti had taken an especial interest in the dialogue in the 1450s and 1460s.[51]

Yet Lapo's statement of the case is clearly different from the *quaestio*-type approaches of Niccolò Palmieri and Fernando of Cordova. Part of this is due to the fact that Lapo was not expressly responding to specific opinions against clerical wealth, as would Jouffroy, Palmieri, and Fernando. But what distinguishes Lapo even more is precisely what delimits the humanistic contribution to theological discussion in general, as Charles Trinkaus saw. When they approached questions that would have been handled in a technical way by their professional contemporaries, humanists felt compelled to present the issues in a way that was readable—readable, that is, in line with their standards of readability.

For an overall evaluation of the defense of wealth, there are other issues that must be considered. One of these is Lapo's subtextual but nonetheless transparent disdain for the extravagance of the curialists. Lapo's arguments were certainly not explicit attacks, but they were disguised in name only, under the rubric of describing the pleasures avail-

---

42). In addition, Jordan had many more stages than Palmieri's three (ibid.). But in Palmieri's first stage, as Palmieri himself says, "in order to eradicate the common opinion . . . that all human happiness was located in earthly goods, . . . it was expedient for Christ—who humbly sought to join man to God—to look down more than it was necessary on wealth." (The Latin text is cited at ibid., 40–41 n. 131: "In hoc statu ad extirpandam opinionem communem, que eo tempore universaliter mentibus hominum inhibita erat, quod in bonis terrenis omnis foelicitas staret humana, cum de retributione finali eterne vite nulla penitus mentio fieret, Christo, qui hominem deo coniungere venerat, expediens fuit magis quam oporteret divitias despicere.") Could it be that for this argument—although certainly not for the formulation—Palmieri's source was Lapo's treatise?

50. At the time of this writing, I have not had access to the entire text, which is edited in M. Mastrocola, *Note storiche circa le diocesi di Civita C., Orte e Gallese,* vol. 3, *I vescovi dalla unione delle diocesi alla fine del Concilio di Trento (1437–1564)* (Civita Castellana, 1972), at 302–6 (cited in Monfasani, "Theologian," 75), but which is better read in the authoritative manuscript (which Mastrocola did not use), MS Vatican City, Biblioteca Apostolica Vaticana, Chis. A.IV.113 (= Monfasani's C), at ff. 7v–46v.

51. See chap. 1, p. 25.

able at the curia. The arguments revealing the excess of certain curialists had even more force because of their veiled quality. In describing the gustatory, sexual, and financial excesses of the curial dandies, Lapo could not help but reveal the extent to which behavior of this sort had permeated the everyday practice of curial life.

These sorts of arguments against clerical wealth—which various Fraticelli had mounted *nudis verbis*—were really the types of things against which Niccolò Palmieri, Fernando of Cordova, and others would later so strenuously argue. That these implicit arguments against wealth (or at least against its misuse) as well as a defense of the acquisition of wealth are present in Lapo's dialogue mark its personal, individual nature as well as a tacit refusal on the part of its author to conform to traditional approaches to then-current intellectual problems. For example, Lapo criticizes the use that many curialists make of their acquired wealth, yet he later defends the acquisition of wealth. In his defense of wealth Lapo rejects what has been characterized as a Stoic conception of the laudability of poverty, yet earlier on in the treatise he had accepted the Stoic idea of the absolute interconnectedness of all virtues. In a philosopher's world all of this would have made him simply inconsistent. But in the world of humanism his strategic acceptance and denial of various parts of different ideological schemata allowed him much. He was able to mount a persistent and consistent critique of curial life while at the same time defending his own interests.

CHAPTER 4

Conclusion

Lapo's life and work reveal that he took part in one of the most flourishing periods of Italian Renaissance humanism. A Florentine, Lapo was, during his short career, a minor character in the age of Leonardo Bruni, Matteo Palmieri, Poggio Bracciolini, Lorenzo Valla, Leon Battista Alberti, Ambrogio Traversari, and others. But by stepping back from the main outlines of his life, perhaps one can arrive at some sort of qualitative judgment. Was Lapo a humanist of "second rank," as one historian has termed him?[1] Lapo perceived himself as ill-starred, and he bemoaned his career more than once in his letters; and the episode of 1436—Lapo's unrealized teaching career at the University of Bologna—would seem to support this picture.

Lapo's ill-starred image, however, highlights the biographer's dilemma in dealing with the source material for Lapo's life. His intellectual development and adult life must be reconstructed for the most part from his self-collected letters. Yet in so doing, one almost inevitably gives credence to the picture of a thinker with fortune against him, simply because our most authoritative source for everything else, the *epistolario*, so describes Lapo, along with providing its more concrete information. The real answer to the question asked earlier is that we cannot make a decisive, qualitative judgment, since those judgments must be made by comparison and the short span of Lapo's career does not allow us the needed material.

Still, Lapo's short *cursus* marks him as a special figure worthy of inclusion in the growing canon of Italian Renaissance humanist literature. As much of an intellectual vogue as was humanism—taken in Kristellerian terms—in early Quattrocento Florence, few humanists knew Greek, and even fewer knew it well enough to translate. That Lapo learned Greek so quickly and so well distinguishes him somewhat in the field and puts him

---

1. Holmes, *Florentine Enlightenment*, 83.

in the company of such elites as Leonardo Bruni, Ambrogio Traversari, Guarino Veronese, and Lorenzo Valla.

Lapo studied Greek under the tutelage of Francesco Filelfo; this professional association opens an illustrative window for us onto the world of humanistic patronage. Filelfo's difficulties with the Medici must have been a contributing, if not the prime, factor in Lapo's alienation from Cosimo, an important source of Florentine patronage. Lapo's complaints concerning the lack of support from his *patria* can be traced, certainly, to this episode, and his dramatic snubbing of Cosimo in Ferrara is indicative not only of Lapo's temper but also of the great importance attached to the *padrone* in the environment of early Quattrocento humanism.

For humanists without independent wealth, there was really no fixed natural place. Their studies could be undertaken only under the auspices of a patron; thus, individual humanists had creatively to carve out individual careers and seek support where they could find it.[2] With Florentine resources closed to him, Lapo sought support at the papal curia and found it in Cardinal Giordano Orsini. But when the cardinal died in 1438, Lapo found himself bereft of a protector and was compelled once again to begin casting about for support. Death—both Lapo's own premature death and the cardinal's untimely death—has obscured our view and prevents us from judging just how much of a success Lapo could have been in the world of the curia.

What we can do is examine the work he left behind. The *De curiae commodis* is Lapo's last lengthy prose work. In presenting the curia's "benefits," Lapo reveals the institution's inner and outer functionings, and in so doing he reveals an insider's knowledge. This, to be sure, was one of his intentions: to show that he *was* a legitimate insider, even if he never had the actual, institutional sanctioning that he desired. But the rhetorical tools of this phase of humanism served him well (and certainly here Fubini's views about humanism's anti-institutional potential must be acknowledged).[3] For although Lapo had an insider's view of the curia, he had an outsider's status, a status, perhaps, that pained him enough to reveal—consciously or unconsciously, intentionally or unintentionally—the manner in which the curia was falling far short of its ideal.

In the *De curiae commodis* Lapo is a cultural critic, but he is a critic of

---

2. This is one reason why the debate concerning the merits of the active versus the contemplative life took on such dimensions in this phase of humanism, since one often had to lead a *vita activa* to arrive at the *vita contemplativa*.

3. See Fubini, "All'uscita dalla Scolastica medievale."

a restricted cultural milieu, the Roman curia. His critique, therefore, is subtle and is not the act of one intentionally burning his bridges. The key to the critique is the Stoicizing passage concerning the virtues (section IV). With a Ciceronian openness to presenting a variety of different philosophical positions, Lapo also reports the view of "Aristotle and others" (IV.16) concerning the virtues. But he advocates the Stoic all-or-nothing approach, that is, that one cannot be virtuous without practicing all of the virtues completely. It is the dialogue's most fully explicated passage and the only major position that goes unchallenged. What can a close reading of the rest of the piece yield in light of this absolutely stated position but that the counterpositions to the criticisms of the curia cannot be taken wholly seriously? If Lapo, while maintaining that the virtues are unbreakably connected, is implicitly, often enthymematically, admitting that viceful abuses of wealth and power do occur at the curia, is he not telling us that the curia is not itself now a virtuous place?

This puts an interesting spin on Lapo's argument in defense of wealth. Lapo proffers the opinion that wealth is to be preferred over poverty since the habitual sins of the wealthy are less extreme than those of the poor (VIII.20). He names the vices to which wealth can lead, depending on personality type: gourmandizing, idleness, extravagance, ostentation, debauchery, and power acquired by bribes (VIII.21).[4] He argues that "even if these sins are to be disapproved of, still, they are not so far from the human condition." Lapo warns that in the right hands wealth can be used properly, in this case, that is, to exercise the virtue of liberality. But this is not the same Lapo we heard before, telling us that the virtues were unbreakably connected. Of course he could have written his dialogue inconsistently, alternately stressing now one position, now another; and if he did write in this fashion, he certainly would not find himself alone in the annals of Neo-Latin literature. But if we wish to see the piece as anything like a consistent whole, the importance of the Stoicizing section on the virtues as a key to revealing a consistent critique must be acknowledged.

It is not unreasonable to assume that Lapo wrote his dialogue when he was on the verge of substantial professional success. Whether that would have come in the curia or in another sphere is impossible to know. It may be the case that Lapo left the curia definitively in his last months. But it is difficult to ignore the fact that, along with the obvious frustration and

---

4. Poverty, in contrast, leads to thefts, plunder, treachery, betrayals, and slaughter (VIII.22).

transparent criticism, there is in the dialogue a real fascination with and admiration for the curia's potential as Christianity's leader.

Lapo's argument in defense of wealth is sincere, and his historicizing of Christ's poverty is original in the environment of humanism. The defense of wealth is long and involved and placed in too strategic a position not to be earnestly meant. The historicizing of Christ's poverty is evidence, really, of the new historical sensibility that was characteristic of this phase of humanism and that helped inform, for example, Valla's criticism of the Donation of Constantine. Lapo may not be completely content with the fact that "those times required one set of morals, these another,"[5] but he is willing to recognize wealth's utility in the curia and uses humanist historical methodology to argue this case.

Finally, there is the issue of humanist self-presentation. Who was Lapo's intended audience? How does he wish them to see him? Lapo could have been trying to write, in an encoded fashion, only for his community of fellow humanists. He then would really be simply tweaking the noses of the highly positioned curialists whom he has grown to despise in the two years of his minor-league curial employment. He would be *stufo*—"fed up"—and ready to leave, but not before taking some parting shots. But a more inclusive reading of the piece as a whole reveals different conclusions. Lapo dedicated his treatise to Francesco Condulmer. There is no reason to assume that this dedication was intended as pure sarcasm. In the final analysis Lapo praises the curia's potential but criticizes the actuality. My belief is that Lapo wrote not only as a well-informed curial actor but also as an outsider who wanted to become an insider.

The *De curiae commodis* is not the parting shot of a fed up hanger-on. It is instead Lapo's last-ditch, highly critical but nonetheless sincere attempt to find a patron who would allow him to join a cultural environment at which he marveled but from which he felt unjustly excluded. Undeniably, there is strong criticism of curial morality. This demonstrates Lapo's desire to be perceived as an in-the-know, concerned insider. But the dialogue's hopefulness about the contemporary council

---

5. It is significant that even after the defense of wealth has been made in full, Lapo has his interlocutor Angelo engage in yet another of the dialogue's criticisms of curial arrogance. It is almost as if there are two sides to Lapo's personality here, the predominant one, undoubtedly, recognizing the real need for curial wealth, the other, perhaps, unwilling to sit silently by and view such a dispassionate mixture of the sacred and the profane without at least some protest.

and its implicit loyalty to the pope regarding the conciliarism question also illustrate Lapo's attempt to show himself as an effective curial propagandist.

Social psychologists have described a cultural phenomenon known as *impression management,* that is, "the conscious or unconscious attempt to control images that are projected in real or imagined social situations."[6] This has been seen as an important governing principle in much social and individual action. One functions as one's own publicist, as it were, and attempts in various ways to achieve one's conscious or unconscious goals through control of the manner in which one is perceived.

My argument regarding the *De curiae commodis* is that Lapo there engages in strategic, self-presenting impression management, to show what a good curial insider he could be if given the opportunity. Beyond this, he himself functions occasionally as a fifteenth-century social psychologist, analyzing the behavior of some of his curial contemporaries based on just these sorts of assumptions about human behavior. Of course, there is no great similarity between Lapo and modern social psychologists, since Lapo assumes an objective moral criterion by which one can judge good and bad. For Lapo, that criterion is the correct practice of the virtues (including those that can be practiced with wealth) toward the end of leading an upright life.

---

6. B.R. Schlenker, *Impression Management: The Self-Concept, Social Identity, and Interpersonal Relations* (Monterey, Calif., 1980), 6.

CHAPTER 5

Introduction to the Latin Text

Sigla

B = MS London, Brit. Libr. Cotton Cleopatra C.V (folia 112–41). Sec. XVI. (*Iter* 4:140b.) See also A.G. Watson, "Thomas Allen of Oxford and His Manuscripts," in *Medieval Scribes, Manuscripts, and Libraries: Essays Presented to N.R. Ker,* ed. M.B. Parkes and A.G. Watson (London, 1978), 279–314, at 300 and 309. B^1 = hand of modern (eighteenth/nineteenth century?) annotator who corrected the text against an authoritative copy. Seen in person.

F = MS Florence, BN Magl. XXIII.126 (folia 65–93). Sec. XV. Autograph. (*Iter* 1:139.) F^1 = Lapo's own hand, correcting himself; F^2 = second hand (folia 95–107); F^3 = possible nonautograph annotating hand. Seen in person.

G = MS Florence, BN Ser. Pan. 123. Sec. XV. (*Iter* 1:145.) G^1 = contemporary annotating hand. Seen in person.

N = MS Naples, BN VIII.G.31. Sec. XV. (*Iter* 1:428.) Seen in person.

P = MS Paris, BN Lat. 1616 (folia 137–62). Sec. XV. (*Iter* 3:215b.) There is a description of this manuscript in P. Lauer, ed., *Catalogue général des manuscrits latins,* vol. 2 (nos. 1439–2692) (Paris, 1940), 90–92. P^1 = contemporary annotating hand. Seen in person. In addition to the information in Lauer, one can add a codicological note. The paper is almost undoubtedly from the 1450s to 1460s and French. Compare the three different watermarks (on, e.g., ff. iii, 26, and 156) with C.-M. Briquet, *Les filigranes,* 4 vols. (nos. 365–88, 1680, and 6911) (Leipzig, 1923). The scribe was surely French; in addition to the look of the hand, the numeration (done in the hand of the scribe) gives this away. At f. 181, for

instance, it is as follows: "CiiiiI," with two small *x*s on top of the small *i*s (so Centquatrevingtun etc.).

V = MS Vatican City, BAV Vat. Lat. 939 (folia 195–215). Sec. XV. For a complete description of this manuscript, see A. Pelzer, *Codices Vaticani Latini*, vol. 2, pt. 1, *Codices 679–1139* (Vatican City, 1931), 368–74. Seen in person.

Sch. = R. Scholz's reading (of V), in his "Eine humanistische Schilderung der Kurie aus dem Jahre 1438, herausgegeben aus einer vatikanischen Handschrift," in *Quellen und Forschungen aus italienischen Archiven und Bibliotheken* 16 (1914): 108–53.
add. = addidit, addiderunt.
canc. = cancellavit.
cod./codd. = codex/codices.
coni. = coniecit.
corr. = correxit.
mar. d. = margine dextra.
mar. inf. = margine inferiore.
mar. sin. = margine sinistra.
mar. sup. = margine superiore.
om. = omisit, omiserunt.

Description of F

The base text of this edition is F, the only manuscript version that is traditionally believed to be an autograph. Although there are ample citations from this manuscript in the work of Luiso,[1] it has nonetheless hitherto not been fully described in any of the standard catalogues. A fifteenth-century paper manuscript, F has 107 numbered folia, plus seven unnumbered (three at the beginning, four at the end), here designated as i, ii, iii, and rear i, rear ii, rear iii, and rear iv, written in two hands (sec. I, ff. 1–93; sec. II, ff. 95–107).
    Folia i and i[v:] blank.
    Folio ii: in a seventeenth-century hand, a table of contents. The page is interesting and deserves to be reproduced in full:

[Later hand] XXIII, 126 *[indicating the Magliabechiano number]*

---

1. See, e.g., Luiso, 273–78, 290 n. 3, 293 n. 1.

[*Seventeenth-century hand:*]
N° 588
Lapi Castelliunculi, Vita Artaxersis 1
et Arati ex plutarco 19
De prefectis equitum ex xenophonte 49
Dialogus de Curie Romane commodis
eiusdem 65
Originale
Eiusdem prefatio in Isocratis oratione ad Demonicum 95
Luciani libelli duo in latinum per ipsum lapum
conversi 101 nel 1438 in circa
Del senatore Carlo di Tommaso Strozzi
1670

The position of the word *originale* indicates that the inventory writer believed that everything up to this point was from the hand of Lapo himself and that there is a change of hands beginning at folio 95 with Lapo's translation of Isocrates' *Oratio ad Demonicum* (cf. infra).

Folio ii^v: blank.

(Folio iii [with iii^v] is one of two vellum folia binding the manuscript; on iii there are inventory numbers.)

Folio iii^v: a partial table of contents and an elegantly fashioned drawing of the melancholic Lapo; at the bottom of the page there is an epigram: "Morì nella cit<t>à di Vinegia, anno MCCCCXXXVIII, del mese d'ot<t>obre d'età d'an<n>i XXXIII di morbo."

Folia 1–18: Plutarch, *Vita Artaxerxis*, trans. Lapo, with preface to Duke Humphrey of Gloucester, 1–2v. See Sammut, *Unfredo*, 168–71, for an edition of the preface, which was finished "ex bononia iii nonas decembris Mccccxxxvii," that is, 3 December 1437.

Translation:

ARTOTERXIS PERSARUM REGIS VITA PER LAPUM CASTELLI-UNCULUM IN LATINUM CONVERSA.

[*inc. f. 3*] ARTOXERXES Ille primus Xerxe patre natus ex persarum regibus tum facilitate humanitate tum maxime animi magnitudine prestitit . . . [*expl. trans. f. 18*] . . . mansuetudinis et clementiae existimationem assecutus est quam non mediocriter auxit ochus, qui immanitate cunctos et crudelitate superavit. FINIS FELICITER P(RI)DIE IDUS OCTOBRIS Mccccxxxvii [*14 October 1437*]. INCIPIT ARATUS EODEM DIE.

Folio 18v: blank.

Folia 19–46: Plutarch, *Vita Arati*, trans. Lapo, with preface to Giuliano Cesarini, 19–20v. See Celenza, "Parallel Lives," for an edition of the preface, which was finished "ex feraria xviii kalendas augusti 1438," that is, 15 July 1438.

Translation:

ARATI SICYONII VITA PER LAPUM CASTELLIUNCULUM LATINUM CONVERSA INCIPIT.

[inc. f. 21] Chrysippus philosophus tritum quoddam veteri sermone proverbium eius credo tristitiam reformidans, convenisse mutatoque verbo leniorem ad partem traduxisse videtur . . . *[expl. trans. f. 46]* . . . Itaque Antigonici regni sublatis haeredibus eius omne genus interiit. Arati autem genus Sicyone et Pellene usque ad nostram pervenit aetatem. FINIS FELICITER ἡμέρα τῇ ὑστάτῃ τοῦ ὀκτοβρίου μημὸς *[lege μηνὸς]* ὥρᾳ ἕκτῃ τῆς νύκτος, ἔτει χιλιόστῳ καὶ τε[ο]τ[α]ρακοσίῳ καὶ τ<ρ>ιακοσίῳ καὶ ἕπτῳ ἀπὸ τῆς τοῦ κυρίου γενέσεως *[31 October 1437]*.

Folia 46v–48v: blank.

Folia 49–62v: Xenophon, *Praefectus equitum*, with preface to Guaspar Villanovensis, 49–50v. See Luiso, 293–95, for an almost complete edition of the preface.

Translation:

XENOPHONTIS SOCRATICI ORATORIS CLARISSIMI PRAEFECTUS EQUITUM INCIPIT FELICITER.

[inc. f. 51] PRINCIPIO QUIDEM CAESIS HOSTIIS A DIIS IMMORtalibus precari oportet, ut dent nobis ea cogitare, loqui, atque agere . . . *[expl. traductio f. 62v]* . . . Est autem consentaneum ipsos magis iis hominibus consulere velle qui non modo quid faciendum sit, cum necessitas instat, sciscitantur, verum etiam secundis in rebus et pro voluntate fluentibus quae possunt religiose casteque deos et colunt et venerantur. Τέλος θεῷ χάριν.

Finis viiii° Kalendas Octobris post horam iiii(a)m noctis bononiae in domo reverendissimi patris Domini F(rancisci) CAR(dinalis) VEN(erabilis) S(ancti) D(omini) N(ostri) Camerarii.

Lapus Castelliunculus ex Xenophonte traduxit ex Greco.

Folia 63–64v: blank.

Folia 65–93: *Dialogus de curiae commodis*. The letters designating interlocutors in the dialogue are written in red ink until section VIII, 4 at f. 85v.

Folia 93v–94v: blank.

Folia 95–101 (F² begins): Isocrates, *Oratio ad Demonicum,* trans. Lapo, with preface to Prospero Colonna, 95–95v. See Luiso, 290–91, for a partial edition of the preface.

Translation:

[inc. traductio f. 96] <C>Um in aliis permultis bonorum atque improborum sentencias et opiniones inter se diferre, demonice, licet intueri tum in usu vite et consuetudine maxime dissidere . . . *[expl. trans. f. 101]* . . . Ac vix ullus poterit impedimenta nature huiusmodi industria diligenciaque superare. Finis Huius operis ysocratis.

Folia 101–7: [Luciani De fletu et De somnio], trans. Lapo, with preface to Pope Eugenius IV, ff. 101–2. See Luiso, 276–78, for an almost complete edition of the preface.

Translations:

[inc. De fletu f. 102] <O>pere precium videtur esse que in fletibus a multitudine fiunt queque c(ir)cuitum observare et que contra a consolantibus eos . . . *[expl. De fletu f. 105]* . . . quod multitudo hominum mortem suppremum terribilem omnium esse opinetur.

[inc. De somnio f. 105] <C>UM PRIMUM essem ad pubertatem etate ipsa provectus et puerili institucioni iam modum statuissem, patet consilium capiebat habitis amicorum colloquiis inquam me petissimum disciplinam perdiscendam traduceret . . . *[expl. De somnio f. 107 but with interrupted text]* . . . Denique ex me brevi rerum omnium . . .

Folia rear i–rear iv: blank.

F, Folio 1–93 as an Autograph Manuscript

The notion that F is an autograph is reasonable. Many things about folia 1–93 (before the change of hands) make F up to that point seem like an author's copybook rather than the work simply of a scribe, even one who corrected himself a lot. First, there are numerous corrections. F is rife with erasures and substitutions for these erased passages. The hand of the writer and corrector in these first ninety-three folia is consistent, and the numerous corrections are also consistently in the same hand. The same symbols for corrections and insertions are used throughout. In addition, at the end of each piece of work in the manuscript, Lapo tells where and when he was when the work was completed ("ego Lapus absolvi" etc.); this information, at least for the De curiae commodis, is lacking in the other manuscript copies of the works. Finally, throughout the manu-

script there are passages as well as individual words written in Greek. Lapo's hand in Greek has been identified, and the Greek in F is written in the same hand.[2] There is thus no reason at this point to doubt the traditional identification of this manuscript as autograph.

A comparison with the readings of the other manuscripts leads to the conclusion that F was seen as an authoritative text that may have been used for an intermediate version, a hyparchetype, now unavailable.[3] V, P, B, G, and N uniformly follow the main corrections in F, corrections that are sometimes somewhat involved. The variations are mainly orthographical, but there are some passages where the scribes seem to have skipped a line, misread a word, or perhaps suggested their own version of a specific text in question.

There are a few suspicious mistakes and particularities that V, P, G, and N share but that are not present in F.[4] Yet it does not seem likely that any of these served as a root for the others in that group, since there are also certain particularities that they do not share.[5] Thus it could be that they were copied from an intermediate version now unavailable. Perhaps this hypothetical hyparchetype was a (dedication?) copy redacted by

---

2. See the Greek *Schriftprobe* of Lapo in P. Eleuteri and P. Canart, "Lapo da Castiglionchio il Giovane (c. 1406–1438)," no. LXXIV in their *Scrittura greca nell'umanesimo italiano* (Milan, 1991). See also D. Harlfinger, *Die Textgeschichte der pseudo-aristotelischen Schrift* Περὶ ἀτόμων γραμμῶν: *Ein kodokologisch-kulturgeschichtlicher Beitrag zur Klärung der Überlieferungsverhältnisse im Corpus aristotelicum* (Amsterdam, 1971), 431; "Die Überlieferungsgeschichte der eudemischen Ethik," in *Akten des 5 Symposium Aristotelicum*, ed. P. Moreaux and D. Harlfinger, Peripatoi I (Berlin, 1971), 1–50, at 50. It is unsurprising that Lapo's Greek hand resembles the early Greek hand of his teacher Filelfo, although there are some distinctions to be made, such as the way each forms the letters ξ, λ, π, and τ; cf. P. Eleuteri, "Francesco Filelfo copista e possessore di codici greci," in *Paleografia e codicologia greca: Atti del II Colloquio internazionale (Berlino-Wolfenbüttel, 17–21 ottobre 1983)*, ed. D. Harlfinger and G. Prato, 2 vols. (Alessandria, 1991), 1:163–79, 2:107–14, at 1:166.
3. For the term *hyparchetype*, see M.L. West, *Textual Criticism and Editorial Technique* (Stuttgart, 1973), 33.
4. Shared by V, P, G, and N: III.28: hodie posuisse videor] posuisse videar hodie *V; * posuisse videor hodie *PGN*. IV.21: suppeditate] suppeditate abunde *VPGNB*. VI.5: cogitis] cognitis *VPGN*. VII.4: enim *om. VPGN*. VII.23: in *om. VPGN*. VII.36: sit] est *VPGNB*. VII.38: invidiam] iniuriam *VPGNB*. VIII.16: L *om. VPGN*. VIII.28: eo *om. VPGN*. VIII.51: assidue *om. VPGN*. VIII.54: conformarit] conformant *VPGN*. IX.2: aut *om. VPGN*. IX.5: admirabilis] laudabilis *VPGN*.
5. Not shared by V, P, G, and N: III.19: semper *om. PGN*. V.5: huius aetatis *om. VGNB; * virum *om. GN*. V.12: ubertatem] libertatem *VPNB*. V.13: hominibus] hominibusque *PGNB*. VI.10: aliquod] quoddam *VPN*. VII.23: reliquis omnibus] omnibus reliquis *PB; * paratissimos] peritissimos *PG*. VIII.1: illis *om. VPGB*. VIII.27: magisque] magis *PGNB*. VIII.39: non] non modo non *PGNB*. VIII.46: reicidendum] recedendum *VPNB*. IX.7: malunt] volunt *VN*.

Lapo himself. If it was, he would have done it soon after he finished his final draft in F, since he died approximately two months later. Basing the text primarily on F, however, is justifiable even if there was an intermediate version that is now lost, since F represents the closest thing we have to a final authorial redaction.[6]

Justification for a New Edition

There has been only one other complete version of the *De curiae commodis,* that of Richard Scholz, the noted scholar of medieval church politics and of the legal history of the church. He based his edition only on V, itself a fascinating manuscript possessing many interesting texts directly relevant to Scholz's own field.[7] Either inadequacies in Scholz's edition or inadequacies in V (since his edition was based only on V) would be justification enough for a new edition of the text. In this case, both situations obtain. As one would expect, there are three types of inadequacies: inadequacies of V itself, inadequacies of Scholz's reading or mistaken conjectures because of inadequacies in V, and basic errors in Scholz's reading.

Examples of the first kind of inadequacy are as follows (ordered according to section numbers):

I.4: deletaeque] delecteque *V.*

I.7: haberis] habere *V.*

II.8: spectarent] expectarent *V.*

II.19: tantum vero abest ut verear me abste convinci] tantum vero abs te convinci *V.*

III.10: iocos] locos *V.*

III.14: principiis] principis *V.*

III.23: moveatur *om. V.* religio] religione *V.* perstringat *om. V.*

IV.13: dementiae] clemencie *V.*

IV.26: expositas] exquisitas *V.*

V.5: huius aetatis *om. V.*

---

6. As mentioned earlier, this is not a diplomatic edition of F. Only occasionally, however, does F not present the best reading; in those cases, the changes are adopted in the text, and F's reading is noted in the apparatus.

7. See the full description of this manuscript in Pelzer, *Codices Vaicani Latini,* cited earlier in this chapter, at siglum V.

V.12: expetendus] expectendus *V*. ubertatem] libertatem *V*.

VI.2: deferuntur] differuntur *V*.

VI.8: scribis *om. V*.

VII.11: praecipuam] precipiam *V*.

VII.29: coquos, fartores, pulmentarios] quos factores pulmentaris *V*.

VII.38: propositum est, ut tecta cuiusquam flagitia detegam, aut mihi *om. V*.

VIII.42: taetris] certis *V*.

Some examples of the second and third kinds of inadequacy are as follows:

I.8: me Kl. Iuliis in] III° Kl. Iulii *sic Sch*. recepissem] recedissem *sic legit Sch*. In this case, Scholz's misreading of the date led him to ignore the fact that the word *me* was present, indicating that *recipere* was to be taken in its reflexive sense, that is, as *se recipere*, "to withdraw to, to retire to." Owing to his misreading of the date, he was forced to read *recepissem* as *recedissem*.

I.9: honestandae] honestam de *sic legit Sch*.

I.10: refectus] reffertus *sic Sch*.

III.10: Omitte] Dimitte *sic Sch*.

III.13: concluseris] conduxeris *sic Sch*.

III.14: remitto] peremitto *sic V*; permitto *sic Sch*.

III.15: ex receptis] exceptis *V*; expetis *coni. Sch*. vi] in *sic legit Sch*.

III.27: videantur] vedeantur *sic V*; reddantur *sic legit Sch*.

IV.9: publico] preco *sic V*; presto *sic coni. Sch*.

IV.22: inuxerunt] inunxerunt *coni. Sch*. 350. improbissimus; curialis bonus, homo *om. Sch*.

IV.26: et praestantissimi *om. Sch*.

VI.11: requirant *om. Sch*.

VII.2: videre in] viderem *sic legit Sch*. et videri *sic coni. Sch*.

VII.21: rerum] verum *sic legit Sch*.

VIII.5: voluntates] voluptates *coni. Sch*. minus] nimis *sic leg. Sch*.

VIII.6: eorum] rorum *sic V*; rerum *sic legit Sch*.

VIII.11: cessatio] cessans *sic legit Sch*.

VIII.13: nimis] minus *sic legit Sch*.

VIII.19: concesseris] censeris *V*; censuisti *coni. Sch*.

VIII.20: quinetiam] quiin et *V*; quin immo et *sic legit Sch*.

VIII.26: abdicandi; si probi, nonne satius est] abdicandi si *[tum vocab-ulum desiderat]* nonne satius est *V;* abdicandi sunt; nonne sanctius est *sic Sch.*

IX.2: gratia *om. Sch.*

IX.11: et turbulentissimos *om. Sch.*

The examples given above constitute a small sampling of the total number of differences. But as one can see, there are a number of substantive variations in V as well as quite a few omissions and misreadings on the part of Scholz, all of which are enough to make the sense fuzzy around the edges at best and to violate the sense considerably at worst.

Lapo as Scribe and Author

F presents us with interesting examples of the process of Renaissance writing. In addition, the manuscript reflects a consistent attitude on the part of its author toward orthography and punctuation, and the text itself shows some of Lapo's stylistic particuliarities.

As mentioned earlier, erasures and corrections in Lapo's hand abound in F. The pursuant changes reflect the process of composition and usually tend toward sharpening the argument and making it more precise. Typically, Lapo, desiring to insert a section into the text, places a symbol in the text that corresponds to a symbol in the margin; next to (or underneath) this marginal symbol there is a small portion of text to be inserted. So that the reader may have an idea of the character of these changes, I offer a few examples (the principle loci of difference are italicized).

The first comes from section III, 2, where the interlocutors are beginning their discussion of happiness. Originally, the passage read:

> L: Beatitudinem dico non humanam, de qua tanta inter philosophos contentio *est, et quam alii in alia re ponendam censuerint;* sed divinam illam quae castis, sanctis, religiosisque viris post mortem ab immortali Deo tribuitur.

> [L: And I'm not talking about a merely human happiness, about which there is so much disagreement among philosophers, *and which some think should be placed in something else.* But it is that divine happiness that immortal God gives to chaste, holy, and religious men after death.]

Revised, however, the text reads:

> *L:* Beatitudinem dico non humanam, de qua tanta inter philosophos contentio *est, cum eam alii in virtute, alii in honoribus, alii in divitiis, alii in bona valetudine, alii in voluptate, alii item alia in re ponendam censuerint;* sed divinam illam quae castis, sanctis, religiosisque viris post mortem ab immortali Deo tribuitur.

> [*L:* And I'm not talking about a merely human happiness, about which there is so much disagreement among philosophers. *Some think the locus of human happiness should be placed in virtue, others in [worldly] honors, others in wealth, others in good health, others in pleasure, while others still think it should be placed somewhere else.* But it is that divine happiness that immortal God gives to chaste, holy, and religious men after death.]

In revising his thought, Lapo has given things a bit more *akribeia* and has also taken greater account of the arguments at the beginning of Aristotle's *Nicomachean Ethics* (I.4–5), where Aristotle discusses his predecessors' opinions about the nature of happiness.

Another place, in section III, 11, shows the same tendency toward greater precision. The interlocutors are in the course of the same argument, that the curia is a good place because it is a concentrated seat of religion. Originally, the passage read:

> *L:* Ita prorsus. In genere enim bonorum quanto maius, tanto praestabilius et melius. *Illud quoque perspicuum,* gratius Deo esse frequentius coli quam rarius, et a plurimis quam a paucis.

> [*L:* Just so. For in the genus of goods, the more of something there is, the more preferable and better it is. *This also is clear,* that to God it is more agreeable to be worshiped more frequently than less and by many rather than by few.]

The revised version reads:

> *L:* Ita prorsus. In genere enim bonorum quanto maius, tanto praestabilius et melius. *Ex hoc* illud quoque perspicuum *fit—cum reli-*

gio Dei sit cultus—gratius Deo esse frequentius coli quam rarius, et a plurimis quam a paucis.

[*L:* Just so. For in the genus of goods, the more of something there is, the more preferable and better it is. In addition, *since religion is the worship of God, this makes* it clear that to God it is more agreeable to be worshiped more frequently than less and by many rather than by few.]

A final notable example from the same argument (at III.13) occurs as Angelo reveals that he understands Lapo's intention, which is to compel him to admit that the curia is a place where there is much religious practice and is therefore good. Originally, the passage had run as follows:

A: Sentio quo me his argutiis tuis concluseris, ut mihi necesse sit huiusmodi esse curiam confiteri; quod si antea percepissem, profecto nunquam effecisses, nec nunc quidem, ut id tibi concedam, a me ulla ratione *extorquere poteris.*

[*A:* I am beginning to understand that your arguments are leading me to a point where I'll have to admit that the curia is just such a place. But if I had understood this earlier, then you never would have carried it through, and certainly now you won't make me admit it with any argument.]

The revised version reads:

A: Sentio quo me his argutiis tuis concluseris, ut mihi necesse sit huiusmodi esse curiam confiteri; quod si antea percepissem, profecto nunquam effecisses, nec nunc quidem, ut id tibi concedam, a me ulla ratione *extorxeris. Quid enim a curia alienius quam religio esse potest?*

[*A:* I am beginning to understand that your arguments are leading me to a point where I'll have to admit that the curia is just such a place. But if I had understood this earlier, then you never would have carried it through, and certainly now you won't make me admit it with any argument. *For what can be more alien to the curia than religion?*]

While most of the changes tend simply toward greater precision and clarity, perhaps here we see a *dopopensiero,* where Lapo decided to take a risk and have Angelo mouth a radical, sarcastic bit of anticurial polemic.

The most important orthographical features (in addition to those noted at the end of the previous section "F as an Autograph Manuscript") are as follows. First, in almost every case of words that with classical orthography are spelled with *ti* followed by an *a, o,* or *u* (e.g., *praestantia, etiam, Veneratio, hospitium*), the words in F are spelled with *ti.*[8] In addition, Latin words that are either transliterated from Greek or have Greek roots and include an upsilon are spelled with a *y.*[9] Finally, Italianizing usages of the initial *h* or lack thereof (as in the word *abundantia* being spelled *habundancia* etc.) are streamlined in F and brought into line with much of what we now consider classical orthography.[10] The aforementioned characteristics thus reflect a fairly consistent concern on Lapo's part for employing a classicizing orthography.

Lapo's punctuation in F is interesting. Like most manuscript punctuation of the period, it is more phraseological than logical and could serve, if looked at from one perspective, almost as instructions for reading the text aloud. To mention just one case, question marks appear often when the voice would be raised interrogatively within an interrogative sentence, not necessarily only at the end of the sentence.

This is not the place for a study of Lapo's Latin prose style, but some salient features do come into relief. First, Lapo presents some interesting wordplay, such as *difficile . . . deficientibus* (II.11); *casu . . . incidi* (II.15); *Deprehensum . . . reprehensio* (II.17); *cognitione dignissimum, cognitumque plurimi* (III.6); and *consentiunt . . . sententia concessuri sunt* (VIII.45).

There are a few features that might be characterized as Italianisms.[11]

---

8. In V and P they are often spelled with *ci;* the rest are haphazard.

9. In most of the rest of the codices they are spelled with an *i.* So, e.g., one will see "tyrannus," "Pythagoras," etc. in F, versus "tirannus," "Pitagoras," etc. in V. The orthography of P and the others in this respect, however, is haphazard. Also, the words *mihi* and *nihil* are spelled in V and often in P and the other codices as "michi" and "nichil," whereas in F they are consistently spelled "mihi" and "nihil."

10. In V, P, G, N, and B this is not so.

11. On Italian humanist Neo-Latin particularities, see S. Rizzo, *Il lessico filologico degli umanisti* (Rome, 1973), passim.

An interesting case shows the vernacular creeping into Neo-Latin usage. Here is the sentence (VII.33).

> *A:* [33] Nec vero privatim tantum et alienae domi hoc exequuntur munus, sed qui paulo lautiores sunt, *apothecas conductas habent* et in publico epulas vendunt.

As we can see, Lapo has here employed a finite auxiliary verb and a participle to express the perfect, just as is done in many modern languages; he uses *apothecas conductas habent* when he could just as easily have used *apothecas conduxerunt.*

Another Italianism occurs when Lapo spells the word *transferamus* as *trasferamus* (II.15), probably exactly how he pronounced it (cf. modern Italian *trasferiamo*).

Lapo's use of the word *confabulonibus* (VII.24) has an Italian feel to it, with the -*on*- part of the word (i.e., confabulo*n*ibus) showing that Lapo means not just storytellers but men who tell very many stories or exaggerated ones. In modern Italian, the word *furbone* is used to describe someone who is not just savvy and clever, *furbo,* but rather overly so. In a modern Italian word formation analogous to our case, the word *mangione* describes someone who likes to eat, *mangiare,* a lot. Here the word to indicate the exaggerated state has no noun but is formed directly from the verb, in the same way, probably, that Lapo forms the word *confabulones* to describe men who like to tell stories, *confabulari,* a lot.

Another interesting instance pops up when Lapo uses the word *carentia* as a feminine nominative singular. The word (essentially the neuter nominative plural present participle of *careo*) is common enough as a feminine nominative singular in medieval Latin but unattested before Chalcidius and Boethius (where it is used to mean something like *privatio,* i.e., Greek στέρησις).[12] The sentence is as follows (VIII.22): "Necessitas enim et bonorum quibus indigemus carentia violentissima omnino res est, . . ." Perhaps Lapo was thinking of the Italian *carenza.*

Lapo presents us with an interesting case of tmesis, when he writes *non enim dum* to express *nondum enim* (III.10).

Finally, there are at least two instances where Lapo shows rhythmic awareness. The first is his quotation of a hexameter translation of

---

12. See, s.v. *carentia,* C. Du Cange, *Glossarium mediae ac infimae latinitatis . . . ,* 7 vols. (Paris, 1840–50) and *Lexicon linguae latinae.*

Odyssey I.3–4 (IV.8): "Varias iactatus in oras et mores hominum multo-rum novit et urbes."[13] The second is Lapo's proverb (IV.22): "Curialis bonus, homo improbissimus; curialis bonus, homo scelestissimus et omnibus viciis cohopertus."[14]

Editing and Translating Principles

I have added section numbers and section subdivisions to the text to facil-itate reference and have given the different sections my own titles, which appear in square brackets at the head of each section. Notes that have to do with variant manuscript readings as well as marginal annotations in the various manuscripts are placed in the apparatus to the Latin text. Explanatory notes and notes relating to Lapo's allusions and quotations are placed with the translation. I have punctuated according to sense. In order not to break the back of a text already overburdened with notes, I have not noted in the apparatus spelling differences among the manu-scripts that do not change the lexical or grammatical meanings of words.

Even the slightest of other variant readings have been noted. This calls for a word of explanation. If a manuscript has *iis* instead of F's *his,* for example, I have always included this sort of admittedly minor difference in the apparatus. Given that we have what amounts to a final authorial, autograph redaction, some might argue that such textual differences are inconsequential. Indeed, if we were dealing with a classical text that would be the case. In other words, if one were editing a classical text and were so fortunate as to have an authoritative autograph (an impossible situation), the rest of the manuscripts would be simply *codices descripti* and could easily be eliminated from anything more than cursory consul-tation in creating an edition. In classical textual criticism one attempts to come as close as possible to the version that the original author intended, and this is also the goal in Neo-Latin textual criticism. However, since

---

13. I have not yet been able to determine whether Lapo used his own translation or an already existing one, although Prof. Walther Ludwig has kindly informed me that Latin translations of the *Odyssey* were much rarer in Lapo's day than those of the *Iliad,* suggesting the possibility that the translation may be Lapo's own.

14. This proverb is unattested in both H. Walther, ed., *Lateinische Sprichwörter und Sentenzen des Mittelalters in alphabetischer Anordnung,* 5 vols. (Göttingen, 1963–67) and idem, *Lateinische Sprichwörter und Sentenzen des Mittelalters und der frühen Neuzeit in alphabetischer Anordnung,* 3 vols. (Göttingen, 1982–86). In the first of the two works, however, there are several proverbial sayings criticizing the curia; see "Curia" and "Curia romana," ad loc.

Renaissance sources are so much nearer to us in time, we can come closer to the historical context of an author's work by having as much information about it as possible—by knowing, in addition to the author's words and intentions, the environments (orthographical, paleographical, and otherwise) in which his or her work was read.[15]

This edition is based on F, and overwhelmingly F's authority has been followed. The edition, however, is not a diplomatic edition of F. I have not used the word *sic* in the text itself, and when I believe that Lapo misspelled a word, as opposed to using what might now seem an unusual late-Medieval/early-Renaissance orthography, I have corrected the text, either indicating the correction with carets <> or correcting the text silently and noting the original reading from F in the apparatus.

I have chosen to maintain certain aspects of F, assuming that they might be of interest to scholars. For instance, in F Lapo indicates all *ae* and *oe* diphthongs either by writing them out or by using an *e-caudata*. Given that he thus notices all diphthongs, and given that in an analogous area, Greek diacritics, Lapo was especially precise (on the advice of his teacher Filelfo), I have decided simply to render the diphthongs in classical fashion, for the sake of consistency.[16] Consistently understanding the diphthong was obviously important to Lapo, and this should be respected in the edition. However, as stated, this is not a diplomatic edition, and I believe that rendering the cedillas literally would simply have marred the text visually and would not have contributed to any greater historical or literary understanding; hence my decision to use classicizing orthography. Not all will be satisfied with this, of course.

There are other particularities. Lapo habitually renders *quamobrem* as *quam obrem* in F and is followed in this practice by V; the other versions are haphazard. I have chosen for the sake of consistency to render this spelling as it is in F, that is, as *quam obrem*. Lapo spells the word *cottidie* for the most part as *quottidie*, sometimes as *quotidie;* I have simply followed F. In two other cases Lapo redoubles consonants, writing *addiunctis* for *adiunctis* (I.11) and *iudiccare* for *iudicare* (II.6). He spells *abs te* as *abste* (II.6, 19), which I have followed. He renders *subactus* as *sub*

---

15. On Neo-Latin in general, see J. IJsewijn, *Companion to Neo-Latin Studies* (Amsterdam, New York, and Oxford, 1977).

16. Lapo's exactitude with respect to Greek diacritics can be seen by examining his Greek hand—it is very rare that one catches him in a mistake. See Celenza, "Parallel Lives," 141. For Filelfo's practices, see M. Cortesi, "Umanesimo greco," in *Lo spazio letterario del medioevo*, pt. 1. *Il medioevo latino*, vol. III: *La ricezione del testo* (Rome, 1995), 457–507.

actus (IV.10). In two cases he uses the letter *x* interestingly, spelling *inusserunt* as *inuxerunt* (IV.22) and *inusta* as *inuxta* (VIII.8).

Lapo's Latin is elegant and functional and is well in line with the Ciceronian standards of his generation. Given this, he often employs long, periodic constructions, which would be impossible to maintain in their integrity in English, so I have often broken up Lapo's sentences into shorter sentences in my translation. I have also tried to steer as skillfully as possible between the Scylla of overliteralism and the Charibdys of trendy but ephemeral locutions. Suffice it to say that my goal has been to provide a translation that is readable but also a reasonable guide to the Latin. I have annotated what seemed to be the most important citations and, where I have been able to discern them, allusions or reminiscences. In section VI of the dialogue, the interlocutors discuss various offices in the curial hierarchy; I have annotated the explicit mentions of various positions and offices. However, for two recent and more complete overviews of the structure of the curia, I refer the reader to the work of John D'Amico and Peter Partner.[17]

Finally, given the malleability of various Latin words, it was necessary to translate the same Latin word differently where it seemed appropriate. For instance, Lapo uses the word *animus* in different ways. When he speaks (in IV.21) of *perturbationibus animi* he seems to refer to the non-material part of a person, so I have translated the word there as "soul." But when, in an angry, hortatory passage (IV.25), he hopes that something might *excitaret* the *animos omnium,* he seems to use the word more generally, so I translate the word there as "spirits."[18] There are other, similar cases where I have tried to let prudence and common sense function as a guide.

---

17. See D'Amico, chap. 1; Partner, *Pope's Men.*

18. In other words, in this case I have borne in mind that for technical, university-based Renaissance philosophers (which Lapo, like most humanists, was not), words like *animus, spiritus,* etc. would have been used with a much more precise meaning.

Lapi Castelliunculi *De curiae commodis* Dialogus

//65// AD CLEMENTISSIMUM PATREM FRANCISCUM CONDOL-
MARIUM SACROSAN<C>TAE ROMANAE ECCLESIAE PRES-
BUTERUM CARDINALEM LAPI CASTELLIUNCULI DIALOGUS
INCIPIT DE CURIAE COMMODIS.[1]

[I. Praefatio]

[1] COMPLURES[2] esse scio, clementissime pater, partim veteres, partim
recentes—et ii quidem gravissimi atque eruditissimi viri—qui Athenien-
sium civitatem, quondam florentissimam urbanis institutis et bellicis,
maxime collaudandam putent; alios qui Spartiatarum principatum caeteris conentur praeferre, sanctissimis Lycurgi legibus constitutum; alios
qui Carthaginensium rempublicam, terrestribus maritimisque rebus
potentissimam, divinis laudibus ad coelum tollant; sed plurimos qui
Romanorum imperium quasi augustius[3] reliquis atque admirabilius non
laude modo,[4] sed etiam veneratione prosequantur. [2] Quas quidem ego
civitates numquam negabo meritissimo laudatas esse et laudari ab
omnibus debuisse; veruntamen ex iis[5] nullam arbitror cum hac Christi
monarchia, quae curia Romana dicitur, nec divinitate originis nec maies-

---

1. AD . . . COMMODIS] Dialogus super excellencia et dignitate curie Romane
supra ceteras policias et curias antiquorum et modernorum contra eos qui Romanam
curiam diffamant *V;* lapi de commodis curie romane *P;* Lapi a castelliunculo de curiae
romanae commodis dialogus *G;* Ad clementissimum patrem dominum franciscum
condolmarium sacrosancte romane ecclesie presbuterum cardinalem lapi castelliunculi dialogus incipit de curie commodis. lege feliciter *N atramento rubeo;* Lapi
casteliunculi dialogus incipit de curie commodis *B.*
2. cum plures *P.*
3. angustius *N.*
4. laude modo] modo laude *N.*
5. his *N.*

102

Lapo da Castiglionchio's Dialogue
On the Benefits of the Curia

HERE BEGINS LAPO DA CASTIGLIONCHIO'S DIALOGUE TO THE
MOST CLEMENT FATHER FRANCESCO CONDULMER, CARDI-
NAL PRIEST OF THE HOLY ROMAN CHURCH, ON THE BENE-
FITS OF THE CURIA.

[I. Preface]

[1] Most clement father, I know that there are many, some ancient, some
recent—and certainly they are the most serious and learned of men—who
think that Athens, a city once most flourishing with civilized as well as
warlike practices, is praiseworthy in the highest degree. There are some
who attempt to place the principate of the Spartans before the others, a
principate founded on the most holy laws of Lycurgus. There are some
who extol to high heaven with praises divine the republic of the
Carthaginians, which was most powerful on land and sea. But I know
that most honor the empire of the Romans with praise and even veneration, as if it were more majestic and more admirable than the rest. [2]
Certainly, I shall never deny that these cities have been praised most
deservedly or that they ought to be praised by all. Nevertheless, I do not
think that any of them can be compared with this monarchy of Christ,
the Roman curia. Think of its divinity of origin, the grandeur, so to

tate, ut ita dicam, regis, nec reliquorum principum multitudine, praestantia, dignitate, nec rerum divinarum observantia, cultu,[6] religione, nec
firmitate sui et stabilitate, nec diuturnitate temporis posse conferri.[7] [3]
Et enim cum illarum nulla unquam diu eodem statu permanserit, haec
sola, numquam mutatis prioribus institutis, non variata administrandi
ratione ac forma, sed servatis semper incorruptis Christi maiorum
patrumque[8] vestigiis, non integra modo ac[9] inviolata, verum etiam aucta
opibus atque amplificata millesimum iam et[10] quadringentesimum
annum transcendit. [4] Nec vero,[11] ut illae, quarum aliae crescentes,
extinctae deletaeque[12] sunt, aliae evectae ad summum aut civilibus dis-
cordiis aut armis hostilibus conciderunt, ita haec[13] oppressa saepius a
sceleratis nefariisque[14] hominibus haud[15] interiit, sed se continuo[16]
erexit[17] et florens pollensque quottidie magis eo ma//65v//gnitudinis, auctoritatis, venerationisque excrevit ut eam omnes Christiani principes,
gentes, nationes reginam suam et dominam fateantur esse[18] eique, cui
divinitus in ea rerum summa permissa est, non ut regi alicui[19] et tyranno
pareant,[20] sed ut Deo in terris religiose[21] obtemperent.

[5] Ex quo perspicue intelligi potest eos omnes quos antea memoravi
principatus, ut humana cetera, fragiles, instabiles,[22] caducosque fuisse et
humano consilio conparatos; hunc autem verum, certum, stabilemque
esse, divino numine institutum et idcirco sempiternum fore. [6] Itaque
quorundam improborum detestabilem procacitatem, ne dicam an amen-
tiam et temeritatem, execrari vehementer[23] soleo, qui in curiam
Romanam veluti in turpissimum aliquem et foedissimum locum petu-

---

6. observantia] observantia et *V.*

7. confiteri *P.*

8. patrumque] que patrum *B.*

9. atque *B.*

10. iam et] atque *B.*

11. non *V.*

12. delecteque *V.*

13. haec *om. V.*

14. *corr. ex* nephariis sceleratisque *F¹.*

15. aut *V.*

16. sed] sed de *V;* sed se *N.*

17. exexit *G.*

18. esse *om. B.*

19. alicuius *B.*

20. pateant *B.*

21. religiose] religiose ut *N.*

22. instabilesque *G.*

23. *corr. ex* vehementer execrari *F¹.*

speak, of its king, the multitude, excellence, and dignity of the rest of the [curial] princes, the observance of divine matters, the worship, the religion, the steadfastness and stability, the durability through time. [3] And indeed, since none of those cities ever has endured in the same state, this city alone, with its earlier institutions unchanged, the contours of its administration unaltered, and the vestiges of Christ and the great church fathers preserved always uncorrupted, has now passed its fourteen hundredth year not only whole and inviolate but even augmented and greater in wealth. [4] And it is not like those cities some of which were extinguished and destroyed as they grew, others of which—even after they had raised themselves to the highest point—fell either to civil unrest or to hostile arms. The church did not perish, even though so oppressed so often by wicked, nefarious men, but rather it stood strong without interruption. It flourished and daily grew more powerful in its greatness, authority, and reverence, and it did so to such an extent that all Christian princes, peoples, and nations confess it their queen and liege lady, to whom the control of all things has been divinely entrusted. Thus they do not yield as to some king or tyrant but rather obey it religiously, as God on earth.

[5] From this one can easily understand that all those principates that I named before were fragile, unstable, and fleeting and, like other human things, established by human judgment.[1] But one can also understand that this principate is true, certain, and stable and, since it was founded by divine command, that it will be eternal. [6] This is why I usually execrate the detestable impudence of certain shameless men, or even—might I say it?—the insanity and heedlessness of those who attack the Roman curia petulantly and rashly, as if they were attacking some scandalous, disgraceful place.[2] They think that all curialists are to be counted as

---

1. For Lapo's "ut humana cetera, fragiles, instabiles, caducosque fuisse et humano consilio conparatos," cf. Cic. *Amic.* 102: "quoniam res humanae fragiles caducae sunt."

2. For Lapo's pairing of *procacitatem* with *petulanter,* cf. Tac. *Hist.* III.11: "tunc procacitatis et petulantiae certamen erat."

lanter et temere invehantur[24] curialesque omnes latronum numero
habendos censeant, et quod in ea nonnullos—quod[25] negari non potest—
nequam homines esse audierint, universos eadem turpitudine et
infamia[26] notent, quasi vero non aliis in locis longe plures nequioresque
inveniantur.[27]

[7] Quam obrem cum ego biennium iam[28] in curia et eo amplius[29] ita
sim versatus ut reliquum aetatis meae in ea statuerim mihi esse vivendum,
meae[30] partis esse putavi illorum comprimere audaciam ac maledicta
refellere susceptoque partis patrocinio me ipsum ac reliquos,[31] qui in
curia caste atque[32] integre vivunt, pro mea facultate defendere apud te,
qui in curia ipsa cum dignitate, auctoritate, potentia, tum[33] prudentia,
abstinentia, integritate, iustitia merito princeps haberis,[34] ut optime
causam cognoscere et aequissime iudicare possis.

[8] Igitur hoc mihi diu facere[35] cupienti commodissimum nuper
maximeque idoneum, ut[36] antea nunquam fortuna, tempus attulit.[37]
Nam //66//[38] cum post obitum[39] summi principis Iordani Ursini, cardinalis integerrimi et[40] religiosissimi viri, ex balneis Senensibus decedens,
quo eram cum illo una profectus, Ferariam me Kl. Iuliis in[41] curiam
recepissem,[42] in Angeli Racanatensis, hospitis et amici mei, domum
diverti, vehementer animo recenti illa calamitate commotus, ab eoque[43]
pro iure veteris hospitii et amicitiae liberaliter benigneque exceptus sum.

---

24. inveheantur *sic F;* invehantur *VGNB.*
25. quidem *V.*
26. infamie *N.*
27. nequioresque] nequiores et *V.*
28. iam *om. N.*
29. et eo amplius] et eo amplius et eo amplius *sic P.*
30. in ea statuerim mihi esse vivendum, meae] *om. G.*
31. non caste vivere in curia *in mar. d. atramento alio N (N²?).*
32. ac *B.*
33. cum *P.*
34. habere *V.*
35. diu facere] facere diu *G.*
36. ut] ut in *G.*
37. attulerit *P.*
38. *in mar. sup. titulus, atramento nigro:* LAPI CASTELLIUNCULI DIALOGUS
DE COMMODIS CURIAE ROMANAE HABITUS FERARIAE. COLLOC. LAPUS
ET ANGELUS. *Titulum cancellavit F¹.*
39. habitum *V.*
40. ac *B.*
41. III° Kl. Iulii *sic Sch.*
42. recedissem *sic legit Sch.*
43. eoque] eo *PB.*

thieves, and they hear that in the curia—and this cannot be denied—there are some vile men. They mark all with the same wretchedness and bad reputation, as if far more and far worse men are not found in other places.

[7] So, since I have been at the curia now for two years and because of this am somewhat more widely experienced—so much so that I have judged that I should live the rest of my life there—I have decided for my part to check their presumption and refute their maledictions. I have also thought that it is my task—having undertaken this defense—to defend in your eyes myself and the rest who live chastely and honestly in the curia, since you are justifiably considered there to be a prince of dignity, authority, and power, of prudence, abstinence, integrity, and justice. [I do this] so that you can know the case in the best manner and judge it most fairly.

[8] A while ago, then, time—in a way that fortune never had—made this task which I have been desiring to do for some time now suitable.[3] For after the death of the highest prince Giordano Orsini (purest of cardinals, most religious of men), I was on my way back down from the baths of Siena where I had traveled together with him. After I had arrived at the curia in Ferrara on the calends of July, I went to stay at the house of Angelo da Recanate, my host and friend, and since I was very moved in spirit by that recent calamity, he took me in generously and kindly,

---

3. For Lapo's "maximeque idoneum, ut antea nunquam fortuna, tempus attulit," cf. Cic. *Fam.* I.2.3: "tempus hoc magis idoneum quam unquam antea."

[9] Quo die apud illum sum pransus, nam casu prandentem[44] offendi, et ipse invitatus accubui, atque inter prandendum, sive ratus—id quod erat—me nonnihil perturbatum esse, sive hoc ex tristitia[45] vultus et taciturnitate mea perspexisset,[46] antea[47] plura questus de inopinato cardinalis casu deque meo incommodo, qui et talem virum et talem amicum amisissem, quo vivo non dubitaret mihi mearum fortunarum patronum et honestandae[48] dignitatis propugnatorem acerrimum numquam defuturum fuisse, me suavissimis et amicissimis verbis consolatus hortatusque est, ut tantum[49] deponerem moerorem iacturamque [rem] illam, etsi magnam, tamen necessariam atque irreparabilem[50] aequanimiter ferrem.

[10] Deinde cum et ego refectus[51] parumper animo excepissem, deploravimus simul ambo[52] casum[53] et orbitatem Romanae ecclesiae, quae gravissimis incommodis ac[54] difficultatibus circumventa suis spoliaretur principibus quo tempore illam afflictam et perditam ad suam obtinendam dignitatem eorum consiliis, ope ac praesidio sublevari maxime oporteret.

[11] Quo confecto sermone, pariter pransi surreximus a mensa et in hortum,[55] qui prope erat, deambulatum descendimus, ubi pluribus[56] inter arbores et vites silentio peractis spatiis fessi quiescendi gratia in herba[57] consedimus, atque ita inter sedentes[58] alius ortus est sermo ex superiore quodammodo ductus, quem ego post mecum repetens disputationis sententias in dialogum rettuli, omniaque ut erant tunc habita exprimere atque imitari conatus tuo nomini dedicavi, addiunctis eodem pluribus quae ad rem pertinebant, quo eorum lectio[59] suavior[60] tibi et gratior redderetur. [12] Quae tu ita legas velim ut, si qua tibi in iis[61]

---

44. *corr. ex* prandendem N^2.
45. tristitia] tristitia mei *N*.
46. prospexisset *V*.
47. antea] ante ea *B*.
48. honestam de *sic Sch.*
49. tam tum *V*.
50. irreprobabilem *V*.
51. reffertus *sic Sch.;* reffectus *V*.
52. simul ambo] ambo simul *P*.
53. causam *NB (et G?)*.
54. ad *V*.
55. *corr. ex* ortum F^1; ortum *VPNB*.
56. plurimus *N*.
57. herbam *N*.
58. sedente *N*.
59. letio *V*.
60. suavio *V;* suaviter *N*.
61. his *VN*.

with the hospitality of old friendship. [9] I had lunch with him that day, for by chance I came on him while he was eating, and since I was invited, I sat down. While we were eating, maybe he was aware that I was somewhat perturbed—which was the case—or perhaps he had noticed this from the sadness of my countenance and my taciturnity. Earlier he had complained much about the cardinal's unsuspected death and about my trouble. I had lost such a man, such a friend, who, when alive, left me with no doubt that I would never be lacking a patron of my fortunes and an ardent champion to defend my worth.[4] With the sweetest and friendliest of words, Angelo consoled me, urging me to put an end to such grief and bear the cardinal's death with equanimity as something that was to be given up and that, although great, was nevertheless necessary and irreparable.

[10] Then after I, too, was somewhat restored in spirit and had taken his advice, together we both bitterly lamented the fall, the want, of the Roman church,[5] which is surrounded by the most serious of troubles and difficulties and is being despoiled by its own princes, at a time when the church—which seems lost and abandoned beyond all hope of maintaining its worth—is greatly in need of being supported by their counsel, wealth, and aid.[6]

[11] After we had finished that talk and had both eaten, we got up from the table and went to walk down to the garden, which was nearby. There, after having walked quite a bit in silence amid trees and vines and having tired ourselves out, we sat down in the grass, to enjoy the quiet. And it was in this way, as we were sitting, that a second discussion arose, which in a certain way proceeded from the preceding one. I have gone over the arguments of our discussion and have re-created it in dialogue form, attempting to express and imitate everything as we had it then. I have dedicated it to your name. Certain things that pertained to the argument have been added to the dialogue, so that in your eyes it would read more elegantly and agreeably. [12] I would like you to read it in such a

---

4. For Lapo's "mearum fortunarum patronum et honestandae dignitatis propugnatorem acerrimum," cf. Cic. *Red. Sen.* 38: "propugnator mearum fortunarum et defensor adsiduus"; *Ad Brut.* I.11.1: "acerrimum propugnatorem communis libertatis."

5. For Lapo's "deploravimus simul ambo casum et orbitatem Romanae ecclesiae, quae gravissimis incommodis ac difficultatibus circumventa suis spoliaretur principibus quo tempore illam afflictam et perditam ad suam obtinendam dignitatem eorum consiliis, ope ac praesidio sublevari maxime oporteret," cf. Petrarch *Sine nomine* VII: "immo casum ac ruinam reipublicae deplorare"; Cic. *De orat.* III.3: "deploravit . . . orbitatem senatus, cuius ordinis a consule, qui quasi parens bonus . . . esse deberet, tamquam ab aliquo nefario praedone diriperetur patrimonium dignitatis."

6. For Lapo's "illam adflictam et perditam," cf. Cic. *Phil.* 3, 25: "homo adflictus et perditus."

parum gravia videbuntur, ea suscepti muneris necessitati[62] attribuas, si qua autem licentius dicta et falsius,[63] benigne accipias nec temere a me[64] maledicendi studio posita esse existimes, sed ex hominum huiusmodi[65] vita ac moribus expressa. Tale igitur ab eo fuit disputationis initium.

[II. Initium et de methodo disputandi]

//66v// A: [1] Cum[66] te contemplor, Lape, et cum vitam ac mores tuos[67] tum eruditionem liberalem considero, vehementer tua causa excrucior animi, et fortunae in te[68] magnopere iniquitati succenseo doleoque; te, quem unice[69] diligam, in haec curiae tempora miserrima ac perditissima incidisse, in quibus scelera, flagitia, fraudes, fallaciae virtutis optinent nomen in precioque habentur, virtuti vero, probitati, rectis studiis[70] honestisque artibus non modo praemium nullum neque honos[71] propositus, sed ne usquam quidem[72] relictus est locus. [2] Imperiti, audaces, largitiosi, sordidi, flagitiosi ubique regnant ac dominantur ceteris; boni autem viri,[73] docti, integri, abstinentes, modesti, temperati, depressi, abiecti repudiatique iacent, nec modo ut pernitiosi et capitales homines repelluntur a rerum maiorum gubernaculis, verum etiam[74] ut taeterrimae et truculentissimae beluae undique ab omnibus expelluntur. [3] Quare non video quid aut tu aut[75] quisquam vir probus et artibus ingeniis[76] eruditus hoc tempore consequi in curia aut[77] etiam sperare[78] possit. Itaque

---

62. necessitate *N.*
63. salius [*i.e.,* sal<s>ius?] *G.*
64. me] me nec *B.*
65. ex hominum huiusmodi] ex hoc uni eius mori *V;* ut homines eiusmodi *N;* ex hominum eiusmodi *G;* ex hominis eiusmodi *coni. Sch.;* hominum eiusmodi *B.*
66. *inter* initium *et* cum *add. rubricam* Angelus et Lapus *G.*
67. *in mar. d. add.* initium disceptationis *N.*
68. in te] vite *V.*
69. unicem *sic FB.*
70. consiliis *N.*
71. *in mar. d.* non infelicitate curie *N.*
72. quidam *V.*
73. *in mar. d.* boni viri *N.*
74. et *V.*
75. aut *om. P.*
76. ingenuis *G;* ingenii *N.*
77. at *G.*
78. sperari *P.*

way that if certain things in it seem to you rather grave, you attribute them to the necessity of the task that was assumed. Moreover, if certain things seem to be said rather presumptuously or falsely, please take them in a good-natured way and think not that I said them rashly, with a zealous desire to say wicked things, but rather that they were said because of the life and character of men of this sort.

And so Angelo began the discussion in this way.

[II: The Beginning and Concerning the Method of Argument]

Angelo: [1] When I think about you, Lapo, and consider your life and character as well as your learning in the liberal arts, I am really tortured in spirit by your predicament. I am earnestly angered at the iniquity of fortune, which has gone against you, and I feel sorry for you. [It troubles me] that you, whom I care for uniquely, have happened on these absolutely wretched and morally bankrupt times of the curia, in which crime, moral outrage, fraud, and deceit take the name of virtue and are held in high esteem. Not only is there no reward or public honor for virtue, uprightness, correct studies, and respectable crafts; there is not even any place left for these things. [2] The unlearned, the rash, the corrupt, the sordid, and the profligate rule everywhere and have power over the others. Moreover, the good men—the learned, pure, abstinent, modest, and temperate men—are neglected, oppressed, abject, repudiated. And not only are they repulsed from the governance of greater things as pernicious and dangerous; they are even driven out everywhere by all as if they were the most foul and savage of beasts. [3] This is why I don't see how you or anyone who is learnedly endowed with craft and skill can follow the curia or even place any hope in it. And so even though to me it is

quamquam[79] me abs te disiungi atque[80] separari non re tantum, sed
etiam cogitatione mihi acerbissimum sit, tamen qui meus in te est[81] amor,
reticere nequeo quae commodis, honori et dignitati tuae conducere arbitror.

[4] Equidem[82] te, mi Lape, et hortor[83] et pro nostra necessitudine
etiam moneo ut haec primum non aliter ac dicuntur[84] a me dici existimes,
sed in meliorem partem ex abundantia quadam amoris dicta accipias,
deinde ea ipsa colligas tecumque diligenter animo meditere, neu te dis-
trahi sinas aliorum consiliis nec promissorum magnitudine capi, quibus
hoc loci maxime abundamus omnes, nec spe dubia et incerta parta tibi,
ac certa[85] abiicias bona, nec praesentia tantum spectes, sed ut[86] vir prudens futura quoque quam longe prospicias et quid //67// haec ad[87] te studia postulent, quid patria, quid maiores tui, quid ante[88] acta vita, quid
denique opinio de te et expectatio[89] civium tuorum efflagitent, cogites, et
quod optimum atque ex tua inprimis dignitate esse censueris, id tibi rebus
omnibus praeferendum putes. [5] Id cum feceris, rectius, ut arbitror,
rationibus tuis consules et te, relicta[90] hac turbulentissima et tumultuo-
sissima vitae ratione, in portum aliquem conferes quietum, et pristina
tua[91] studia temporibus intermissa revocabis contendesque aliquid
scribere atque edere quod et caeteros iuvet et tibi ipsi ad posteros immortalem gloriam propaget. Hoc opinor tibi fore et ad quietem animi, cuius
te rei cupidissimum[92] esse numquam negabis, aptius acommodatiusque
et cum ad[93] extimationem[94] hominum, tum ad memoriam nominis
uberius.

L:[95] [6] Laudo te merito, Angele, et unum prae ceteris diligo ac meae

---

79. quamquam *om. N.*
80. ac *GNB.*
81. est] est et *G.*
82. Equidam *sic V.*
83. ortor *G.*
84. ac dicuntur] *om. G.*
85. parta tibi, ac certa] *om. N.*
86. ut *om. G.*
87. a *PNB.*
88. quid ante] quidam *V.*
89. expectio *N.*
90. *in mar. sin.* consulit quod reli<n>quatur curia *N.*
91. tua] tua tua *sic N.*
92. *in mar. sin.* m( ) quies animi et *N.*
93. ad *om. G.*
94. existimationem *PGB.*
95. L *om. P.*

the bitterest of things to be opposed to you and be separated from you (not only in actual fact but also in thought), nevertheless, my feelings are on your side and so I just cannot be silent about things that I think might lead to your advantage, honor, and worth.

[4] Really, my dear Lapo, I urge you and because of our friendship I even warn you: first, do not think that these things that I have said are said otherwise than the way in which they are intended; then, take them as the better part of an abundance of my aforementioned affection toward you. Finally, I want you to gather these very things up and meditate on them diligently. Do not be distracted by the advice of others or be taken in by the vastness of their promises with which all of us here are all too familiar. You shouldn't, with doubtful hope and uncertain possessions, cast aside goods that are certain. Rather, as a prudent man, you should look as far as possible to the future and consider as most important whatever your studies ask of you. Think about what your homeland, your elders, your previously transacted life, and, finally, your fellow citizens' opinion and expectation of you spur you on to do. You should judge whatever is best using your worth as a measure, and you should think that this is what must be put before all things. [5] Once you have done this—rightly, I think—then be mindful of your own arguments and, having left behind this restless and confused type of life, direct yourself to any restful harbor. Then you will summon up once again your earlier studies, interrupted by the times, and seek to write and publish something that will help others. This will earn you immortal glory in the eyes of posterity. I also think that it will be conducive to the repose of your soul. And you will never deny that this is what you desire most, as something more suitable and fitting, both for the judgment of men and, more widely, for the memory of your name.

Lapo: [6] I praise you as you deserve, Angelo, and care for you above

laudis meaeque dignitatis cupidissimum quottidie magis esse perspicio. Nec me fugit, ut est amicissimi viri officium, eumdem te meis incommodis aeque ac tuis graviter angi.[96] Quae autem abste dicta sunt, tam mihi iucunda fuere, quam quod gratissimum et iucundissimum, nec dubito illa ex optimo animo et ardentissimo quodam amore omnia esse deprompta, nec vero fas esset aut a te aliter fieri aut me de coniunctissimo homine aliter iudiccare. [7] Sed nolim mihi hoc tantum tribuas ut mea causa, si quid indignum tibi pati[97] videor, iniquitati temporum et fortunae potissimum succensendum putes, tametsi opinor in eo quoque te amice agere, nec mihi assentatum[98]—quod vicium longe a tuis moribus abhorret[99]—sed benivolentia mei esse deceptum. [8] Etenim si nequam homines et indigni, ut tu[100] dicis, honores et praemia assequuntur, dignissimi vero et honestissimi viri despiciuntur ab omnibus nec ullam dignitatis suae partem obtinere possunt, in caeteris //67v// est id[101] indignius ferendum quibus fortasse, quod ad maiores spes animo[102] spectarent[103] maioremque de se expectationem suis meritis excitassent,[104] plura atque ampliora debentur, mea vero causa non magnopere fortunae iniquitas incusanda est. [9] Ego enim imbecillitatis meae satis conscius et, illius mobilitatem ac rerum humanarum mutabilitatem saepius expertus, perfacile ista contemno, meamque sortem, qualiscunque est, modo honestam, satis egregiam mihi contigisse duco, eamque sedato animo ac molliter fero. Levia enim quaedam et[105] ea perpauca, non ad splendorem vitae et ostentationem, sed ad[106] explendam naturae necessitatem appeto. [10] Ex his si quid mihi detrahitur aut minus pro voluntate conceditur, non subirascor fortunae, sed indignitati meae totum[107] attribuo et me ipsum hac ratione consolor.

[11] Postremo, quod iubes ut relicta curia in ocium me et studium referam, facerem et quidem[108] haud invite, si facultas esset. Sed est id pri-

---

96. arrigi *V.*
97. pati *om. N.*
98. absentatum *P.*
99. abhorreret *V.*
100. tu *om. N.*
101. id *om. N.*
102. animos *G.*
103. expectarent *V.*
104. excitasset *P.*
105. ut *V.*
106. ad *om. B.*
107. tantum *V.*
108. quidam *V.*

other men, and I see that more and more every day you truly desire that I be praised and valued. And it does not escape me that you are troubled by my difficulties just as if they were your own, as is the duty of a great friend. And what you said was as pleasant for me as could be, and I have no doubt that everything you said was prompted by the best of intentions and by a most impassioned love—and it wouldn't be right that it happen in any other way or that I judge otherwise about my closest friend. [7] But I would not want you to give me so much credit that for my sake—if I seem in your view to be treated unworthily—you feel compelled to become especially angry at the iniquity of fortune and the times. Even so, I do think in this case that you are doing it for friendship's sake and that you are not flattering me—a vice that would be far from your character.[7] Rather, it seems to me that you were deceived because of your goodwill toward me. [8] Granted, as you say, detestable and unworthy men attain honors and prizes while the most worthy and respectable are despised by all and cannot obtain any share of the distinction they deserve. Now in the case of some, perhaps, this unfairness is rather difficult to tolerate. After all, since these men in their heart looked toward greater goals and had, based on their own merits, stirred up greater hope for themselves, they were owed more and wider things. But in my case, really, one shouldn't blame fortune's unfairness. [9] For I am well aware of my own weakness and have often experienced its fickleness as well as the changeableness of human affairs. Given this, I have no trouble esteeming lightly those unimportant things.[8] In fact I think that my lot, of whatever sort it is, has been honest and praiseworthy enough for me, and I bear it calmly, with a sedate spirit. In fact all I want are trifles—and few at that—not for the splendor and showiness of life, but for nature's necessity, which, after all, must be fulfilled. [10] If one of these things is taken away from me or given somewhat less than willingly, I do not become angry at fortune. Rather, I attribute everything to my unworthiness and console myself in that fashion.

[11] Finally, as to what you strongly advise—that I leave behind the curia and return to leisure and study—I would do this willingly if there

---

7. For Lapo's "quod vicium longe a tuis moribus abhorret," cf. Cic. *Catil.* I.20: "id quod abhorret a meis moribus"; perhaps Cic. *Cael.* 10: "longe ab ista suspicione abhorrere debet."

8. For Lapo's "perfacile ista contemno," cf. Livy VI.41.8: "Parva sunt haec; sed parva ista non contemnendo."

mum factu difficile, deficientibus[109] domesticis[110] copiis ad ocium perse-
quendum in hac praesertim tanta confusione et perturbatione rerum
omnium, in qua nusquam bono viro animo quieto, nusquam ocioso[111]
esse liceat. [12] Deinde non video quid sit causae, cur mihi discessum e
curia suadere coneris. Qua quidem in re nequeo satis te admirari; ac nisi
existimarem aut amore mei inpulsum aut inscitia et ignoratione[112] pro-
lapsum, non possem hoc tuum consilium, ut levissime[113] dicam, non
summopere improbare qui tam cupide loquaris, nec videris quid curia sit,
in qua tam diu verseris, satis nosse nec quid coneris attendere. [13] Quid
est, obsecro, quod me a curia abducere debeat? Quid quod non me[114]
retinere aut, si alibi terrarum vitam agerem, ad eam allicere atque adhor-
tari[115] queat? Numquid //68// a[116] sanae mentis homine vel ad bene beat-
eque, tum ad splendide magnificeque vivendum vel ad opes et copias
comparandas vel etiam, si ita vis, ad perfruendas voluptates desiderari
atque expeti[117] potest, cuius non in curia quam largissime copia sup-
petat?

A:[118] [14] Longe mihi contrarium videtur esse,[119] nec vero nunc arbitror te ita sentire, ut loqueris, sed sive aucupandae tibi gratiae studio sive
ingenii exercendi causa[120] hanc disceptationem inducere, quae quidem
mihi haud iniucunda erit, maxime cum simus ociosi. Quam obrem perge,
quaeso, ut instituisti, ac mihi proba haec quae dicis.

L: [15] Minime omnium istuc[121] a me requiras velim! Non enim consilio nec de industria, ut tu putas, in huiusmodi disputationem veni, sed
casu et ex tempore incidi, nec vero ea mihi est[122] vis ingenii nec tanta facultas dicendi atque copia, ut id me facturum ausim polliceri aut[123]
praestare ullo modo possim. Quare malim tibi hisce de rebus assentiri,
quam hoc tantum onus suscipere. Sed haec iam missa faciamus quae,

---

109. deficientibus] deficientibus quidem *N*.
110. domesticis *om. G*.
111. ociose *B*.
112. ignorancia *B*.
113. benignissime *B*.
114. non me] non mea *G*; in ea non *B*.
115. abhortari *N*; exortari *B*.
116. o *sic P*.
117. expecti *V*.
118. A *om. P*.
119. videtur esse] esse videtur *G*.
120. gratia *N*.
121. istud *V*.
122. mihi est] est mihi *N*.
123. an *G*.

were a way. But first of all it is difficult to do, since I lack domestic wealth for pursuing studious leisure.[9] And this is especially so in such confusion and disorder of all things, where a good man cannot be tranquil in spirit and at leisure. [12] So I just do not see the reason why you try to persuade me to leave the curia; certainly, in this matter I cannot wonder at you enough. And if I did not think that you either were motivated by friendly love for me or had fallen into awkwardness and ignorance, then I could not (if I may speak most frivolously) *not* reprove you in the highest degree, you who speak so foolishly and do not see what the curia is—a place where you have been for so long and where you have not even tried to wait it out enough to know. [13] I ask you, what is there that should take me away from the curia? What is there that could not keep me around or that if I were to lead my life elsewhere in the world could bind me to that other life and encourage me to favor it? Is there anything that can be desired or sought after by a man of sound mind either as far as living well and soundly goes—not to mention with splendor and magnificence—or as far as becoming wealthy goes, or even, if you so wish, as far as thoroughly enjoying worldly pleasures goes, that is not available in the curia in the greatest dimensions possible?

A: [14] The contrary seems to me to be the case, by far. But I also don't think that, at this point, you really believe what you have said. Instead I think you have come up with this discussion either out of zeal for increasing your esteem or as an exercise for your mental ingenuity; and it certainly won't be unpleasant for me, especially since we are at leisure. Because of this, then, I ask of you: go on as you have begun and prove what you say to me.

L: [15] The one thing I wish you didn't ask of me! Indeed, I did not come to this sort of disputation knowingly or intentionally, as you think. Rather, I happened on it extemporaneously and by chance. Really, I do not have that power of mental ingenuity, or even such a great wealth of speaking ability, that I would dare to promise or even in any way be able to excel in doing the task. So for this reason I would rather give in to you on these matters than take up such a great burden. But now let us forget

---

9. With "domesticis copiis" Lapo alludes to his lack of success in finding patronage in Florence, his native city.

utcumque[124] se habeant, nec[125] disputatione nostra corrigi nec aliter immutari possent, et sermonem hunc nostrum alio tra<n>sferamus.[126]

A: [16] Nequaquam istuc hodie tibi[127] per me licebit facere, nec ego te hinc abire aut a me passum digredi[128] patiar, quandoquidem[129] coepisti et meam[130] spem, meum animum erexisti, quoad cumulatae[131] satis huic expectationi meae feceris.

L: [17] Deprehensum me plane[132] esse sentio et praeter opinionem[133] meam in maximam difficultatem conpulsum, ut aut mihi amicissimi viri voluntas offendenda sit aut inprudentiae et ineptiarum reprehensio subeunda. Verum quoniam te ita velle intelligo, cui nihil a me honeste denegari potest, ad rem ipsam aggrediar et desiderio tuo potius quam existimationi meae serviam, ac si alterutrum evenire necesse est, malim in suscipiendo et satis faciendo parum prudens quam in recusando ingratus atque inhumanus videri. [18] Igitur sic //68v// agamus: ego te interrogabo, tu, ad ea quae percontatus fuero quod videbitur respondebis ac nisi fallor, ex hac sententia te depellam, ut curiam non modo prudentibus viris non fugiendam esse, sed enixius exquirendam censeas.[134]

A: [19] Socratico[135] more, ut videris, mecum agere vis et me meis responsionibus irretitum convincere. Sed faciam quod iubes, et tibi in omnibus morem geram, modo ex te quod cupio audiam, tantum vero abest ut verear me abste convinci,[136] ut id vehementer exoptem, quod intelligo convicto mihi vitam posthac[137] in curia multo iucundiorem futuram.

[III. De Deo excultando curiae]

L: [1] Quare, ut a potioribus ordiamur, responde, si placet, putesne ullum[138] bonum maius aut praestabilius aut expetibilius esse quam id

---

124. utrumque *P.*

125. ne *PG.*

126. transferamus *VPNB.*

127. istuc hodie tibi] tibi hodie istuc *N.*

128. disgredi *P.*

129. quandoquidem *canc. ad* quando, *tum in mar. d. add.* quidem *B².*

130. meam] in eam *GN.*

131. quoad cumulate] que adcomulate *V.*

132. me plane] plane me *VP;* sane me *GN.*

133. vero de perplexitate *in mar. d. B¹.*

134. censas *V;* annuas *sic legit Sch.*

135. Socratis *P.*

136. tantum vero abest ut verear me abste convinci] tantum vero abs te convinci *V.*

137. hac *B.*

138. illum *VG;* illum *B corr. ad* ullum *B¹.*

about these things, since our discussion could not correct or change them in any way, however they may be. Let us change the direction of our argument.

A: [16] By no means will I let you do this today. I will not allow you to leave here or permit you to part until you have completely satisfied this expectation of mine, since, having begun, you raised my hope and my spirits.

L: [17] I feel trapped, in over my head, forced into the greatest of difficulties. As a result, either the will of my dearest friend will be displeased, or I shall have to suffer the charge of imprudence and foolishness. Of course I understand that you—to whom I can in good faith refuse nothing—wish it thus: that I attack the argument itself and that I cater to your desire rather than to my good name. But if one of the two things has to happen, I would rather seem somewhat less than prudent in taking up this argument and satisfying you than seem an inhuman ingrate in my refusal. [18] Therefore let us proceed this way: I shall ask you questions, and you will respond what seems best to the things that I shall ask. And if I am not mistaken, I shall wean you away from this opinion. The end result will be that you think not only that the curia is not to be fled by prudent men but that it is rather to be sought after more than earnestly.

A: [19] You wish to handle me in the manner of Socrates, it seems, and refute me after I have become entangled in my own responses. But I shall do what you ask and humor you in all things. May I only hear from you what I desire. In fact, far from shrinking from being convinced by you, I fervently long for it, understanding that after I am convinced, my life in the curia will be much more agreeable.

[III. On Worshiping God at the Curia]

L: [1] Well then, let's begin with what is most important. If you would, answer this: do you think that there is any good that is greater, more preeminent, or more desirable than that which is highest, self-sufficient, and

quod est summum per se sufficiens, nullius externae[139] opis indigum, sed ex omni[140] parte perfectum et cumulatum atque extremum bonorum omnium, a quo omnia sint et quo omnia referantur, quo parto omnis nostra cupiditas terminatur?[141]

A: [2] Nullum arbitror.

L: Hoc autem non negabis beatitudinem esse.

A: Minime.

L: Beatitudinem dico non humanam, de qua tanta[142] inter philosophos contentio est, cum eam alii in virtute, alii in honoribus, alii in divitiis, alii in bona valetudine, alii in voluptate,[143] alii item alia[144] in re ponendam[145] censuerint;[146] sed divinam illam quae[147] castis, sanctis, religiosisque[148] viris post mortem ab immortali Deo tribuitur.

A: [3] Ne in hoc quidem abs te dissentio.

L: Huiusmodi beatitudo quid erit aliud[149] quam ipse immortalis Deus?

A: Nihil.

L: Quam quidem tum assecuti videmur cum ex hac mortalium vita ad meliorem vitam migramus adeptique immortalitatem ac divinitatem quandam Deo perpetuo fruimur[150] et cum eo coniunctissime vivimus.

A: [4] Verissimum.

L: At[151] secundum et huic proximum bonum illud mea quidem sententia vere habendum est, quo id nobis comparatur et quo sine ad illud pervenire non possumus.[152]

A: Nihil verius.

L: [5] Hoc enim //69// nisi esset, frustra insita atque ingenita nobis foret tanta summi boni cupiditas, qua inflammamur[153] omnes atque

---

139. exterre *G.*
140. ex omni] omni ex *G.*
141. terminetur *G.*
142. tanto *sic P.*
143. alii in divitiis, alii in bona valetudine, alii in voluptate] alii in voluptate, alii in diviciis, alii in bona valetudine *P;* voluptate] voluntate *B.*
144. alii *B.*
145. ponebant *V;* ponere *legit Sch.*
146. consuerint *V.*
147. quae *om. G.*
148. religiosisque] religiosis *P.*
149. quid erit aliud] quid erit quid erit aliud *sic N;* quid aliud erit *B.*
150. fruimus *sic G.*
151. Ad *V.*
152. *in mar. s.* frustra *F;* possumus] possimus *G.*
153. inflammantur *G.*

needs no outside help, is perfected and complete in every part, and is the highest extreme of all good things, from which all things exist and to which all things return, toward the acquisition of which our every whim is directed?

A: [2] I think there is no greater good.

L: And you will not deny that this good is happiness.

A: Not in the least.

L: And I'm not talking about a merely human happiness, about which there is so much disagreement among philosophers. Some think the locus of human happiness should be placed in virtue, others in [worldly] honors, others in wealth, others in good health, others in pleasure, while others still think it should be placed somewhere else.[10] But it is that divine happiness that immortal God gives to chaste, holy, and religious men after death.

A: [3] I certainly don't disagree with you about that.

L: Will happiness of this sort be anything other than immortal God himself?

A: Nothing at all.

L: Certainly, we seem to have reached this happiness when we depart this life of mortals in favor of a better one. Then, fit out, in a way, for immortality and divinity, we enjoy the presence of God in perpetuity and live with him in a most closely joined fashion.

A: [4] That's very true.

L: But there is also a second good and one that is proximate to this one [i.e., God]. In my opinion one certainly must obtain this second good, since it makes the primary good available to us. Without it we cannot attain to the primary good.

A: Nothing is truer.

L: [5] Now this wouldn't be the case if this great, innate, inborn desire for the highest good that is in us were in vain. It is a desire with which all of us are aflame and by which we are all inspired. If the way and method

---

10. Cf. Cic. *Fin.* V.5.14.

ince<n>dimur.[154] Incognita enim via ac ratione nunquam eo quo intendimus potiremur.[155] Frustra autem dicere absurdum omnino et contra naturam esse[156] videtur, quippe cum ab ipsa, ut ita dixerim, parente omnium natura non ad ludum et ad iocum, sed ad beatitudinem generati simus.[157] [6] Necesse est igitur esse aliquod[158] medium quo ad illud ultimum perducamur, atque id ipsum, si quod[159] est, preciosissimum[160] esse et maximum atque cognitione dignissimum, cognitumque plurimi[161] ab hominibus faciendum et omni diligentia retinendum.

A: [7] Vehementer tibi assentior; sed quod[162] id tandem sit medium quo ad beatitudinem pervehimur, cupio ex te cognoscere.

L: Rem quaeris tu quidem haud[163] vulgarem neque[164] contemnendam et, quanquam a multis non ignoratam, a paucis tamen excultam, nonnullis etiam[165] invisam.

A: Concedo ita esse. Quid tum? Profer in medium quam rem hanc tam divinam atque admirabilem putes[166] esse.

L: [8] Religionem equidem.

A: Iam pridem istuc ipsum, me hercule, tacitus cogito, ac si me quispiam rogasset, aliud nihil quam religio<nem> respondissem.

L: Recte tu quidem respondisses, sed quam obrem?

A: Quoniam memini me et legisse saepius et a peritis quoque hominibus audisse nonnumquam: religionem esse verum immortalis Dei[167] cultum, quod nos Deo religet et admirabili quadam caritate devinciat.

L: [9] Ex Apollinis haec oraculo edita mihi esse videntur!

A: Irrides.[168]

---

154. incendimur *VGNB*.
155. poterimus *sic legit Sch.*
156. esse] esse esse *sic N*.
157. sumus *V*.
158. aliquid *V*.
159. quid *V*.
160. spetiosissimum *G*.
161. plurimum *legit Sch.*
162. quid *coni. Sch.*
163. aut *V*.
164. neque] neque tam a paucis *N*.
165. et *V*.
166. putas *B*.
167. immortalis Dei] Dei immortalis *G*.
168. Irridens *B*.

were unknown, we would never be able to go where we aimed to go. In fact to say it is in vain seems wholly absurd and contrary to nature, especially since it is from nature—who is, if I may speak in such a way, the parent of all things—that we are all born. And we are born not to trifles or jokes but rather to happiness. [6] And so it is necessary that there be some mean by which we are led to that end. It is also necessary that this mean itself, if it is anything at all, be something very valuable, optimally great, and most worthy of investigation. It should be made known to many men and be preserved with all watchfulness.

A: [7] I strongly agree with you.[11] But I desire to know from you what that mean is, finally, by which we are drawn toward happiness.

L: Certainly, what you seek is no common thing, nor should one look down on it. Although many know about it, nonetheless it is practiced by very few and even begrudged by some.

A: I agree that that is the case, but what then? Come out with this thing you consider so divine and admirable.

L: [8] Religion, of course.

A: For a long time now, by Hercules, this is what I have thought without saying it, and if someone had asked me, my answer would have been nothing other than religion.

L: And of course you would have answered correctly. But why?

A: Because I remember that I have read rather often and have also heard sometimes from learned men that religion is this: the true worship of immortal God that binds us to him and obliges us to a remarkable kind of charity.[12]

L: [9] Those words seem to me to have come from the oracle of Apollo!

A: You laugh.

---

11. For Lapo's "Vehementer tibi assentior," cf. Cic. *Div.* I.105: "cui quidem auguri vehementer assentior"; *De orat.* I.262.

12. Perhaps cf. August. *De civ. D.* X.1.

L: Minime[169] vero, sed doctrinam istam tuam admiror, ac iam nunc primum perspicio olim te dissumulasse et astute nimis et callide ad[170] huiusmodi concertationem me impulisse, ut[171] siquid adversus curiam dixissem incautus,[172] efferes in vulgus magnamque ex eo mihi conflares invidiam; //69v// sed fortunae a me gratia est habenda, quod in hanc partem oratione delatus sim!

A: [10] Omitte,[173] inquam, iocos[174] atque illuc revertere unde digressus es, nec velis me diutius suspensum expectatione tenere. Non enim dum video quo pertineat haec tua tam longa et tam alte repetita oratio.

L: Videbis propediem, si te mihi parumper ad audiendum dedideris. Quoniam igitur haec mihi abs te omnia[175] concessa sunt, religionem rem optimam esse ac maxime preciosam, quae homines immortali Deo conciliet carosque exhibeat, illud quoque concedas oportet, quanto maior religio est, tanto preciosiorem esse, et quanto quis magis religioni studeat, tanto Deo cariorem fieri.

A: [11] Quis hoc non videat, quod maius sit bonum, id esse praestantius, et qui quod est maius assecutus fuerit, eum[176] esse meliorem?

L: Ita prorsus. In genere enim bonorum quanto maius, tanto praestabilius et melius. Ex hoc illud quoque[177] perspicuum fit—cum religio Dei sit cultus—gratius Deo esse frequentius coli quam rarius, et a plurimis quam a paucis.

A: [12] Perspicuum nempe, ut dicis!

L: Addam etiam: a sacris hominibus quam a prophanis, a[178] maioribus et in maxima aliqua dignitate positis quam a privatis sacerdotibus.

A: Fateor.

L: Et magnificentius etiam quam parcius.

A: Probe.

L: Et a multis simul nationibus quam ab una.[179]

A: Certe.

L: [13] Consequens ergo est, ut locum in quo frequentius et a pluribus

---

169. Minime] Minime me *sic Sch.*
170. ab *B.*
171. et *V.*
172. incautius *PG.*
173. Dimitte *sic Sch.*
174. locos *V.*
175. abs te omnia] omnia abste *B.*
176. esse *sic N.*
177. illud quoque] quoque illud *G.*
178. et *B.*
179. A:Probe. . . . una *om. G.*

L: Why, not at all. On the contrary I admire this erudition of yours, and I see now for the first time that you were dissimulating before and that in an exceedingly astute and cunning fashion you were leading me into this kind of controversy. Thus, had I said anything heedless against the curia, you would let everybody know about it and stir up ill will against me. I should thank fortune that I've been led to this point by our argument.

A: [10] Please, will you spare the humor and return to where you were when you digressed—if, that is, you don't want to hold me in suspense too long. Because I still do not see where this terribly long and repetitive oration of yours is going.[13]

L: You'll see very soon if you just give me a little time to be heard. Now then, because you have conceded all these things to me—that religion is the greatest and most valuable thing, which reconciles men to immortal God and shows that they are beloved to him—you also have to concede this: that the greater religion is, the more valuable it is, and that the more someone adheres to religion, the more beloved he becomes in the eyes of God.

A: [11] Who wouldn't see that the greater a good is, the more outstanding it is, and that whoever has pursued what is greater is better?

L: Just so. For in the genus of goods, the more of something there is, the more preferable and better it is. In addition, since religion is the worship of God, this makes it clear that to God it is more agreeable to be worshiped more frequently than less and by many rather than by few.

A: [12] Extremely clear, as you say!

L: I might also add: by sacred men rather than by the profane, by those who are greater and placed in positions of the highest authority rather than by private priests.

A: I'll admit that.

L: And in a more magnificent fashion rather than in a poorer one.

A: Right.

L: And by many peoples at the same time rather than by one.

A: Of course.

L: [13] Consequently, then, a place in which God is worshiped more

---

13. For Lapo's "tam longa et tam alte repetita oratio," cf. Cic. *Sest.* 31: "oratio tam longa aut tam alte repetita."

et a dignioribus et magnificentius Deus colitur et a pluribus una nationibus eum caeteris praestantiorem et Deo gratiorem nobisque ad beate
degendam vitam aptiorem esse dicamus.

A: Sentio quo me his argutiis tuis concluseris,[180] ut mihi necesse sit
huiusmodi esse curiam confiteri; quod si antea percepissem, profecto
nunquam effecisses,[181] nec nunc quidem, ut id tibi concedam, a me ulla
ratione extorxeris. Quid[182] enim a curia alienius quam religio esse
potest?

L: [14] Ut lubet. Non enim vim[183] afferam nec te pigneribus cogam,
quanquam ex rebus hoc a te concessis[184] //70// efficitur et in[185] eo fidem
tuam requirere possim,[186] quod ab initio pollicitus sis, morem te mihi
esse gesturum. Verum[187] hoc quoque perlibenter et facile remitto[188] tibi.
Negatis enim a te iis[189] disputationis principiis,[190] disputatio tota tolletur
et ipse magno onere levabor.

A: [15] Iam muto sententiam, et quod ex receptis[191] a me conficitur,
etsi minus probem, disputationis gratia concedam atque admittam fate-
borque curiam, ut videris velle, locum esse non praestantem solum, sed
etiam praestantissimum Deoque gratissimum et ad beate vivendum
inprimis accomodatum. Modo non, ut mathematici[192] solent, qui ex
superioribus tantum dictis et concessis quod propositum sit demon-
strant,[193] sed pro tua consuetudine, locis pluribus et rationibus, id pla-
nius mihi facias, ut, cum ad concedendum vi[194] argumentationis impel-
lar,[195] orationis etiam copia et suavitate adducar.[196]

L: [16] Faciam id[197] ut potero. Ad nostrum igitur munus pensumque

---

180. conduxeris *sic Sch.*
181. affecisses *P.*
182. Quod *V.*
183. vim *om. G.*
184. confessis *N.*
185. in *om. N.*
186. possum *VP.*
187. Verum] Verum ego *B.*
188. peremitto *sic V;* permitto *sic Sch.*
189. hiis *P.*
190. principis *V.*
191. ex receptis] exceptis *V;* expetis *coni. Sch.*
192. methamatici *sic N.*
193. demonstrant] de monseant *sic G.*
194. in *sic legit Sch.;* in *G.*
195. inpellor *VG.*
196. suavitate adducar] suavitate adducat *V;* suaviter adducam *GN.*
197. id *om. G.*

frequently, by more and worthier people, in a more magnificent fashion, and by many peoples at the same time—we may say that this place is more outstanding and more pleasing in God's eyes and is for us more suited to carrying on our life in a holy fashion.

A: I am beginning to understand that your arguments are leading me to a point where I'll have to admit that the curia is just such a place. But if I had understood this earlier, then you never would have carried it through, and certainly now you won't make me admit it with any argument. For what can be more alien to the curia than religion?

L: [14] As you wish. Now I won't use force, nor will I compel you with pledges[14]—even though I could make you comply with what you have already conceded and I could ask for your good faith. After all, at the outset you did promise you would comply with me. But I shall happily and easily give up. After all, if you have rejected the principles of argument, the entire disputation will be done away with and I shall be relieved of a great burden.

A: [15] All right, now I'll change my opinion and concede what follows logically from what I have pledged—even if I don't really approve. For the sake of argument I shall admit and even confess that the curia, as you seem to want it, is a place that is not only outstanding but even most outstanding and pleasing to God, in addition to being well-suited to living well. Now make all this clearer to me, but not like the mathematicians usually do, who argue from "what has been said above" and "conceded thus far" and then demonstrate what has been propounded. Instead do it in your customary manner, with many arguments and theories—so that necessity compels me to concede your arguments and I am persuaded both by the abundance of the oration as well as by its rhetorical sweetness.[15]

L: [16] I'll do what I can. Let's return, then, to our allotted task.[16] If

---

14. For Lapo's "pigneribus cogam," cf. Cic. *Phil.* I.12: "coguntur enim non pignoribus, sed gratia."

15. This request pays attention to the genre of rhetorical argumentation called the *sorites*—or "heap"—argument, where persuasion is achieved by a gradual mounting up of different arguments, so that the listener is persuaded not only by the quality but also by the quantity of points made.

16. For Lapo's "Ad nostrum igitur munus pensumque redeamus," cf. Cic. *De orat.* III.119: "me . . . ad meum munus pensumque revocabo."

redeamus. Si divini cultus religio nos delectat, quis est usquam locus in terris cum curia romana in hoc genere comparandus?

A: Perge ad reliqua.

L: Ubi enim tantum sacerdotum reperias numerum?

A: [17] Haud mirum. Ceterae enim regiones,[198] conventus, civitates suos habent tantummodo sacerdotes, quibus ad rem divinam utuntur. In curiam autem sacerdotes[199] partim religione et visendi pontificis studio, partim dignitatis consequendae cupiditate, partim aliis de causis ex omnibus paene orbis terrarum partibus confluunt. Sed quid ad rem? Quasi vero Deus non meritis[200] hominum vitae sanctimonia, integritate, religione, iustis precibus, sed vulgo, ut pecudum et multitudine delectetur?

L: [18] Nunquam id ego dixerim, ac si quis dicat supplicio dignum puto. Hoc unum affirmare non dubitem, primum, in parvo numero paucos esse bonos,[201] etiam si omnes boni forent; ex magna vero multitudine probatissimos viros plurimos existere posse. [19] Quinetiam, quantum humano ingenio assequi possum, sic statuo ac iudico multitudinem non pessimam //70v// sacerdotum quam non optimam paucitatem Deo cariorem esse, cum acceperimus[202] ex veteribus sacrarum historiarum monumentis illum a multitudine semper[203] coli voluisse, siquidem cultus et honos (de nobis[204] enim hominibus[205] coniecturam facio)[206] etiam a quovis habitus delectare solet, [20] et nostris quoque divinis legibus sapientissime comparatum est,[207] omne sacrificium, vel a sceleratissimo sacerdote, modo rite factum, verum, integrum, absolutum, intactum atque intemeratum sacrificium Deoque acceptum esse habendum, quod maximo argumento est Deum ipsum, non dico non magis bonorum religione moveri, sed nullius cultum recusare, sed debitum sibi honorem ab omnibus[208] exhiberi velle exhibitumque accipere atque exhibitori placari.[209] [21] Quare dubitare non possumus colentium multitudinem,

---

198. religiones *B.*

199. quibus ad rem divinam utuntur. In curiam autem sacerdotes *om. G.*

200. mentis *G.*

201. bonos *om. G.*

202. accepimus *coni. Sch.*

203. semper *om. PGN.*

204. de nobis *om. B.*

205. nominibus *sic G.*

206. facis *V.*

207. est] est et *V.*

208. omnibus] omnibus sibi *P.*

209. placare *P.*

we love the sacredness of divine worship, what place anywhere on earth could you compare in this sort of thing with the Roman curia?

A: Go on.

L: For where else might you find such a great number of priests?

A: [17] No wonder, since other regions, alliances, and cities have merely their own priests whom they use for religious matters. But priests flow into the curia from nearly all corners of the world, partly because of religion and a zealous desire to see the pope, partly to pursue high office, and partly for other reasons. Still, so what? As if God were delighted not by the merits of men, not by holiness of life, integrity, religion, or just prayers, but instead by the crowd, as if by a multitude of sheep.

L: [18] I would never say anything of the sort, and if someone does say it, I think him worthy of punishment. This at least I would not hesitate to affirm: first, in a small number [of men], there are few good men, even if they were all good; but in a great multitude there can exist very many most upright men. [19] In fact—as far as I can follow it with human ability—I am convinced and I judge that a multitude of priests who are not the worst is more pleasing to God than a paucity of priests who are not the best. [This is so] since we learn from the old traditions of sacred scripture that God always wanted to be worshiped by the multitude. Certainly, if I make a conjecture about us human beings, worship and veneration are usually pleasing, whoever carries them out. [20] This is also most wisely established by our divine laws: that every sacrifice, even if it is made by the most corrupt of priests, provided that the ritual is done correctly, is a sacrifice that is true, integral, absolute, intact, and inviolate and is to be deemed as accepted in the eyes of God.[17] This is the greatest argument that God himself—and I am not saying he is not more moved by the religion of *good* men—refuses the worship of no one. Rather, he wants the honor owed to him to be displayed by all. He accepts this displayed honor and is reconciled to the one who displays it. [21] For this reason we cannot doubt that a multitude of worshipers—in which it is

---

17. The locus classicus of this anti-Donatist position stressing the efficacy of the sacraments (whatever the vessel of their transmisson) is found in Augustine's anti-Donatist works; see Augustine, *Traités anti-Donatistes*, 5 vols. (Paris, 1963–65), especially vol. 2 (1964), *De baptismo libri VIII*, ed. G. Bavard, at VI.4–5 (pp. 412–14).

in qua plures esse bonos necesse est et sacrificia, cultus, cerimonias, fre-
quentissime celebrari atque innovari, ipsi immortali Deo, in cuius haec
honorem fiunt, esse gratissimam.[210]

A: Probo magnopere quae abs te modo in hanc[211] sententiam dispu-
tata[212] sunt, et erectior multo sum atque attentior ad ea quae sequuntur
redditus.[213]

L: [22] Iam vero sacerdotum in curia dignitas tanta est quanta maxima
hominibus tribui potest. Est enim hic primum[214] pontifex maximus, qui
Dei obtinet locum et quo post illum maius nihil habemus, qui non
humano consilio, sed divinitus atque adeo[215] Dei voce et auctoritate con-
stitutus est.[216] Est patrum cardinalium pulcherrimum amplissimumque
collegium, qui apostolorum explent ordinem et pontifici non praesidio
modo maximis in rebus gerendis atque administrandis, sed etiam decori
et ornamento esse videntur. [23] Sunt archiepiscopi, epiescopi, patriar-
chae, protonotarii aliique paene[217] infiniti ordines, omnes maxima dignitate et auctoritate ad Dei cultum instituti et inventi, qui cum in unum vel
ad sacrificium vel ad quamvis rem divinam obeundam //71// conierunt et,
sedente pontifice maximo in augusta illa pontificum sede collocato,
cuncti ex ordine assederunt ac divini illi hymni ac psalmi disparibus vari-
isque vocibus decantantur, quis est tam inhumanus, tam barbarus, tam
agrestis, quis[218] rursus tam immanis, tam Deo hostis, tam expers religionis, qui haec aspiciens audiensque non moveatur,[219] cuius non mentem
atque animum aliqua religio[220] occupet et stupore perstringat[221] et dul-
cedine quadam deliniat?[222] [24] Cuius non oculi mirifice aspectu ipso
pascantur oblectenturque? Cuius non aures incredibili cantus suavitate et
harmonia mulceantur? Quo quidem[223] spectaculo quod[224] in terris pul-

---

210. gratissima *G*.
211. ver( ) com( ) su( ) al( ) *in mar. d. B¹*.
212. deputata *G*.
213. redditus *om. N*.
214. primo *B*.
215. a Deo *coni. Sch.*; a deo *P*.
216. est *om. G*.
217. paene *om. G*.
218. qui *P*.
219. moveatur *om. V*.
220. religione *V*.
221. perstringat *om. V*.
222. deliniat] deliniatur *PN*; delineat *B*.
223. quidam *V*.
224. quid *coni. Sch.*

necessary both that there are many good men and that sacrifices, worship, and ceremonies are celebrated and renewed amid the greatest concourse—is most beloved in the eyes of immortal God himself, in whose honor these things happen.

A: I greatly approve of the opinions you have just discussed, and I have been rendered much more resolute and attentive to the things that follow.

L: [22] Now then, in the curia, the worth of the priests is already the highest men can have. First of all, there is the pope, who takes the place of God: after him we have no greater. He has been given power not by human counsel but divinely and has been placed at such a high point that he has the voice and authority of God. There is the noble and esteemed college of cardinals, who fulfill the role of the apostles and seem to be for the pope not only an aid in both accomplishing and administering the grandest affairs but a graceful, becoming ornamentation as well. [23] There are archbishops, bishops, patriarchs, protonotaries, and an almost infinite number of other categories, and all of them have been created and devised with the greatest worthiness and authority for the sake of worshiping God. When they have come together either for the sacrifice of the Mass or for carrying out any other religious matter, and when the pope is sitting—after he has been stationed in that majestic papal seat—and when all those in their proper place have been seated, and when those divine hymns and psalms are being sung by different, varying voices—well, who is so inhuman, so barbarous, so boorish, or who, on the other hand, is so horrible, inimical to God, and unknowing of religion, that on seeing and hearing these things he is unmoved? [Is there anyone] whose mind and spirit a certain feeling of religion does not grasp, stupefy, and captivate with delight? [24] Is there anyone whose eyes are not marvelously nourished and delighted by the very aspect of the thing, whose ears are not soothed by the unbelievable elegance and harmony of the song? What, then, on earth is known to be more beautiful than this spec-

chrius, quod[225] maius, quod[226] divinius, quod[227] admiratione,[228] quod[229] memoria[230] ac literis dignius reperitur, ut non homines modo, qui intersunt et quibus hoc natura datum est, sed ipsius[231] etiam parietes templi et[232] exultare quodam modo[233] et gestire[234] laetitia videatur?

A:[235] [25] Vera narras, et, medius fidius, ipse praesens interdum ita afficior ut cogitatione abstrahar et non humana illa neque ab hominibus[236] acta videre, sed sublimis raptus ad superos, ut de Ganimede veteres poetae fabulis prodidere, deorum mensis videar interesse.

L:[237] [26] Haud iniuria. Harum[238] enim rerum tanta admiratio ac religio et fuit semper, hodieque, hoc Eugenio pontefice maximo, non in Italia solum, sed ad remotissimas etiam oras et[239] regiones[240] fama pervasit, ut, cum divisa iam diu Christi religio foret eiusque homines inter se non sententiis tantum atque opinionibus, sed capitali quoque odio dissiderent,[241] nunc primum tot post secula Byzanthinum imperatorem una et Thraces, Indos, Ethiopes, taceo alios orientis reges,[242] principes, nationes, ad pacem, concordiam, unionem cum orientalibus ineundam attraxerit; [27] quae cum //71v// propediem, nisi infestum aliquod numen inpediat, futura videantur,[243] si nulla[244] mihi esset alia causa frequentandae curiae, satis haec una magna cuique ac probabilis existimari deberet, ut hunc tantum, tam varium, tam celebrem hominum atque adeo genitum[245] concursum, tantum tam admirabilem consensum, antea nunquam auditum

---

225. quid *coni. Sch.*
226. quid *coni. Sch.*
227. quid *coni. Sch.*
228. admiratione] admiratione quod admiratione *sic P.*
229. quid *coni. Sch.*
230. memoria *om. Sch.*
231. ipsi *G.*
232. et *om. GB.*
233. quodam modo] quod admodum *N.*
234. gestari *V;* egestire *B.*
235. A *om. V.*
236. omnibus *V.*
237. L *om. V.*
238. Nam *N.*
239. ac *V.*
240. religiones *PN.*
241. dissederent *V.*
242. regis *V.*
243. vedeantur *sic V;* reddantur *sic legit Sch.;* videant *G.*
244. ulla *B.*
245. gentium *PNB.*

tacle, greater, or more divine? What is there that is worthier of wonder, remembrance, or being recorded in writing, so that not only men (who take part in these matters and to whom nature has given them) but also the walls of the church building itself seem to revel in a certain way and be transported with happiness?

A: [25] What you say is true, by God, and when I am there, at times I am so affected that I am lost in thought and seem to see things neither human nor by humans transacted. Uplifted and seized into the heavens, I seem to be present at the tables of the gods, as the ancient poets in their fables spoke of Ganymede.[18]

L: [26] Justifiably so. After all, there has always been so much admiration and worship of these things [at the curia]. And today, now that Eugenius is pope, the [church's] reputation has spread not only in Italy but even to the remotest shores and regions. Of course, it is true that the religion of Christ has been divided now for a long time and that the people who comprise the church disagree among themselves—and it is not just that they disagree about feelings and opinions; they do so with a life-endangering hatred! Even with all this, now, for the first time after all these centuries, the report of these things has brought [here] the Byzantine emperor as well as the Thracians, Indians, Ethiopians (and I pass over the kings, princes, and peoples of the East), for the sake of entering on peace, concord, and union with the Easterners. [27] Since it seems to be about to happen any day now—unless impeded by some hostile spirit—if there were no other reason for me to be frequenting the curia, then this one great reason would have to be thought believable enough: that I, being present, might see what would seem unbelievable to those who are not here. I might see, that is, this coming together of men that is so great, so variegated, so famous, so engendered by God, and such a great and admirable unanimity that the likes of it has never been heard of

---

18. Ganymede, because of his great beauty, was taken up by Zeus to live with the gods in Olympia. The locus classicus is in Homer's *Iliad* (XX.231), but different aspects of the Ganymede legend were known from a host of Latin sources as well.

aut lectum, qui absentibus incredibilis videatur, praesens aspicerem et communi omnium plausu et gaudio[246] fruerer.

A: [28] Vehementer sum tua oratione delectatus et uberrimum ex hac disputatione fructum me percepisse sentio, quod de veteri mea[247] sententia paulatim dimoveri incipio maximamque partem diuturni erroris mei per te hodie posuisse videor.[248] Fit enim nescio quo modo ut quae unicuique rei insint vicia, statim appareant, lateant bona diutius obscurenturque ab illis ut prodire atque in lucem emergere nequeant. Sic mihi olim curiae vitia ante oculos quottidie versabantur,[249] tot vero ac tanta bona quasi caligine ac tenebris circunfusa haud videbam, quae nunc omnia illata a te luce orationis aspicio et plura multo maioraque[250] superesse intelligo.

L: [29] Nihili est ergo deinceps explanatione mea opus. A me enim aditu[251] ianuaque patefacta, reliqua quae superesse dicis tu ipse pro tua diligentia, si paulum modo invigilare volueris, facile cognoscere poteris.

A: [30] Immo[252] nunc magis est opus multo quam antea, et negocii etiam plus incumbit. Ut enim viator penitus ignorans viam, raro aberrat, quod nunquam fere sine duce iter ingreditur, edoctus autem qua sibi eundum sit, si careat duce, in avia[253] saepe et difficilia loca inducitur, sic ego antea totius rationis ignarus et[254] hebes in eo uno tantum versabar errore, nunc autem initiis cognitionis perceptis, si praeceptione[255] tua destitutus essem, in varios et inextricabiles errores inciderem. Quare perge, obsecro,[256] quousque ad exitum incolumem me perduxeris.

[IV. De prudentia et aliis virtutibus acquirendis curiae]

L: [1] Non recuso equidem, //72// sed vellem aliquid proferres[257] in medium[258] ex iis[259] quae te reliqua percepisse dixisti.

---

246. gladio *V.*
247. me *B.*
248. hodie posuisse videor] posuisse videar hodie *V;* posuisse videor hodie *PGN.*
249. quottidie versabantur] versabantur quotidie *G.*
250. multo maioraque] multoque maiora *G;* multo maiora *N.*
251. auditu *V.*
252. Admodum *N.*
253. in avia] inania *VB.*
254. ut *V.*
255. perceptione *V.*
256. queso *canc. ad* obsecro *in mar. s. B¹.*
257. proferre *G.*
258. me *P.*
259. hiis *P.*

or read about before. Thus I might rejoice in the common applause and joy of all.

A: [28] I am truly delighted by your speech and feel that I have taken away from this discussion the ripest of fruits, since little by little I am beginning to be nudged away from my prior opinion and seem, thanks to you, to have done away with most of this long-standing error of mine. For it happens—and I don't know how—that whatever vices are present in a certain thing appear on the spot, while the good things lie hidden for quite some time, obscured by the vices. The result is that the good things cannot find a way out into the light of day. So to me, previously, the vices of the curia were occurring before my very eyes every day, and I just really didn't see the great multitude of good things, which were overwhelmed as if by a dark haze. Of course now I see all of these good things—which you have brought forth by the light of your oration—and I understand that they stand out over and the bad, since they are so many more and so much greater.

L: [29] Well then, further explanation on my part would be pointless. After all, since I have opened the door for you, you yourself, with your own diligence, could easily figure out the rest of the things that you say remain, if only you choose to stay awake for a little while.

A: [30] Not at all; in fact now there is much more need than before and it is even more pertinent. Before, when I was completely ignorant of the whole discourse, I was like a traveler who doesn't know the way at all and thus rarely makes a mistake. For the traveler does not undertake a journey without a guide, since, if he is informed as to how to go but has no leader, he is often led into trackless, dangerous places. I was a dull-witted creature who was thoroughly engaged in that one error, but now that I have just begun to understand, if I were deprived of your instruction, I would fall into many different, inextricable errors. So please, go on, until you have led me to a safe way out.

[IV. On Prudence and the Other Virtues to Be Acquired at the Curia]

L: [1] Of course I won't refuse. But I do wish you would come out openly with one of those [good] things that you said you thought remained.

A: [2] Illud est inprimis, quod ex dictis tuis potissimum colligo, videri mihi nos faciliorem quodam modo et expeditiorem ad superos aditum habituros esse. Siquidem ibi praesente pontifice praecipuo Dei beneficio et munere et meritorum praemia immortalia et delictorum remissio et venia tribuatur, itaque non dicam mortem usquam²⁶⁰ expetendam²⁶¹ esse, sed, sicubi moriendum est, ut certe est, in curia mori quam alibi malim, ubi moriendi ratio tutior et sanctior.

L: [3] Et bene etiam²⁶² prudenter moderateque vivendi²⁶³ oportunitas maior.

A: Quonam pacto?

L: Dicam. Num²⁶⁴ prudentiam ducem bene vivendi et magistram appellare solemus?

A: [4] Rectissime, quippe qua honesta, turpia, iusta, iniusta, aequa, iniqua, commoda, incommoda, utilia inutiliaque dignoscimus eaque²⁶⁵ seiungere abinvicem²⁶⁶ ac separare, tum quae²⁶⁷ probemus eligere, contraria fugere aspernarique valemus; ad haec praeterita meminisse, quae instant²⁶⁸ sapienter gerere, quae impediunt, ut ventura sunt,²⁶⁹ multo antea providere, et si qua secum ferant incommoda, declinare.

L: [5] Quid? Quod eadem virtute maxime a ceteris animantibus²⁷⁰ distare videmur,²⁷¹ hac eadem supra homines attolli et proxime ad Deum accedere? Nam²⁷²—quod nullum aliud animal potest—quod in rebus decorum, quis ordo, quae convenientia sit perspicimus et hominibus dubiis suarum rerum²⁷³ et incertis et in aliqua difficultate constitutis salutaria consilia damus veritatisque cognitionem attingimus. Haec autem virtus duabus rebus praecipue comparatur.

A: [6] Quibus?

L: Longitudine aetatis et usu atque experientia rerum.

---

260. usque *V.*
261. expectendam *V.*
262. etiam] et iam *V.*
263. moderateque vivendi *om. G.*
264. Non *B.*
265. Qeaque *V;* omniaque *coni. Sch.*
266. adinvicem *VPGB.*
267. tum que] cum equa *V.*
268. instantur *V.*
269. sunt *om. G.*
270. animalibus *coni. Sch.*
271. videmus *P.*
272. Non *B.*
273. suarum rerum] rerum suarum *B.*

A: [2] Well, first of all, the most important thing I infer from what you said is that it seems to me that we shall have in some way a simpler and more unhindered passage to the upper world. Certainly with the pope present and by the special privilege and gift of God, we receive immortal reward for our merits and remission and forgiveness for our sins. So I am not saying that death is to be sought out. But since there is no doubt that we have to die, I would rather die in the curia than anywhere else, since in the curia there is a safer and holier way of dying.

L: [3] As well as a greater opportunity to live prudently and moderately.

A: How so?

L: I'll tell you. Don't we usually call prudence the guide and teacher of living well?

A: [4] That's very true, since by prudence we discern things that are decent and indecent, just and unjust, fair and unfair, advantageous and disadvantageous, and useful and useless. We learn how to separate these things from one another and divide them up. After this we can choose what we approve of and avoid and reject the contrary. We can also remember the past, deal wisely with the present, and foresee well in advance the things to come and any future impediments. And if any of those things might bring difficulties along with them, we can turn them down.

L: [5] What do you mean? That the same virtue that seems to separate us in the highest degree from other animals raises us above men and makes us come closer to God? For—as no other animal can—we see the beauty, the order, and the harmony that exists in things. We give helpful advice to those who are doubtful and uncertain of their affairs as well as to those who have wound up in some kind of difficulty. And we attain to an understanding of the truth. Moreover, we acquire this power by two things.

A: [6] Which ones?

L: Length of age and everyday practice and experience with things.

A: Sic arbitror et verissimum illud puto esse, quod //72v// apud Aristotelem legisse me[274] memini: iuvenem mathematicum et phisicum[275] esse posse, prudentem vero nisi senem ac natu grandiorem non posse, quod duo illa sint in senibus, quae iuvenes aduc per aetatem assequi nequiverunt.

L: [7] Philosophari mihi videris!

A: Tua id praeceptio effecit.

L: Utinam id praestare mea[276] praeceptio posset; sed vereor ne, si hoc verum est, quoniam iam adeo profecisti,[277] perbrevi magistrum exsuperes.

A: Ita ne iocaris mecum?

L: [8] Existimo igitur Aristotelem Homeri poesim legisse atque illum imitatum esse, qui, cum in Ulyxis persona prudentem virum fingere vellet, sic scripsit: "Varias iactatus in oras[278] et mores hominum multorum novit et urbes;" eadem videlicet erroris longitudine et varietate locorum atque hominum notavit. Huius preciosissimae rei consequendae gratia numquam ego cuiquam Calypsen, Circem,[279] Pheaces, Lystrigones, Syrenas, Ciclopes, inferos ut[280] Ulyxi petendos censuerim. Nam quae ille diuturno errore, summo vitae discrimine consequutus est,[281] haec omnia abunde tibi Romana curia suppeditabit. [9] In ea enim una rerum multitudinem, varietatem hominum, magnitudinem causarum reperias.[282] Nihil enim fere[283] maximum inter Christianos agitur, de quo non consulatur[284] pontifex maximus, in quo non eius interponatur auctoritas. Sive enim de bello sive de pace sive de foederibus ineundis sive de matrimoniis inter summos orbis reges et principes deliberatur[285] sive aliqua inter eos vertitur[286] controversia, cuncta ad illum deferuntur et in curia

---

274. legisse me] me legisse *P.*
275. phisicum] phisicum et phisicum *sic P.*
276. praestare mea *om. G.*
277. perfecisti *N.*
278. in oras] in horas *V;* moras *G.*
279. Artem *sic B.*
280. et *G.*
281. est *om. V.*
282. reperies *coni. Sch.*
283. fore *G.*
284. consolatur *VNB.*
285. deliberantur *G.*
286. aliqua inter eos vertitur] aliqua vertitur inter eos *P.*

A: I think so too, and I believe that what I remember reading in Aristotle is very true: that a young man can be both a natural philosopher and a mathematician, but that a man cannot be prudent unless he is an old man, someone greater in age. This is because present in old men are those two things [you mentioned] that as youths they couldn't yet acquire, given their age.[19]

L: [7] You seem to me to philosophize!

A: Well, your teaching brought it about.

L: I wish my teaching could have been responsible for it. But if this is true I am afraid that you are fast superseding your master, since you have already come this far.

A: Really, are you jesting at my expense?

L: [8] Well then, I think that Aristotle read the poem of Homer and that he imitated him. When Homer wanted to portray the prudent man in the person of Ulysses, he wrote as follows: "Having been cast onto various shores, he came to know the cities and customs of many peoples";[20] that is, Homer denoted the same things [mentioned earlier] by the length of wandering and variety of places and men. I never thought that for the sake of pursuing this most precious thing [i.e., this virtue], anyone—like Ulysses—had to seek out Calyps, Circes, the Phaeacians, the Laestrygones, the Sirens, the Cyclops, and Hades. After all, what he gained by long wandering and with extreme danger to his life—well, the Roman curia will offer you all of it in abundance. [9] There, together, you would find a multitude of things, a variety of men, and a great number of inducements. For among Christians almost nothing of great importance is done on which the pope is not consulted or in which his authority is not in some way involved. Whether it is a deliberation concerning war, peace, or striking treaties, or marriages among the greatest kings and princes of the world, or even if it concerns some controversy that occurs among these great leaders, all things are deferred to the pope, and they

---

19. Angelo is confused. In the *Nicomachean Ethics* (VI.8), Aristotle does not say that a boy can be both a mathematician and a natural philosopher but not a wise man. Rather, he says that a boy can be a mathematician but not a natural philosopher or a wise man, since the latter two require *empeiria*, or experience. The general point, however, for the goals of the discussion, is clear: the curia provides useful experience of the world, since many different peoples and customs can be observed there.

20. See Hom. *Od.* I.3–4.

ut[287] in[288] publico[289] aliquo foro[290] agitantur. [10] Itaque necesse est eum qui in hac tanta frequentia versetur rerum atque hominum multa videre, multa audire, //73// multa discere, multa etiam[291] ipsum agere, plurimorum item nec vulgarium nec imperitorum hominum colloquio, sermone, et consuetudine uti, plurimorum mores et vitae instituta agnoscere, cum nonnullis etiam familiaritates amicitiasque coniungere. Ex quibus omnibus sibi quod libeat probandi, improbandi, legendi, reiiciendi, dimittendi, sumendi, corrigendi, emendandive[292] potestas permittitur, ut, tametsi natura hebetior sit, modo non negligens, paulo[293] tamen diutius tritus in curia et sub actus[294] summo[295] saepe viros ingenio superet.

A: [11] Hoc mihi ita esse facillime persuadeo. Complures enim proferre possum adulescentes profectos nuper in curiam[296] qui cum egregia indole essent, ita peritos magistros diligentesque invenere[297] ut paucis mensibus in viros evaderent, nec vero Tiresiae nec Cenei tam celerem formae mutationem arbitror fuisse nec tantam. Quod minime mirum. [12] Sunt enim in curia Romana homines quidam non usu modo rerum maximarum imbuti, sed etiam inusitata quadam admirabili atque inaudita disciplina praediti et ad instituendos adolescentes accommodata, cuius[298] ego nomen ne proferam veluti Eleusina illa mysteria religione impedior. Sed quid reliquae[299] virtutes? Nullusne[300] in curia illarum est usus, nulla exercitatio,[301] nullum munus?

L: [13] Permulta. Difficile est enim quempiam esse prudentem, quin idem et iustus et fortis et temperans sit. Quis enim iniustum aut ignavum et timidum aut intemperantem, prudentem audeat appellare? Quae omnia summae dementiae[302] et insaniae vitia videntur esse.[303]

---

287. et *N*.
288. ut in *om. V*.
289. preco *sic V*; presto *sic coni. Sch*.
290. aliquo foro] foro aliquo *B*.
291. et *V*.
292. emendandi *N*.
293. paula *V*.
294. *lege* subactus; sublatus *V*.
295. summos *G*.
296. curia *N*.
297. inven( )e *V*; invenire *legit Sch*.
298. quorum *coni. Sch*.
299. reliquie *V*.
300. Nulliusne *G*.
301. exercitatio] exercitatio et *P*.
302. clemencie *VP*.
303. videntur esse] esse videntur *B*.

are all discussed in the curia as if it were a kind of public forum. [10] This is why it is inevitable that whoever is involved in such frequent contact with men and affairs sees many things, hears many things, learns many things, and also himself does many things. He takes advantage of the talk, conversation, and social interaction of many men—and these are men who are not common or unlearned—and he knows the customs and manners of living of many and forms acquaintanceships and friendships besides. From all of these things, he is granted the power of approving and disapproving what he wishes, of choosing and rejecting, of letting go and taking back, as well as the power of correcting and emending. The result is that even if he is by nature somewhat dim-witted—and as long as he is not negligent—after being worn down and broken in for a while in the curia, he often conquers men of the highest cleverness.

A: [11] I'm actually quite easily convinced by this. For I can name quite a few very young men who have advanced recently into the curia and, while they had great natural ability, have come upon teachers who were so skilled and diligent that in a few months they emerged as men, so that I think that not even Tiresias or Caeneus changed their form so swiftly or in such a great degree.[21] And really it's no wonder. [12] For there are some in the Roman curia who are not only imbued with practice in the greatest affairs but also endowed with a certain unaccustomed, marvelous, and unheard-of teaching system, one well suited for training very young men. I am impeded by scruple from revealing its name, as if it were the famous Eleusinian mysteries. But what about the rest of the virtues? In the curia isn't there any practice of them, any training in them, any function for them?

L: [13] Of course. After all, it is difficult for someone to be prudent without at the same time being just, brave, and temperate. Really, who would dare to call the prudent man unjust, or ignorant and cowardly, or intemperate? All of these vices seem to be characteristic of the highest folly and insanity.

---

21. Tiresias and Caeneus were two ancient mythological figures who were said, in some versions of the legends surrounding them, to have changed sexes completely. Lapo would have known about Caeneus from Virg. *Aen* VI.448–49: "There goes Caeneus as a companion, once a young man, now a woman, straightaway she has been changed into her old form" [It comes et iuvenis quondam, nunc femina, Caeneus / Rursus et in veterem fato revoluta figuram]. Cf. also Servius ad loc. For Tiresias, Lapo would have known the story from Ovid *Met.* III.316–40. There he would have read the story that Tiresias, on seeing two snakes copulating, hit them with a stick and thereafter was changed into a woman. When the same thing happened later on, Tiresias was changed back into his original, masculine form.

[14] Virtutes autem omnes, cum ab uno fonte et capite manent, uno societatis vinculo continentur inter se, officiis tamen ab invicem distinguntur. Sic qui //73v// agit ea quae sunt prudentiae, prudens,³⁰⁴ quae iustitiae, iustus, quae fortitudinis, fortis, quae temperantiae, temperans dicitur, quae omnia si in uno³⁰⁵ complecti volumus, virum illum bonum appellamus.³⁰⁶ Itaque necesse est qui prudentiam sive quanvis aliam³⁰⁷ virtutem habeat, eum virtutes omnes habere; cui una desit, deesse omnes.

[15] Ex quo non³⁰⁸ temere videntur Stoici illum viciis omnibus inquinatum putasse cui aliquid ad summam virtutem deficeret,³⁰⁹ nec quicquam interesse aut differre Socratem,³¹⁰ summum philosophum et sanctissimum virum, a Phalari, scelestissimo crudelissimoque tyranno, quoniam neminem bonum habendum ducerent nisi sapientem, nec sapientem quenquam,³¹¹ nisi in quo perfecta et absoluta virtus foret; quam cum minus assecutus Socrates videretur, aeque ipsum ac Phalarim vitio obnoxium et perinde ut illum improbum esse.

[16] Sed Aristoteles et alii³¹² de virtute accuratius disputant. Duo ponunt virtutum genera, quorum alterum in pervestigatione³¹³ et cognitione veritatis, alterum in actione versetur, illud intellectivum, hoc morale vocitant; quos secutus Cicero in primo De officiis libro: Duo, inquit, sunt officiorum genera, quorum unum quod pertinet ad finem bonorum, quod Graeci κατόρθωμα,³¹⁴ nos perfectum officium possumus appellare, alterum ad³¹⁵ institutionem vitae communis, quod medium officium nuncuparunt. [17] Quae duo genera veteres quidam philosophi solo sapientiae nomine contineri statuunt, et eas omnes virtutes in unum collectas et inter se coherentes sapientiam dicunt. Qui vero ex iis³¹⁶ vir-

---

304. prudens *om. P.*
305. uno] unum *V; post* uno *add.* animo *inter lineas B.*
306. appellans *V.*
307. quanvis aliam] quavis aliam *N;* aliam quanvis *B.*
308. nunc *B.*
309. difficeret *V.*
310. societatem *N.*
311. nisi sapientem nec sapientem quenquam] nisi sapientem quempiam *V;* nisi sapientem nec sapientem quempiam *PN.*
312. alii] alii qui *B.*
313. in pervestigatione] impervestigatione *G.*
314. καθορτωμα *F;* κατόρθωμα *om. VPGN cum spatio vacuo; om. B sed sine spatio;* κατόρθωμα *add. Sch., recte.*
315. ad *om. V.*
316. hiis *PB.*

[14] Besides, all of the virtues, even though they flow from one source and one point of origin and are contained among themselves, singularly bonded in relationship, nonetheless are distinguished one from another in their duties. Thus whoever does those things that are characteristic of prudence is said to be prudent; whoever does those things that are characteristic of bravery is said to be brave; whoever does those things that are characteristic of temperance is said to be temperate. If all of these things are gathered together in one man, then we call that man good. And so it is necessary that someone who possesses prudence or any other virtue possess all the virtues. Whoever is lacking one lacks them all.

[15] Because of this it seems that the Stoics were not being rash to have thought that the man who is lacking anything toward the attainment of the highest virtue is polluted by all vices. Nor were they rash in thinking that nothing distinguished or differentiated Socrates—who was the greatest philosopher and the most holy of men—from Phalaris, who was the wickedest and cruelest of tyrants. For they thought that no one was to be considered good unless he was wise and that no one was wise unless there was complete, absolute virtue in him, and since it seems that Socrates had not attained this, they thought that Socrates himself was practically subject to vice, just like Phalaris, and that Socrates was as wicked as Phalaris.[22]

[16] But Aristotle and others argue more precisely about virtue. They set forth that there are two genera of virtue. One of these turns on the investigation and cognition of truth, the other on action. They call the first genus "intellectual virtues" and the second "moral virtues." Cicero followed them in the first book of the *De officiis*. He says that there are two genera of duties. One of these pertains to the end of goods, and the Greeks called it κατόρθωμα [katorthōma]; we can call it "complete duty." The other comprises the principles of common life, and they called it "middle duty."[23] [17] Certain ancient philosophers judge that these two genera are contained under the single name of wisdom, and they say that all these virtues are collected together and, hanging together among themselves, constitute wisdom. They mean that whoever is completely com-

---

22. Perhaps an allusion to the fact that Socrates yielded lustfully to Alcibiades (?); perhaps cf. Plut. *De fortuna . . . Alexandri* 12.
    23. Cf. Cic. *Off.* I.7–8, and see chap. 2 supra.

tutibus totus conglutinatus[317] est, sapientem et esse et[318] appellari volunt. Sapientiam autem ipsam divinarum humanarumque rerum scientiam esse diffiniunt. Ex quibus colligi potest existimasse[319] //74// illos unam tantum esse virtutem[320] quam qui nactus[321] esset, sapientem eundemque bonum virum esse, cui pars aliqua deesset, eum nec sapientem nec bonum.

[18] Ut igitur ad propositum reducatur oratio, si quis vel natura duce vel[322] doctrina vel usu et pertractatione rerum vel alia quapiam ratione prudens evaserit, illi continuo virtutes reliquae comitentur[323] oportet, aliter non erit prudens, quanquam etiam[324] separatim non minores nec pauciores contineat[325] curia oportunitates reliquarum virtutum parandarum, quam conparandae, retinendae augendaeque prudentiae. [19] Ex eadem enim diversitate rerum et copia, quibus gerendis prudentes efficimur, discimus neminem laedere nisi provocati, insontes ab iniuria prohibere, aeque omnibus ius dicere, fidem datam non fallere, quod suum est unicuique tribuere, quae iustitiae officia sunt; praeterea non confidere nimium nec temere desperare, res magnas ac[326] arduas spectare[327] atque appetere, despicere humiles, pericula laboresque cum ratione utilitatis suscipere eademque[328] constantissime tolerare, nec secundis rebus efferri[329] nec perturbari adversis et tumultuantem de gradu deiici,[330] quae a fortitudine proficiscuntur. [20] Nec minus assuefimus[331] rationem ducem sequi eidemque appetitus subiicere atque oboedientes praestare, contemnere voluptates, cupiditates[332] nostras facile continere, in omnibus[333] vitae partibus decorum gravitatemque servare et, ut Pythius Apollo praecipit, nihil nimis. Quae omnia a temperato modestoque viro inprimis desiderare solemus. Haec igitur, ut vides,

---

317. conglutinans *V.*
318. et *om. B.*
319. extistimasse] existimans se *V;* existimas se *N.*
320. esse virtutem] virtutem esse *B.*
321. natus *G.*
322. et *B.*
323. committentur *V.*
324. quanquam etiam] etiam quanquam *N.*
325. continet *G.*
326. et *N.*
327. espectare *V.*
328. eademque] ea denique *N.*
329. offerri *N.*
330. clerici *V.*
331. assuescimus *G.*
332. cupiditates *om. P.*
333. hominibus *G.*

posed of these virtues is wise and is called wise. Indeed, they define wisdom as the very knowledge of divine and human things, from which we can gather that they thought that virtue was very much one thing and that whoever has obtained it is wise and good, whereas whoever is lacking even a part of virtue is neither wise nor good.

[18] So (to return to the point of the conversation), if someone emerges as a wise man—whether because he is led by nature or custom and everyday dealings with things or because of any other reason—then he must be accompanied by the remaining virtues. Otherwise he will not be prudent, although the curia too has neither lesser nor fewer opportunities for coming by the remaining virtues than for acquiring, maintaining, and increasing prudence. [19] For from the same diversity and abundance of things that make us prudent when we do them, we learn never to injure anyone unless provoked, to protect the innocent from injury, to judge all equally, not to break a promise, and to render to each his own—all of which are the duties of justice—and, moreover, not to trust excessively or to despair rashly, to aim toward and desire great and arduous things, to look down on humble ones, to take on dangers and difficult tasks for utility's sake and to tolerate these same things with the greatest constancy, and not to be carried away by things that are favorable, or be disturbed by adverse circumstances, or be dislodged from one's place of battle in times of confusion—these things come from bravery. [20] Nor are we less accustomed [in the curia] to follow reason as our leader and to subordinate our appetites to reason, showing that we are obedient to reason; to despise pleasures; to contain our desires with ease, and in all parts of our life to preserve decorum and seriousness and, as Pythian Apollo ordered, "nothing in excess."[24] We usually think that all of these things are needed above all by the man who is temperate

---

24. Apollo is sometimes known as Pythian Apollo because his temple was known as the "palace of Python." The traditional classical proverb "Nothing in excess" (Latin "nihil nimis," Greek μηδὲν ἄγαν) was found in various forms in a host of sources. Included among these are Pindar fr. 216; Ter. *Hau.* 519; Cic. *Fin.* III.73.

parari in curia possunt, si quis illis vigilanter studeat. Quae quidem[334] si magna atque adeo maxima et preciosissima sunt bona dubitare non potes,[335] plurima nos ex eis[336] commoda, emolumenta, utilitatesque[337] percipere.

A: [21] Est quidem,[338] ni fallor, ut dicis. Non tamen arbitror ad ea bona licere omnibus aspirare.

L: Certe omnibus //74v// volentibus, dico, ac perquirentibus nec adiumentis et praesidiis naturae destitutis. Sunt enim quidam ita remisso animo ac[339] abiecto, ingenio vero ita hebeti ac tardo, plerique ita negligentes, desidiosi, stupidi aut ita delicati et molles, nonnulli calidi in consiliis, rapidi et perturbationibus animi adeo obnoxii, adeo praeposteri alii natura ac perversi, complures sic corruptis et inquinatis moribus ut, etiam si omnes a curia sibi facult<at>es[340] suppeditate[341] fuerint, in illorum tamen quos dixi numerum venire non possint.

A: [22] Hos[342] equidem homines, si splendorem curiae, si decus pristinum, si honestatem[343] recuperare et retinere cupimus, veluti pestes quasdam ac labes hominum procul a curia abigendos et in ultimas terras exportandos censeo, qui inutiles sibi, reliquis perniciosi, curiae universae dedecorosi sunt. Suis[344] enim[345] probris ac flagitiis magnam illi nobisque omnibus notam atque infamiam inuxerunt.[346] Ex quo iam apud omnes homines in sermone ac proverbio usurpatur sine exceptione aliqui: "Curialis bonus, homo improbissimus; curialis bonus,[347] homo scelestissimus et omnibus viciis cohopertus." Itaque me pudet iam, puto item bonos omnis[348] et esse et dici curiales.

L: [23] Scio, me hercule, vera istaec esse quae dicis, et quidem[349] ita esse vehementer indoleo. Atque utinam id quod dixisti modo in mentem

---

334. equidem *V.*
335. potest *VG.*
336. ea *sic codd.*
337. utilitatisque *V.*
338. equidem *V.*
339. et *PGN.*
340. facultates *VPGNB.*
341. suppeditate] suppeditate abunde *VPGNB.*
342. Nos *P.*
343. honestate *V.*
344. suis] sinis *aut* suus *V.*
345. etiam *N.*
346. inunxerunt *coni. Sch.;* iniunxerunt *P; corr. in mar. d. ad* induxerunt *G.*
347. improbissimus; curialis bonus, homo *om. Sch.*
348. hominis *coni. Sch.;* omnes *N.*
349. quia *G.*

and modest. These things, then, as you see, can be acquired in the curia, if one seeks them out watchfully. Certainly, if these goods are great things, or even the greatest and most valued things, you cannot doubt that we receive many benefits, profits, and advantages from them.

A: [21] Of course, if I am not mistaken, it is as you say. Still, I don't think everyone is permitted to aspire to these goods.

L: I say that it is permitted to all who are willing and who search eagerly for these things and who are not lacking in nature's assistance and aid. There are some, after all, who are so remiss and abject in spirit, so dull and laggardly in intelligence, more who are so negligent, idle, and stupid, so soft and effeminate, some who are hot-tempered in their judgment as well as quick to anger and are so subject to perturbations of the soul, others who are so wrongheaded and perverse in nature, many who are so corrupt and polluted in character, that even if they had for themselves all of the curia's possibilities in abundance, they still could not come into the number of those whom I have mentioned.

A: [22] Well I certainly think that these men should be driven far away from the curia as plagues and disgraces to humankind and expelled to the ends of the earth, if we want to recover and then retain the curia's splendor, original beauty, and honor. These men are useless to themselves, destructive toward others, and disgraceful to the whole curia. Indeed, because of their shameful and outrageous acts, they have branded the curia as well as all of us with a great and widely known mark of shame. Because of this, now everyone, without any exception, in everyday speech and proverbially, uses this phrase: "Good curialist, wickedest of men; good curialist, most corrupt of men, overwhelmed by all vices." And so, by now I am ashamed—and I think that all good men are ashamed—to be curialists and to be called such.

L: [23] By Hercules, I know what you say is true, and it bothers me immensely! If only what you said would find its way into the mind of the

veniret ei qui summae rei praeest, ut hos³⁵⁰ impurissimos et perditissi-
mos³⁵¹ homines, quibus ob impunitatem facinorum referta sunt omnia,
suppliciis, ignominiis, exilio, morte multaret! [24] Melius profecto sibi,
melius dignitati suae, melius existimationi curiae, melius curialium qui
honeste vivere cupiunt commodis salutique consuleret. Cederent
improbi, cederent, inquam,³⁵² curia, cederent magistratibus,³⁵³ cederent
dignitatibus, cederent hoc amplissimorum et illustrissimorum virorum
cetu et frequentia, quem paene iam totum suis sceleribus nequissimis
inquinarunt!³⁵⁴ Respirarent tandem aliquando boni seque attollerent
meritis! Potirentur honoribus et digna suis operibus praemia //75//
reportarent! Esset enim virtuti, esset honestati honos.

[25] Haec consuetudo, si serpere ac³⁵⁵ prodire inciperet, animos
omnium hac spe proposita ad laudem, ad³⁵⁶ gloriam, ad digni<ta>tem
maxime excitaret³⁵⁷ et ab improbitate deterreret, cum nonnisi bonis artibus ad honores³⁵⁸ et amplitudinem aditum patere intuerentur; pro faci-
norosis honestos, pro intemperantibus temperatos, pro luxuriosis
modestos, pro corruptis integros, pro sceleratis viros sanctissimos
haberemus. Itaque iure³⁵⁹ tum floreret³⁶⁰ curiae Romanae nomen et eius
imperii dignitas pontificisque maiestas gravis haberetur.

[26] Quae quidem³⁶¹ contra nunc fiunt³⁶² omnia. Nam quae miseria
tanta est ut cum hac curialium comparari conferrique possit? Tot honestissimi et praestantissimi³⁶³ viri, quot in curia Romana sunt, paucorum
vicio ac turpitudine contemnuntur despiciunturque ab omnibus, gravi
diuturnaque invidia flagrant.³⁶⁴ In pontificis iam maximi caput audaces
ac temerarii homines insultant eidemque et reliquis cladem aliquam
atque exitium quottidie moliuntur; bona fortunasque ecclesiae sceleratis-

---

350. hos *om. G.*
351. periclitissimos *V.*
352. inquit *P.*
353. magratibus *N.*
354. inquinarunt] inquinarunt et *N.*
355. et *N.*
356. et *P.*
357. extitaret *N.*
358. honeres *sic F;* honorem *G.*
359. iure *om. G.*
360. flereret *V.*
361. quidam *V.*
362. nunc fiunt] fiunt nunc *P.*
363. et praestantissimi *om. Sch.*
364. flagitant *corr. ad* flagrant *in mar. d. B¹.*

one at the head of the whole institution. Then he might punish with torture, dishonor, exile, and death these most impure, desperate men with whom the whole [institution] is packed because of their unpunished crimes! [24] Certainly it would be better for him [the pope] to think about his own interests, his own worth, the reputation of the curia, as well as the safety and success of the curialists who desire to live honorably. These disgraces should retreat—retreat, I say—from the curia, retreat from the magistracies, retreat from their dignified status, retreat from the company and concourse of such widely accomplished and illustrious men, which [company] they have almost completely defiled with their most wicked crimes. The good might at last catch their breath and raise themselves up by their own merits. They would take possession of honors and bring home rewards worthy of their own works. Then virtue and honorable dealing would have their honor.

[25] If this habit began gradually to wend its way in and then grow, it would particularly stir up the spirits of all—once this hope had been conceived—to praise, glory, and dignity. It would also deter them from wickedness, since they would clearly see an opportunity for honors and high rank only by means of liberal culture. Instead of criminals we would have honest men, instead of the intemperate we would have temperate men, instead of the excessive we would have modest men, instead of the perverse we would have pure men, and instead of the corrupt we would have the most holy of men. Then the name of the Roman curia would rightfully flourish, and its dignity of empire as well as the grave majesty of the pope would be obtained.

[26] Of course, everything that happens now at the curia works against this goal. Really, what wretchedness is there that is so great that it could be likened or compared to that of the curialists? Despite the existence at the curia of quite a number of honorable, outstanding men, still, just as many are hated and despised by all because of the vice and filthiness of a few; they are subjected to a fire of envy that has long oppressed them. The audacious and the rash call down insults on the head of the pope. Every day they hurl one disaster or another on him and the rest. We see that the goods and fortunes of the church have been exposed to the most corrupt of thieves for the purpose of pillage and devastation,

simis[365] latronibus praedae ac populationi expositas[366] esse videmus
eorumque armis vexari ac diripi omne patrimonium dignitatis; ac nisi his
illorum[367] audaciae occurratur, subito extremum propediem curiae
excidium imminere videtur.

[27] Quare arbitror tempus iam instare omnibus[368] excitari atque
assurgere tantisque et prementibus[369] et futuris incommodis prospicere
ac providere. Commune est enim hoc malum, communis metus, commune periculum, communi praesidio haec tanta calamitas tanquam
aliquod commune incendium repellenda est. Serpit enim in dies magis
atque ingravescit morbus et altius radices agit. Curandus est igitur atque
opprimendus anteaquam se ad interiora insinuet, cum nullum salutis
remedium reperiri[370] poterit.

A:[371] [28] Sed iam querelis sit modus,[372] praesertim nihil profuturis.
Nam et ad institutum nostrum non pertinent et etiam periculosae sunt
propter improborum multitudinem, ne quis ista in se dici existimet.
//75v//

L: Obsequar voluntati tuae meque[373] ad propositum sermonem
referam, ac si hae[374] querelae meae tibi iniucundae fuerunt, memento[375]
te earum incoandarum[376] auctorem et principem fuisse. Sed ego fortasse
a te provocatus dolore et indignatione longius sum provectus, in quo
mihi debes ignoscere.

A:[377] Haec hactenus.

[V. De clarissimis otiosis curiae]

L:[378] [1] Illuc propero, quo iubes. Ne igitur putes negociosis[379] tantum

---

365. scelarissimis *F;* sceleratissimis *VPGNB.*
366. exquisitas *V;* expositas *om. G.*
367. illorumque *coni. Sch.*
368. omnis *sic B.*
369. preeminentibus *V;* p( )ntibus *P.*
370. inveniri *B.*
371. A *om. V.*
372. morbus *G.*
373. neque *P.*
374. ve *G.*
375. memento] me merito *GN.*
376. incoandarum *suprasciptum est F¹ (aut F³?).*
377. A *om. V.*
378. L *om. V.*
379. negociis *B.*

and we see that the entire patrimony has been ruined and stripped of its worth by force of their weapons. And unless we hasten to meet them and their audacity, it seems that soon, any day now, the ultimate annihilation of the curia is at hand.

[27] This is why I think the time is now at hand for all of us to be aroused, to rise up and look toward and provide for future troubles, which are so great and so pressing. For this is a shared evil, a shared grief, and a shared danger; this great calamity should be repelled by a shared defense, as if it were a common fire. For the disease creeps onward day by day. It grows more serious and plants its roots more deeply. It must be cured and extinguished, before it finds its way into the curia's inner reaches. Because if that happens, no remedy will be found to guarantee the curia's health.

A: [28] But now let that be the extent of the complaints, especially since they will be of no use. They do not pertain to the point of our discussion, and they are also dangerous precisely because of the multitude of wicked men. One of them might think they are directed specifically against him.

L: Let me bend to your will and bring myself back to the point of our talk. If these complaints of mine were harsh in your eyes, remember that you were their originator and author. But perhaps, provoked by you, I have been carried a bit too far by a suffering and indignation for which you ought to pardon me.

A: Enough of that.

[V. On the Famous Men of Intellectual Leisure at the Curia]

L: [1] I hasten to your command. Now I wouldn't want you to think that

hominibus[380] in curia locum esse, ociosis aut[381] nullum, si quis esset qui animo ab hac turba curiae negociisque abhorreret et se cuperet in ocium studiumque transferre, qua in re maxime peritorum copia desiderari et quaeri solet, a quibus instrui atque erudiri et quibuscum iis de rebus, quae in studio sibi praecepta sunt, comunicare ac loqui possit, illi ego nullum commodiorem curia locum neque aptiorem requirendum censeo.

[2] Ad quancumque enim te artem liberalem mente et cogitatione converteris, in ea tot perfectissimos ac summos viros una Romana curia habet quot arbitror in cunctis aliis civitatibus ac rebus publicis reperire difficillimum foret. Non proferam hoc loco sacrae theologiae professores, quorum[382] studia cum his[383] nostris nulla socie<ta>te iunguntur. [3] Non commemorabo physicos, mathematicos, astronomos, musicos, civilis vero[384] ac pontificii[385] iuris interpretes silentio praeteribo, qui quamquam et ipsi magno curiae ornamento praesidioque sint eorumque industriae curiae pars maxima committatur,[386] non afferunt tamen huic facultati meae aliquid, ex quo fructum quempiam aut delectationem capere possim. Illos tantum modo enumerasse contentus ero quos mihi et studia haec humanitatis[387] et consuetudo vitae devinxerit.[388]

A: [4] Quid? Graecosne etiam tacitus pertransibis?

L: Certe ita, quoniam tibi, ut reor, incogniti sunt, nec perpetuo versantur apud nos. Quorum tamen sunt quidam eorum regem sequuti ita eruditi homines, ita suis disciplinis omnibus ornati ut[389] cum maioribus suis mea[390] quidem sententia //76// conferendi sint. Horum ego sermonibus cum intersum, quod saepissime contingit, in Academia illa veteri ac Lycio versari videor.

A: Transi istos atque ad nostros veni; quos quidem, etsi ego omnes et agnosco et diligo, attamen de illorum laudibus et quo quenque genere excellere putes, aliqua abs te in medium proferri velim.

---

380. hominibus *om. VG.*
381. autem *coni. Sch.*; autem *PB.*
382. quorum] quorum sacra *P sed* sacra *canc. (P¹?).*
383. iis *V.*
384. vero *om. B.*
385. pontificis *sic N.*
386. conmutatur *N.*
387. virtutis *B.*
388. deiunxerit *V;* coniunxerit *coni. Sch.;* devinxerint *P.*
389. et *V.*
390. mea] in ea *P.*

the curia is a place only for outwardly active men and not for men of intellectual leisure. Let us imagine a man whose spirit shrank from the curia's confusion as well as from its worldly duties. Let us say that he wanted to change his position to one of study and intellectual leisure. For that purpose one usually needs and seeks out a great number of learned men; from them one can be instructed and educated, and with them one can communicate and speak about those things that one has learned through study. For that man, I think you couldn't ask for a more advantageous or well-suited place than the curia.

[2] In fact, to whichever of the liberal arts you turn your mind and imagination, the Roman curia has in one place quite a number of the most complete, best men. The number in fact is so great that I think it would be extremely difficult to find it in any other city or republic. I shall not refer, here, to the professors of holy theology, whose studies have no real kinship to those of ours. [3] I won't mention the natural philosophers, mathematicians, astronomers, and musicians, and I shall pass over in silence the interpreters of civil and canon law. Although they are like a great beautification and fortification to the curia, and though the largest share of the curia is entrusted to their industriousness, still, they do not contribute anything to this special area of mine—any fruit, that is, the likes of which I can taste. I shall be content to have enumerated only those whom these studies, the humanities—as well as everyday social intercourse—have bound closely to me.

A: [4] What then? Will you really pass right over the Greeks in silence?

L: Certainly so, since I think they are unknown to you and since they are not always with us. Nonetheless, certain of them who have followed their king here[25] are men of such learning and are so beautifully well versed in their respective academic disciplines that—certainly in my judgment anyway—they must be compared with their ancient forebears. When I am present at one of their talks, which happens quite often, I seem to dwell in that ancient Academy or in the Lyceum.[26]

A: Pass them by and come to our own. Even though I know and love all of them, nevertheless, I would like you to offer something in praise of them and something about which branch of the humanities you think each of them excels in.

---

25. Lapo refers here to the number of learned Greeks who came west for the ecumenical Council of Ferrara-Florence (1438–39), among whom were the famous Cardinal Bessarion (c. 1403–72) and Gemistos Plethon (c. 1360–c. 1452).

26. I.e., Plato's Academy and Aristotle's Lyceum.

*L.:*391 [5] Veniam ac primum omnium ad392 Ambrosium393 monacho-
rum huius aetatis394 principem, virum395 ea vitae sanctimonia, ea integritate, ea religione, tanta doctrina, tanta humanitate, tam eximia dicendi
copia ac suavitate praeditum ut phoenix quaedam hac aetate nostra, non
nata inter homines, sed e coelo delapsa merito atque optimo396 iure exis-
timari397 possit; Christophorum Garathonium, Coroniensem episcopum,
virum et Graecis et Latinis litteris apprime eruditum; Poggium398 Florentinum, pontificis399 maximi a secretis, in quo summa inest cum400 eru-
ditio,401 eloquentia, tum singularis gravitas salibus402 multis et403 urban-
itate condita; [6] Cincium Romanum, sic omnibus praesidiis virtutis,
doctrinae, eloquentiae cumulatum ut eo civitas sua, etiam si prisca illa
maiorum gloria maneat, non iniuria gloriari possit; Flavium404 Foro-
liviensem, virum non prudentem modo et gravem, verum etiam, ut405
duo superiores sui ordinis, doctum et in scribenda historia exercitatum,
cui non nihil nostri homines debere videntur, quod maiorum consuetudinem referre ac renovare aggressus est et horum temporum res gestas
historiae monumentis prosequi ac posteritati commendare.

---

391. in laude ali(orum) *in mar. s. B¹.*
392. et *B.*
393. *in mar. s.* Ambrosius monachus *G¹.*
394. huius aetatis *om. VGNB.*
395. virum *om. GN.*
396. *in mar. s.* Cristophorus garathonius *G¹.*
397. estimari *P.*
398. *in mar. s.* Poggius florentinus *G¹.*
399. *In mar. sin.* no(ta) hic de pogio *P¹.*
400. tum *P.*
401. erudicione *coni. Sch.;* eruditione *G.*
402. salibi *V.*
403. *in mar. sin.* Cincius cives romanus *G¹.*
404. *in mar. sin.* Blondus seu flavius *G¹.*
405. etiam ut] quoque et *V.*

L: [5] Let me come then first of all to Ambrogio, the prince of the monks of our day.[27] He is a man who is endowed with a sanctity of life, a purity, such scruples, such learning, such humanity, such an excellent abundance and eloquence of speaking ability, that he can deservedly and most rightfully be judged a kind of phoenix in this age of ours, a phoenix not born among men but fallen from heaven. There is also Christoforo Garatone, the bishop of Corona, who is excellently learned in both Greek and Latin literature.[28] As the pope's domestic secretary there is Poggio of Florence, in whom there is not only the highest erudition and eloquence but also a unique gravity, seasoned with plenty of great wit and urbanity.[29] [6] There is Cencio the Roman, who is so packed with all the armaments of virtue, learning, and eloquence that that city of his can justifiably take pride in him, even if it still retains the ancient glory of its ancestors.[30] There is Flavio of Forlì, a man who is not only prudent and serious but also—just like the two of his rank previously mentioned [i.e., papal secretaries]—learned and well versed in the writing of history. We are indeed in his debt, since he has undertaken to relate and recover the ancients' way of life and describe at length the deeds of our own times in works of history, leaving them behind for posterity.[31]

---

27. Ambrogio Traversari (1386–1439), general of the Camaldulese order. Among many other things, he was a famous humanist translator; and among his many accomplishments can be listed translations of various church fathers and a famous translation, probably done in the late 1420s, of Diogenes Laertius's *Lives of the Philosophers*. This latter translation gave thinkers in the fifteenth century a greater and fuller picture of the history of ancient philosophy than was previously possible.

28. A bishop from Treviso, Garathonius—also known as Garatone da Treviso—paid, in Constantinople, for the copying of a manuscript of Diodorus Siculus (by the humanist Chrysococcus). He was thus the first to introduce the Greek text of Diodorus to Italy and the world of the papacy of Eugenius IV. He held the offices of *scriptor* and *secretarius*. See Hoffman, 2:111.

29. Poggio Bracciolini (1380–1459) is most famous as a book hunter; this pupil of the famous humanist chancellor Coluccio Salutati made his most important discoveries during the Council of Constance (1414–18), among them the *De architectura* of Vitruvius and the *De rerum natura* of Lucretius. During the course of his life, he held a number of curial offices, including *abbreviator, scriptor,* and *secretarius.* See Hoffman, 2:110.

30. Cencio de' Rustici (c. 1390–c. 1445) was a humanist translator, whose translations into Latin include, among other works, the pseudo-Platonic *Axiochus,* which he dedicated to Cardinal Giordano Orsini. See J. Hankins, *Plato in the Italian Renaissance,* 2 vols. (Leiden, New York, 1990), 82, 509. Cencio was an apostolic secretary from 1417 until his death, and he held the office of *scriptor* from 1411 until 1443, when he gave the office up to his son Marcellus. See Hoffman, 2:110.

31. Flavio Biondo (1392–1463) was perhaps the most famous fifteenth-century historian of ancient and medieval Italy. He became an apostolic secretary in 1433. See Hoffman, 2:111.

[7] Assunt duo reliqui, Iohannes Aurispa et Andreas[406] civis meus ex eodem ordine, praestantes viri, et ita bonis artibus instructi ut nulla[407] iis recedere[408] videantur. In quibus non praetermittam[409] Rinuccium Castiglionum, cui ego ob eius maximas virtutes, libe//76v//ralem eruditionem, suavissimos[410] mores et singularem in me amorem cum summe afficior, tum ex iis[411] qui a me[412] commemorati sunt neminem praeferendum putem; [8] et aequalem meum Baptistam[413] Albertum, cuius ingenium ita laudo ut hac laude cum eo neminem comparem, ita admiror ut magnum mihi nescio quid portendere inposterum videatur. Est enim eiusmodi ut ad quancumque se animo conferat facultatem, in ea facile ac brevi ceteris antecellat. Sunt alii mihi[414] his similes complures et vitae socii et studiorum comites et quasi aemuli, quos[415] commemorarem libenter si satis ii noti forent aut se in horum numero habendos ducerent. [9] His igitur ego tot tantis, tam[416] eruditis, tam excellentibus viris amicissime utor, his delector, his perfruor, ab horum lateribus, quoad honeste possum, numquam discedo. Quae vitae consuetudo, si perpetuo mihi concessa sit, maiorem nullam ab immortali Deo felicitatem optarem.

---

406. *in mar. sin.* Aurispa, Andreas *G¹*.
407. ulla *B.*
408. recedere] re cedere *P.*
409. *in mar. sin.* Ranuccium *G¹*.
410. suavissimus *V.*
411. ii *V;* hiis *P.*
412. me *om. N.*
413. *in mar. sin.* Baptist(a) albertus *G¹*.
414. multi *VPB.*
415. quo *G.*
416. tam *om. B.*

[7] There are two others of the same rank: Giovanni Aurispa[32] and Andrea [of Florence],[33] my fellow citizen. Both of them are outstanding, and they are both so well instructed in the liberal arts that nothing seems to pass them by. And don't let me pass over Rinuccio da Castiglione.[34] On the one hand, he is a man to whom I am most highly bound, on account of his great virtues, his wide learning in the liberal arts, his most elegant manners—and his unique affection for me. On the other hand, he is a man before whom I think no one from those I have already named should be placed. [8] There is also Battista Alberti,[35] who is the same age as I. I so praise his genius that I would compare no one with him. I wonder at his genius to such an extent that it seems to bespeak I know not what for the future. For his genius is of this sort: to whichever area of study he puts his mind, he easily and quickly excels the others. There are many others known to me who are similar to these men, who are their associates in life and companions in studies and almost their rivals [i.e., in excellence]. I would be quite willing to mention them, if they were well known enough or thought that they, too, should be counted in the number of the men I have already named. [9] I am, then, on very close terms with these men who are so many, so learned, and so outstanding. I am delighted by them, I enjoy them fully, and I never stray from their sides, insofar as this is honorably possible. If this way of life were given to me in perpetuity, I would ask no greater happiness of immortal God.

---

32. The Sicilian-born humanist Giovanni Aurispa (1376–1459) is a fascinating character of the early Quattrocento. He is most well known, justifiably, for his manifold interaction with the Byzantine world, which included his tireless activities as a book collector, as well as his efforts as a translator. He became an apostolic secretary in 1437. See Hoffman, 2:111.

33. Andrea da Firenze was a papal secretary from at least the beginning of the pontificate of Eugenius IV, i.e., 1431 (see Hoffman, 2:111). He did an Italian prose translation of the *Aeneid*, essentially a prose translation of the *Romance of Aeneas*.

34. Rinuccio da Castiglione was a curialist who in his lifetime would hold three curial positions: *scriptor, custos cancelleriae apostolicae*, and *secretarius*. He was named to the first two offices under the pontificate of Eugenius IV, although both after Lapo's death. He was named to the post of secretary under the pontificate of Calixtus III (1455–58). See Hoffman, 2:79, 114.

35. Leon Battista Alberti (1404–72), humanist and polymath, is well known for his numerous works in a number of fields, among which are his treatises *De pictura* (On painting) and *De architectura* (On architecture) and his treatise on family life, *I Libri della famiglia*. At the time of Lapo's writing, Alberti was associated with the papal chancery.

[10] In hac[417] eruditissimorum virorum copia duo tantum desider-
arunt[418] a me ac summo studio requiruntur, illi videlicet litterarum
fontes, illa lumina[419] aetatis nostrae,[420] illa ornamenta doctrinae et eloquentiae: Franciscus Philelfus, praeceptor meus, et Leonardus Arreti-
nus,[421] qui haec studia nostra suis laboribus et vigiliis maxime[422] et[423]
ampliarunt et illustrarunt. Hi si ad superiores aliqua forte[424]
accesserint,[425] nihil mihi et ad rationem studiorum et ad vitae suavitatem
deesse arbitrarer.

[11] Nec solum ad studia doctrinae ac litterarum, sed etiam ad reliqua
tenuiora non desint in curia socii. Sive enim quis ad ludendum sive ad
aequitandum sive ad venandum conferre se cupiat, plurimos ubique eiusdem[426] rei studiosos inveniat.

A: [12] Peroptanda quidem sunt haec, et expetendus[427] maxime is[428]
locus, qui huiusmodi ubertatem[429] et copiam afferat. Nihil est enim in
vita //77// iocundum quod solus agas. Solitudo enim ipsa gravissima est et
omnem adimit vivendi iucunditatem.

L: [13] Iam vero cupidis splendoris ac nominis propagandi, quam
scimus cupiditatem in maximis animis praestantissimisque ingeniis
plerunque innasci solere, praecipueque cum se vel doctrinae liberalis
studiis vel rei militari vel aliae cuivis[430] praeclarissimae facultati
dediderint,[431] tantum affert Romana curia campum quantum nec
Athenarum civitas Alexandro Macedoni, a qua ut laudaretur, confessus

---

417. *in mar. d.* no(ta) leornard *[sic]* aretino *P¹*.
418. desiderantur *G*.
419. *in mar. d.* Franciscus philelphus *G¹*.
420. vestre *N*.
421. *in mar. d.* Leonardus aretinus *G¹*.
422. maximis *V*.
423. et *om. P*.
424. sorte *sic B*.
425. accesserent *sic F*; accesserint *VPGN*.
426. ubique eiusdem] eiusdem ubique *V*.
427. expectendus *V*.
428. his *V*; hic *coni. Sch.*
429. libertatem *VPNB*.
430. cuius *B*.
431. dederint *VN*.

[10] In this great crowd of most learned men I feel the absence of only two and I long for their presence with the utmost urgency: namely, those founts of letters, those ornaments of learning and eloquence, Francesco Filelfo,[36] my teacher, and Leonardo of Arezzo.[37] They have greatly expanded and adorned these studies of ours with their vigilant labors. If these men were by some chance to be added to the aforementioned above, I would think that I were missing nothing as far as the knowledge of studies and the agreeableness of life goes.

[11] And it is not only that there are companions in the curia for the pursuit of learning and literature. One would also find companions for the remaining, lighter things. For if someone desires to devote himself to gaming, horsemanship, or hunting, he would find many there—everywhere—who are desirous of the same thing.

A: [12] Certainly, these things are exceedingly desirable. A place that offers a richness and abundance of this sort of thing should be sought out in the highest degree. Really, nothing that you do alone in life is enjoyable. For solitude is itself the gravest of things and takes all the fun out of life.

L: [13] Well then, the Roman curia already offers a field of play to those who want splendor and the propagation of their name, and we know that this desire is usually born in the greatest of spirits and most outstanding of intelligences, particularly when they have given themselves to studies of liberal erudition or the military arts or to any of the other most outstanding areas of study. The Roman curia offers this to an extent that even the city of Athens could not offer to Alexander of Macedon, who admitted that he had declared war on the whole world, on

---

36. Francesco Filelfo (1398–1481) was an immensely learned humanist scholar who in the 1420s went to Constantinople for six years to study Greek, in the same fashion as Guarino Veronese and other early humanist pioneers. Filelfo was in Florence from 1429 to 1434 as a teacher at the Florentine *studium,* where he ran afoul of Niccolò Niccoli and Carlo Marsuppini and subsequently—or perhaps, consequently—of the Medici. Although Lapo missed Filelfo at the curia at the time of his writing, Filelfo would become a papal secretary later, during the pontificate of Nicholas V (1447–55).

37. Leonardo Bruni Aretino (1369–1444) was one of the most influential humanists—if not the most influential humanist—in the Florence of the early Quattrocento and was that city's chancellor from 1427 to 1444. His translations (among the most famous are Aristotle's *Nicomachean Ethics* and *Politics*), his histories, and his prose rhetorical works gave strength and direction to the already rooted humanist movement. Bruni was missing from the curia at the time of Lapo's writing but had during his career held important curial offices, including *secretarius,* abbreviator, and *scriptor.* See Hoffman, 2:107.

est se toti orbi terrarum bellum diis, hominibus[432] indixisse,[433] nec
Olympia Themistocli, ubi ab universa simul Graecia laudatum se esse
gloriatus est, affere potuerunt. Illorum enim laus unius civitatis atque
unius nationis testimonio contenta fuit.

[14] Hoc autem est theatrum maximum et amplissimum, in quod spec-
tatum nationes plurimae convenerunt, in quo praeclarum nihil geri potest
quod non iis[434] omnibus innotescat, omnium laudibus illustretur. Ad
hunc communem plausum et approbationem accedit etiam eorum laus,
quos supra dixi, eruditorum, quae maximi facienda est. [15] Nam quae a
vulgo ac multitudine proficiscitur, delectat illa quidem et stimulos ad res
gerendas affert,[435] sed quoniam opinione quadam inani et[436] temeritate
excitatur, non iudicio et consilio,[437] labitur brevi et concidit; [16] itaque
a prudentibus iure contemnitur, quippe qui a laudatis tantum viris laudari volunt. Quae quidem laus altissime defixis[438] radicibus tenetur et
solida stabilisque est et infinita saecula duratura nec vetustate[439] cor-
rumpi potest nec ex memoria hominum oblivione deleri.

A: [17] Eleganter et copiose prosecutus es quae ad beate vivendum
spectare dixisti. Sed quoniam te non fugit quod placet peripateticis divitias etiam et copias ad beatitudinem //77v// pertinere, iam ab hac honesti
cogitatione recedamus, quae quaestuosis fortasse hominibus contem-
nenda esse videatur, et de praemiis ac quaestibus Romanae curiae aliquid
agamus.

[VI. De divitiis acquirendis curiae]

L:[440] [1] Hoc in loco ne me magnopere commovet id, quod a multis saepe
inprobari audivi, in curia Romana ad honores et dignitates consequendas

---

432. hominibusque *coni. Sch.;* hominibusque *PGNB.*
433. induxisse *V.*
434. his *V.*
435. afferret *N.*
436. ac *V.*
437. iudicio et consilio] consilio et iudicio *P.*
438. de fixis *P.*
439. vetustate *hoc verbum illegibile in F, hoc modo:* [....]s[..]te; vetustate *codd.*
440. L *om. P.*

gods, and on men, in order to be praised by this city. Nor could the Olympic games offer this to Themistocles even though there he took pride in the fact that he was praised by all Greece at once.[38] After all, their praise was content with the testimony of one city and of one nation.

[14] But this is the greatest and most esteemed of theaters, and many peoples have come here to watch. Nothing admirable can be done here that does not draw everyone's notice and is not illuminated by everyone's praises. To this common applause and approbation is added the praise of those learned men I mentioned before, which must be valued as the greatest thing. [15] For the praise that springs from the crowd and the multitude is certainly delightful and does offer stimuli toward accomplishing things. However, because it is spurred on by a kind of banal opinion and rashness and not by sound judgment and wise counsel, it soon totters and falls. [16] This is why the prudent rightly despise the praise of the crowd, since they want to be praised only by men who themselves have been praised. Certainly this kind of praise is held very deeply by fixed roots. It is solid and stable and will last for infinite centuries, and it can be neither corrupted by age nor blotted out from the memory of men by forgetfulness.[39]

A: [17] You have described elegantly and abundantly the things that you said pertain to living well. But since you have not failed to notice that the peripatetics are in favor of abundant wealth toward the end of happiness, now let us turn from this idea of the "honorable," which seems perhaps destined to be disdained by men greedy of gain, and say something about the rewards and financial opportunities of the curia.

[VI. Concerning the Wealth to Be Acquired at the Curia]

L: [1] Well, under this heading, I am deeply concerned indeed by an attack that I have often heard made by many: that in the Roman curia

---

38. The dramatic episode of the entire crowd at the Olympic Games turning to stare at Themistocles is related in Plut. *Them.* XVII.

39. Cf. Cicero's letter to Cato *Fam.* XV.6.1: "'I am happy,' says Hector, in Naevius, I believe, 'that I am praised by you, father, a man who has been praised.' For agreeable indeed is the praise that one receives from those who themselves have lived in praise" ["Laetus sum laudari me," inquit Hector, opinor, apud Naevium, "abs te, pater, a laudato viro." Ea est enim profecto iucunda laus, quae ab iis proficiscitur, qui ipsi in laude vixerunt].

gratiae, largitioni, corruptelae faciliorem aditum esse quam doctrinae, probitati, integritati. Non enim quid agatur, sed quid statutum sit, spectare oportet. [2] Maiores enim nostri haec haud fomenta viciorum, sed virtutum ornamenta esse voluerunt; quae si quando ad indignos aut minus dignos deferuntur[441] fortunae, id totum tempori, hominibus, non curiae vicio adscribendum est. Illud tamen, ut arbitror, negabit nemo: ea ipsa, utcunque illis[442] utantur homines, esse amplissima maximamque in curia facultatem esse, qua se quisque, modo[443] ne iners[444] ignarusque sit, vel ad altissimum dignitatis gradum attollere possit.

[3] Quo in genere magna mihi[445] exemplorum copia est, si velim eos modo omnis percensere, qui memoria[446] nostra ex obscuro loco et humili ad summum fastigium[447] evaserunt, quos brevitatis causa praetermittam et simul, ne cui invisa oratio mea esse videatur. Deinde esse etiam nonnullos honestissimos ordines, ut[448] ab secretis pontificis maximi, causarum auditores, advocatos, procuratores, ad quos nisi periti illarum rerum et industrii accedere atque aspi<ra>re[449] non possint.

A: [4] Quid? Quod[450] eos[451] ipsos, qui ad honores et dignitates non probatis nituntur artibus, haud hebetes et rudes[452] necesse est? Callidi est enim, solertis, astuti, versuti malitiosique ingenii cognoscere eorum naturas quibus se potissimum conciliare studeant et animos[453] penitus, mentes, //78// consilia omnia, cogitationes, libidines, cupiditatesque perspicere, qua disciplina, quo victu, qua consuetudine domestica sint, quos domi rerum suarum curatores, quos ministros,[454] quos cubicularios habeant, quibus secreta, quibus pecunias committant, quibus amicis intimis familiaribus utantur, et quantum unicuique credant, et ad quod ministerium et quaestum eorum operam et industriam exigat;[455] [5] et his

---

441. differuntur *V.*
442. illis *om. N.*
443. mo *sic N.*
444. in eis *N.*
445. mihi *om. G.*
446. moria *V.*
447. fastidium *P.*
448. et *P.*
449. aspirare *VPN.*
450. Quid? Quod] Quidquid *B.*
451. quod eos *quasi illegibilia in F;* quod eos *codd.*
452. rudes] rudes esse *PB.*
453. amicos *V.*
454. quos ministros *om. P.*
455. exigant *coni. Sch.*

influence, bribery, and corruption provide easier access in attaining office and rank than do learning, uprightness, and purity. Really, you have to look not at what is done there but rather at what was intended. [2] After all, our honored elders wanted these things [office and rank] to be not incitement to vice but rather ornaments of virtue. If sometimes fortunes are handed over to the unworthy or to those who are not so worthy as they might be, the whole business has to be ascribed to the age and the men, not to the vice of the curia. Nevertheless, I do not think anyone will deny this: that the things themselves are there and most abundant, and that however men use them, there is in the curia the greatest possibility for anyone, provided he is not lazy and ignorant, to be able to raise himself to the very highest level of personal honor.

[3] As far as this type of thing goes, I have a great number of examples—if only I wanted to go through them all—of men who from obscure and humble origins arrived at the highest rank. For brevity's sake I shall pass over these altogether, so that my speech does not seem malicious to anyone. Then, also, there are certain highly honorable groups: the important men in the papal household, auditors of legal cases, lawyers, and prosecutors. Unless those of humble origins are highly learned and diligent in their fields, they cannot join or even aspire to those groups.

A: [4] Why, must those who strive after honors and offices by unapproved skills be dull and uncultured? It is, after all, characteristic of men of cunning, skillful, crafty, and tricky—as well as knavish—intelligence to know the natures of those whom they desire especially to win over. They perceive the deepest recesses of their spirits and minds; all of their intentions; their plans, longings, and desires. They know their routine, the food they eat, their domestic habits, whom they have in their homes as managers of property, as servants, as valets; they know to whom they entrust their secrets, their money, whom they associate with as friends, close associates, and companions; they know how much they trust each one and to what employment and business each one of these devotes his time and energy. [5] And having thought about these things, they apply

cogitis[456] ad illos expugnandos[457] quasi machinas admovere,[458] hos[459] frequentare, illis blandiri, alios simulatione amicitiae, alios forma, alios lenociniis,[460] alios muneribus capere. Haec omnia qui efficere possunt, non probi illi quidem, sed tamen sagaces maximeque ingeniosii et diligentes habendi sunt neque hac gloriolae[461] parte defraudandi, quod se per laborem et industriam conentur attollere ac superioribus adaequare.

L: [6] Sed reliquos quaestus perscrutemur qui omnibus iis qui curiae negocia obeunt quot, quanti, quam multiplices expositi sint enumerare difficile esset. Quot enim ordines in curia sunt, tot ad lucrum et ad quaestum patent viae, quibus non mediocres, sed prope maxime opes divitiaeque parantur. Nam ut omittam patres cardinales—de pontifice enim quis dubitat?—ac sedis apostolicae protonotarios, quos nullus ignorat lucrari plurimum? Quis nescit praefectus Romanae curiae, qui camerarius vulgo dicitur, sub cuius iure et imperio tota est curia, omnes civitates, provinciae, homines qui inditione ecclesiae continentur, quos proventus et quantos habeat? [7] Quis ab libellis pontificis maximi, quem vicec<anc>ellarium,[462] quis ii qui supplicationes pontifici deferunt, quos referendarios[463] vocant, quis ab[464] secretis, quis cubiculari, quis apos-

---

456. cognitis *VPGN.*
457. reprobandos *corr. in mar. d. ad* expugnandos *B¹.*
458. admovet *V;* admo//65v//admovere *N.*
459. has *V.*
460. lenociniis *om. cum spatio vacuo N.*
461. glorie *VP;* glorioso *sic B.*
462. vicecancellarium *VPGNB.*
463. deferendarios *V.*
464. a *V.*

what amount to stratagems in order to capture them by storm, to be in their company, to flatter them; they try to take some of them in by feigned friendship, others by personal appearance, others by pandering, and still others with presents. Now the ones who can do all these things—they are certainly not upright men. Nevertheless, they must be considered savvy, very clever, and very diligent, and they are not to be cheated out of their share of a little glory, since they do try to raise themselves up through work and industriousness and to become equal to those who are higher.

L: [6] But let us take a good look at the rest of the financial opportunities. It would be difficult to count the number, importance, and diversity of opportunities set before those who take part in the curia's business. Really, as many groups as are in the curia, just so many ways lie open that lead to financial gain and advantages, and to not just middling wealth but the greatest riches and financial reward. I shall omit the father cardinals—and who can have doubts regarding the pope?—and the protonotaries of the apostolic see;[40] is there anyone who doesn't know how much they can earn? Who does not know of the earning potential—and amount of it—that is possessed by the prefect of the Roman curia? He is commonly called the "chamberlain," and he has complete control and charge of the whole curia—all of the cities, provinces, and men who are contained within the taxing power of the church.[41] [7] Who does not know about the pope's bookkeeper, whom they call the "vice-chancellor"?[42] Or about the ones who are in charge of the papal petitions, who are called the "referendarii"?[43] Who does not know of the ones in the

---

40. Part of the general administrative branch of the curia (the papal chancery *[cancelleria]*), protonotaries *(protonotarii)* served directly under the vice-chancellor (or *vicecancellarius*); there were both functionary and honorary protonotaries, and they could have charge of the preparation of certain papal letters. See D'Amico, 25; Re, *La curia,* 281–82.

41. The "chamberlain," or *camerarius,* was the head of the curia's financial branch, the "apostolic chamber," or *camera apostolica.* See D'Amico, 24.

42. The "vice-chancellor," or *vicecancellarius,* was the head of the papal chancery, as the office of chancellor had dissolved. See Hoffman, 1:20; Re, *La curia,* 279–80; D'Amico, 25.

43. The *referendarii* served in the judicial branch of the curia (see D'Amico, 23). They could function as mediators between the pope and those presenting supplications, i.e., requests for grace. In the early fifteenth century they gained quite a bit of power; during the papacy of Eugenius IV they even acquired the power to sign the supplications themselves, although this had to be done in the presence of the pope. See Re, *La curia,* 227–28; Hoffman, 1:69–79 and *ad indicem.*

tolici aerarii quaestores, quos appellant clericos, quis praetor aerarii, id
est auditor camerae,[465] quis qui in foro //78v// causas iudicant, quanto in
lucro compendioque versentur? [8] Quem fugit advocatis, procura-
toribus, causidicis, scribis,[466] signatoribus, et litterarum apostolicarum
scriptoribus quantae pecuniae cumulentur? Taceo reliquos, qui sunt
paene[467] innumerabiles, lucrandi opifices, e quibus nemo est, ne[468] nunc
quidem, cum imminuta lucra et exhausti omnes pecunia sunt, qui non
suis sumptibus in curia ample et magnifice[469] vivere possit.

A: [9] Sunt huius generis plura quae a te non sine causa praetermissa
arbitror esse. Sed unum illud cuipiam non immerito admirandum videri
potest, unde ad tantos quaestus suggerantur pecuniae?

L: [10] Nequaquam admirandum est, si quis diligenter consideret. In
curia enim Romana omnes omnium christianorum episcopatus,
archiepiscopatus, reliquaeque[470] sacrae dignitates, multi etiam profani
magistratus non sine magna mercede conferuntur et causae ac controver-
siae iudicantur. Quare nemo horum petendorum, nemo iudicii ac litis
contestandae gratia in curiam venit qui nesciat plurima sibi impendenda
esse, qui non plurima impendere possit, ex quo fit ut infinitae[471] undique
in curiam pecuniae, ut[472] in commune aliquod[473] aerarium congerantur;
nec tamen ex ea quicquam[474] praeterquam tabellas, ceram, sigilla,
plumbum, ac lora asportari videmus. Itaque omnes hae pecuniae iis[475]
quos dixi superius dividuntur et in eorum quaestum vertuntur.

---

465. quaestores, quos appellant clericos, quis praetor aerarii, id est auditor cam-
erae] id est autor camere, questores, quos appellant clericos, quis pretor erarii, id est
autor camere *sic N.*
466. scribis *om. V.*
467. paene *om. G.*
468. nec *B.*
469. et magnifice *om. N.*
470. relique *V.*
471. infante *P.*
472. et *V.*
473. quoddam *VPN.*
474. quisquam *B.*
475. hiis *P.*

pope's household or of the "cubicularii"[44] or the quaestors of the apostolic treasury, whom they call "clerics"?[45] Who does not know about the praetor of the treasury—that is, the auditor of the papal chamber?[46] Who does not know about the ones who judge public cases? Who does not know how much they are involved in matters of money and compensation? [8] Is there anyone who is not aware of how much money the lawyers, procurators, advocates, clerks, signatories, and apostolic letter writers heap up? I shall pass over the rest of the profit takers, who are almost innumerable. Of their number there is certainly no one who cannot live nobly and splendidly at the curia at his own expense, even now when funds are short and everyone is out of money.

A: [9] There are more things of this sort, which I think you passed over not without cause. But isn't there that one thing about which everyone must wonder, and with reason, namely, where the money for all these jobs comes from?

L: [10] One mustn't wonder about it at all, if one were to think about it carefully. After all, in the Roman curia, all the episcopates, archiepiscopates, and the rest of the sacred dignities, as well as many secular magistracies, are conferred with great financial profit. Cases and controversies are judged [in the same way]. This is why no one who comes to petition at the curia, no one who comes for the sake of a judgment or to bring a lawsuit, does not know that he must pay dearly, and why no one does come who is unable to do so. Because of this, it happens that an infinite amount of money from all over is gathered into the curia, into a kind of common treasury. And still, we see nothing that is brought away from this, save for documents, wax, a seal, lead, and leather bindings. And so, this money is divided up by those men we were talking about before and is turned to their advantage.

---

44. There were various kinds of *cubicularii*, and they had many functions, which generally centered around personal service to the pope; see Hoffman, 1:160–61, especially n. 4. Interesting here is Lapo's Latin phraseology "quis ab secretis, quis cubiculari." Hoffman distinguishes three different types of *cubicularii*. The third type took care of personal service to the pope in the papal chamber (1:160–61 n. 4). According to Hoffman, it was only during the reign of Pope Sixtus IV (1471–84) that this branch of the office was divided into two types: there were then the *cubicularii extra cameram* and the *cubicularii secreti*, the latter of whom took special care of the pope's personal needs (even the pope's barber, e.g., was among this number). But this did not mean that those who held these offices had unimportant positions; they were close to the pope and often had considerable influence (ibid.).

45. The "clerics of the chamber," or *clerici camerae*, worked in various aspects of curial fiancial management. Their number grew during the Western Schism (1378–1417); there were a total of twenty-five during the papacy of Martin V and sixteen during the papacy of Eugenius IV. See Hoffman, 1:110–14; D'Amico, 24.

46. The "auditor of the chamber," or, to use the full Latin title, *auditor causarum curiae camerae apostolicae*, dealt with judicial and disciplinary matters inside the the chamber and often, more widely, in the curia itself. See Hoffman, 1:24.

A: [11] Hinc licet intelligamus quibus de causis tot homines tam amplas, tam repente divitias sibi et copias paraverunt; at erunt, credo, nonnulli qui his⁴⁷⁶ parum moveantur rebus. Et tum⁴⁷⁷ quod lauti opulentique sint, tum quod industria careant—quod in iis⁴⁷⁸ hominibus⁴⁷⁹ saepe contingit—non divitias maiores, sed divitiarum comites et asseclas,⁴⁸⁰ voluptatem ac delectationem, requirant.⁴⁸¹ *//79//*

[VII. De voluptatibus curiae]

*L:*⁴⁸² [1] Haud frustra requirent. Aut enim Romana in curia aut alio nullo in loco talia reperire poterunt. Etenim si visui⁴⁸³ auditu<i>ve,⁴⁸⁴ qui sunt acerrimi reliquorum⁴⁸⁵ sensuum et maxime proprii humanitatis, delectantur,⁴⁸⁶ his⁴⁸⁷ ipsis obiciuntur in curia infinita atque innumerabilia genera voluptatum.

*A:*⁴⁸⁸ Quibus rebus hos sensus maxime delectari existimas?

L: [2] Nemo fere est qui modo⁴⁸⁹ aliquid sentiat qui ignoret magnitudinem rerum, speciem, novitatem, ac varietatem auditui visuique iucundissima esse solere,⁴⁹⁰ quae hoc loco cuncta exuberant. Primum quid videre in⁴⁹¹ terris maius, quid divinius, quid speciosius quam Christi vicarium, quam apostolorum successores, quam illum conspectum⁴⁹² et consessum, de quo paulo ante locutus sum, possumus?

*A:*⁴⁹³ [3] At⁴⁹⁴ illud multo admirabilius ac monstri similius est aspicere paludatos et galeratos proceres, eodem ipsos pallio et beluato⁴⁹⁵ adoper-

---

476. iis *N.*
477. cum *V.*
478. hiis *PB;* his *G.*
479. omnibus *VP.*
480. assedas *V;* asseclas *coni. Sch. recte.*
481. requirant *om. Sch.*
482. L *om. V.*
483. visui] in sui *sic P.*
484. auditu<i>ve] auditui ve *VG;* auditui ne *P;* aditui ve *sic N;* auditui que *B.*
485. aliquorum *G.*
486. delectentur *N.*
487. iis *N.*
488. A *om. V.*
489. *in mar. d.* De voluptate auditus *F.*
490. esse solere] solere esse *V.*
491. videre in] viderem *sic legit Sch. et* videri *sic coni. Sch.*
492. consessum] conspectum tum *N;* concessum *B.*
493. A *om. Sch.*
494. At] [ ]d *sic V;* at *coni. Sch, recte.*
495. belvam *sic F et PGNB;* bellua *V.*

A: [11] From this we can understand why so many have furnished themselves so swiftly with such magnificent and abundant fortunes. But there will be some, I suppose, who aren't much excited by these things! Because they are [already] distinguished and wealthy, and because they lacked industriousness—something that happens often with these men— they seek not greater wealth but rather the allies and followers of wealth: pleasure and delight.

[VII. Concerning the Pleasures of the Curia]

L: [1] And they won't seek after these things in vain. For if they cannot find things like that in the Roman curia, they will not be able to find them anywhere else. Really, even if it is only the visual and auditory senses that are delighted—which are the most penetrating of the senses and the most proper to humanity—in the curia infinite and innumerable types of pleasures are thrown in their way.

A: Which things do you think delight these senses the most?

L: [2] There is almost no one with any sense who does not know that a magnitude of things and their beauty, novelty, and variety are usually the most pleasurable for the ear and eye. In this place all of them abound. First of all, what on earth is visible that is greater, more divine, or more beautiful than the vicar of Christ, than the successors of the apostles, than that spectacle and assembly that I discussed a little earlier?

A: [3] But it is much more wonderful and marvelous to see noblemen clothed in military uniforms, helmeted, and covered with cloaks that are

tos,[496] apparitorum catervis per curiam stipatos incedere et sacerdotum ac comitum turbam longo ordine subsequentem.

L:[497] [4] Ad haec quid magnificentius, quid illustrius intueri quam alios[498] principes qui frequentant curiam comitatu maximo et ornatu? Postremo, quid pulchrius, quid dignius, quid magis decorum, magis regium quam maximorum regum legatos et oratores summis de rebus ad pontificem missos, quorum cum alii maneant, alii absoluto legationis munere decedant, alii accedant? Eorum quottidie magnus est numerus; atqui, cum huiusmodi hominum maxima semper in curia Romana multitudo[499] versetur, hoc inprimis tempore ob hanc concilii unionisque celebritatem maior ac multo maxima est. [5] Quis est enim christianus princeps qui honorificam legationem non miserit? Nec de //79v// illis modo loquor qui nostrae sectae[500] ac religionis sunt, sed de ipsis etiam orientalibus, qui nobis antea maxime infensi erant, qui partim legatos miserunt, partim etiam ipsi venerunt, partim venturi putantur, ut tantae tam novae, tam spectatae rei, quanta futura est, interesse possint. [6] Venit enim Bysanthinus imperator, nunquam ante hoc tempus non dico[501] in curia, sed in Italia visus. Hunc omnium orientalium gentium ac nationum, apud quas Christi colitur nomen, sacerdotes, antistites, legati, interpretes plurimi consecuti sunt, quorum varietas linguae, morum, cultus, habitus, incessus, corporum denique ipsorum non delectationi modo, sed etiam risui,[502] admirationi sunt.

A: [7] Est ita profecto. Nam ego huiusmodi homines[503] numquam sine risu aspicio. Etenim video alios prolixa ad pectus barba, densa coma, capillo crispo, horrido et inculto, cuiusmodi Spartiatas Lycurgi legibus fuisse accepimus, quo terribiliores essent, si quando manus cum hoste consererent; alios detonsa parumper barba, semiraso capite; picto alios supercilio,[504] horum partim pilleis[505] et iis[506] quidem[507] dissimilibus,

---

496. odopertos *P.*
497. L *om. Sch.*
498. illos *B.*
499. multitud *P (forsitan Gallicismus).*
500. secrete *N.*
501. non dico] dico non *P.*
502. usui *sic N.*
503. homines *om. B sed add. in mar. d. B¹.*
504. supericilio *sic F;* supercilio *codd.*
505. pileis *coni. Sch.*
506. hiis *P.*
507. qui *corr. ad* quidem *B¹.*

ornamented with figures. They advance through the curia accompanied by throngs of servants, along with a crowd of priests and counts who follow in a long line.

L: [4] As for these things, what is more magnificent or brilliant to see than the other princes who frequent the curia with a huge and distinguished attendance? Finally, what is more beautiful, becoming, elegant, or royal to see than the legates and orators of the greatest kings, who have been sent to the pope about the most important matters? Although some of them remain, others leave after completing the task of their legation, and others still are added. There is a great number of them every day; but although the crowd of men of this sort who dwell in the Roman curia is always enormous, still, now most of all, because of the council of union's fame, there is an even greater crowd—indeed, the number is at an all-time high. [5] After all, is there any Christian prince who has not sent an honorable legation? And I am not only talking about those who are part of our religious confession but also about the Eastern princes who earlier were quite ready to attack us. Some of them have sent legates, some have come themselves, and some are thought to be on the way, so that they can take part in whatever new and eagerly awaited things the future brings. [6] Indeed, the Byzantine emperor has come—I say, before now he has not been seen in Italy, let alone in the curia. He has been followed by priests, high priests, legates, and many translators from all the Eastern peoples and nations among whom the name of Christ is worshiped. The variety of their language, their character, their adornment, their dress, their bearing, and, finally, their bodies themselves leads not only to delight but also to laughter and wonderment.

A: [7] It *is* so. I mean, I never look at men of that sort without laughing. I see some of them with a beard that goes down to their chest, a thick hairdo, and curly, wild, and disordered hair. It is the same kind of thing that we have learned was characteristic of the Spartans (by the laws of Lycurgus), so that they would be all the more terrifying were they ever to come in contact with the enemy.[47] Others have their beard just about shorn off and a half-shaved head, and still others have painted eyebrows. Of these, some wear felt caps—which are certainly different from one

---

47. Plutarch (*Lys.* I.2–3) relates that the reason the Spartans let their hair grow and the reason that they wore it in the style they did was to seem more fearful to the enemy.

partim mithris[508] erectis in summo avium[509] pinnis[510] aut aureo aliquo redimiculo, manicatisque tunicis utuntur, ut de Phrygibus poeta inquit: "Et tunicae manicas et habent redimicula mithrae."

[8] Rex eorum eodem modo quo illi amictus et ornatus est, praeterquam quod purpura indutus[511] est, et pro pilleo[512] thyaram gerit more Persarum regum, quam, ut[513] apud Persas, ferre nisi regibus nulli permissum est, in cuius summitate est gemma permagna et lucens, in auro illigata.[514] Taceo reliquos omnes, inter se habitu, cultu, forma ipsa[515] corporis et figura rebusque omnibus dissimillimos, plerosque aspectu ita ridiculos ut nemo sit adeo severus //80// et tristis qui risum aspiciens contineret.[516]

L: [9] Quid dicemus de nostris, id est, de iis[517] qui in curia Romana iam antea versantur, Gallis, Germanis, Pannoniis, Scotis, Britanis, Illyriis, qui iam et communione Latinae linguae et diuturno commertio nobis familiares sunt facti. Inter quos quanta morum vitaeque dissimilitudo sit quivis facile perspicere potest; non dico quam diversae artes atque artifices, quam varias merces, gazas, nummos, signa, tabulas ornamentaque alia eae[518] nationes secum in curiam invehant.

[10] Quibus quid visu pulchrius, quid iucundius, quid delectabilius aut cuiquam ad pascendos oculos optabilius dici fingive[519] potest? Qui[520] denique spectandi[521] cupidis locus eo ipso, in quo haec sunt, potius incolendus?[522] Etenim si Solonem Atheniensem, clarissimum philosophum[523] et sapientissimum legum latorem atque ex septem sapientum numero unum, decennium peregrinatum esse accepimus; si Democritum physicum constat inter doctos[524] omne aetatis suae tempus peregrinando

---

508. mithus *sic N.*
509. anium *sic N.*
510. punis *V.*
511. inductus *G.*
512. pileo *coni. Sch.*
513. et *B.*
514. alligata *G.*
515. ipsa *om. G.*
516. continetur *V;* contineat *coni. Sch.*
517. hiis *P;* his *GN.*
518. hee *P.*
519. fingive] fingi ne *N.*
520. quis *PGN.*
521. spectandis *P.*
522. colendus *VPG.*
523. *in mar. d.* Solon *F.*
524. *in mar. d.* Democritus *F.*

another—and some wear headbands with feathers of birds on top. Or they might wear some kind of golden band and long-sleeved tunics, just as Virgil said about the Phrygians: "Their tunics have sleeves and their headbands gold."[48]

[8] Their king is decked out and beautified in the same way that they are, except that he is clothed in purple, and for a hat he wears a tiara in the manner of the Persian kings,[49] just like the one that no one among the Persians but the king can wear. At the top of this tiara there is a truly giant and luciferous gem, bound around with gold. I shall not mention all the rest, who really do differ among themselves in dress, in adornment, in their actual physical shape and figure, and in all things. Most of them look so ridiculous that there is no one so serious and sad that he would contain his laughter on seeing them.

L: [9] What might we say about our own, that is, about those who have already been living in the curia? There are French, Germans,[50] Hungarians, Scots, English, and Illyrians, who are already familiar to us both because of the common use of the Latin language and because of long-standing commercial intercourse. Among them there is a difference in manners and lifestyles that is so great anyone could easily see it. I shall not even mention how many different crafts and artisans, how many varied kinds of merchandise, treasures, coins, statues, paintings, and other accoutrements, these peoples bring with them into the curia.

[10] What is more beautiful, agreeable, or delightful to see than these things? What can be more delightfully described or even imagined for feasting the eyes? Finally, for those who are desirous of seeing all this, what better place is there to live than that place itself where all of these things exist? And indeed, let us recall that Solon of Athens—the most famous of philosophers, wisest of lawgivers, and first of the Seven Wise Men—traveled around for a decade; that Democritus the natural philosopher spent all of his time traveling around among learned men;

---

48. Virg. *Aen.* IX.616.
49. Cf. Plut. *Them.* XXIX.5.
50. The total number of Germans listed in the Vatican registers as belonging to the curia during the entire pontificate of Eugenius IV (1431–47) was 1,170. See C. Schuchard, *Die Deutschen an der päpstlichen Kurie im späten Mittelalter (1378–1447),* Bibliothek des deutschen historischen Instituts in Rom 65 (Tübingen, 1987), at 35 and passim on the whole question.

consumpsisse; [11] si Pythagoram[525] Samium et Platonem, illum philosophorum principem,[526] Egyptios, Caldeos, Magos, Gymnosophistas adi-
isse memoriae proditum[527] est, omnes vivendi atque spectandi[528] cupiditate
pellectos, cui haec omnia uno in loco et uno quasi sub aspectu intueri liceat,
quae illis tanto tempore, labore, impensa, periculo conquisita[529] sunt, illi
non praecipuam[530] quandam et singularem felicitatem contigisse dicemus?
Itaque necesse est, qui visu maxime moveatur, ex his tot, tantis, tam variis,
tam diversis rebus mirificam voluptatem percipere. Et tu me, homo prudens,
consulendo[531] et hortando ab eiusmodi loco conaris abducere?

[12] Nec[532] tamen cum[533] tot ac tanta videantur pauciora, sed longe
plura audiuntur in curia. Quottidie enim fere recentes aliquae[534] assunt
legationes, quottidie nova quaedam literis, nunciis, rumoribus perferun-
tur, //80v// nullus toto anno dies atque adeo hora labitur qua non sug-
geratur aliquid, nihil in universo terrarum orbe geritur quod non continuo sciatur in curia. Nec enim fieri aliter potest, ubi ea hominum
frequentia ac multitudo sit, qui domesticorum litteris et nunciis de rebus
patriae certiores fiant.

[13] Ubicunque[535] igitur sis in curia, novi aliquid[536] audias. Quocunque
te vertas, in circulos,[537] colloquia, sermones, et confabulationes hominum
incidas, qui advenienti tibi ultro occurrant, qui abs te nunquid audieris per-
contentur, qui vel invito[538] quae ipsi noverint nuncient, nonnulla etiam ex
tempore quae probabilia videantur confingant,[539] quae, tametsi[540] vera non
sint, tantisper tamen, dum nesciantur,[541] specie veritatis oblectant.

[14] Quod si quando instituto sermone de rebus levioribus devenitur
ad[542] iocum et dicacitatem,[543] (magna est enim[544] omnibus in curia

525. *in mar. d.* Pythagoras *F.*
526. *in mar. d.* Plato *F.*
527. traditum *PN.*
528. expectandi *VBG.*
529. consita *B.*
530. precipiam *V.*
531. consuetudo *sic N.*
532. *in mar. d.* De voluptate auditus *F.*
533. tamen cum] cum tamen *V.*
534. aliquae *om. G.*
535. Ubique *P.*
536. novi aliquid] aliquid novi *P.*
537. circulo *sic Sch.*
538. invito] in vitio *N.*
539. confingat *G.*
540. tametsi] tam si *B.*
541. *aut* resciantur *F;* resciantur *PB.*
542. ac *V.*
543. dicatitatem *sic F;* dicacitatem *codd.*
544. enim *om. VPGN.*

[11] that Pythagoras of Samos and Plato the prince of philosophers went to the Egyptians, the Chaldeans, the magi, and the gymnosophists; and that all of them were enticed by a desire to live and to observe.[51] To the one who can observe in one place and almost with one glance all of these things—which those men obtained with so much time, labor, expense, and danger—shall we not say that an outstanding and unique happiness has befallen him? Well then, anyone who is especially moved by the visual must feel a marvelous pleasure, owing to these things, which are so many, so great, so varied, and so diverse. And you, a prudent man, are trying with your advice and exhortations to draw me away from a place of this sort?

[12] And still, even though one sees much of importance in the curia, one hears not less but more by far. Really, almost every day some sort of newly arrived legations are present. Every day some news is conveyed by letters, messengers, and rumors, and no day or even hour in the whole year goes by in which something is not suggested. Nothing that is done in the whole world is not known directly in the curia. Nor can it happen otherwise where there is this throng, this multitude of men who are informed about matters in their homeland by the letters and messengers of their servants.

[13] Wherever you are in the curia, then, you hear some bit of news. Wherever you turn, you happen on the conversational circles, talks, speeches, and tall tales of men who of their own accord run to meet you as you arrive. They ask you whether you have heard anything. They talk about what they themselves know, even to an unwilling listener, and also extemporaneously make up some things that seem probable. Even if these things are untrue, they nevertheless give pleasure for a little while, under the guise of truth, as long as they are not known [to be falsehoods].[52]

[14] But whenever a conversation about lighter matters comes up, if it turns toward jests and raillery (for a great liberty and license is allowed

---

51. Pythagoras, Democritus, and Plato are mentioned together in Cic. *Fin.* V.49–50; Cic. *Tusc.* IV.44; Val. Max. VIII.7 ext. 2–4.

52. Cf. this description of someone who invents news with Theophrastus's *Char.* VIII (ed. Jebb no. XX), λογοποιίας (Newsmaker), a work that Lapo himself translated from the Greek; see the edition of the translation in K. Müllner, "Zur humanistischen Übersetzungsliteratur: Fortsetzung," *Wiener Studien* 24 (1902): 216–30.

Romana obloquendi ac maledicendi libertas licentiaque permissa) nemini parcitur, non modo absenti, sed ne praesenti⁵⁴⁵ quidem. Invehitur pariter in cunctos magno risu et cachinno omnium. Cenae, popinae, lenocinia, largitiones, furta, adulteria, stupra,⁵⁴⁶ flagitia in medium proferuntur.

[15] Qua ex re non voluptas tantummodo, sed etiam illa vel maxima capitur utilitas, quod, cum ita vita ac mores omnium⁵⁴⁷ ponantur tibi ante oculos, nullus⁵⁴⁸ (tota curia cuiusmodi sit) latere te possit. Quocirca si quando tibi ab illis gratia ineunda est, ut peritus medicus, habeas quasi medicamenta quaedam prompta ac parata, quae ad cuiusque morbum adhibere queas, ut nunquam tibi, si illis recte uti volueris, repulsa sit ab ullo perferenda quo nescio an quicquam melius ei qui inter homines versari commode cupiat //81// aut optabilius possit esse. [16] Quemadmodum enim neque fabrum bonum neque architectum⁵⁴⁹ esse quis dixerit cui sint incognita instrumenta quibus indigeat ad suum artificium; ita qui hominum, quibus utitur ad omnia, mores non teneat, is non dico in vita rudis et ignarus, sed vix homo, mea quidem sententia, est habendus. Itaque, cum hoc incommodum ne subeatur curia praeest,⁵⁵⁰ non tantum in ea plura audiendi, sed sapientius etiam vivendi et cautius facultas erit.

A: [17] Confert vero, ut a⁵⁵¹ te dicitur, plurimum hominum quibuscum verseris mores cognoscere. Nam cum reliquis in rebus rudem videri turpe est, tum in vita decipi, errare, labi foedissimum simul et perniciosissimum est, quam quidem peritiam si curia afferre potest, merito laudatur.

L: [18] Potest certe, si quis alius⁵⁵² potest locus. Sed⁵⁵³ reliquas prosequamur voluptates, ne veluti Tantalus ille, de quo habetur in fabulis,⁵⁵⁴ in maxima rerum affluentia collocati⁵⁵⁵ nihil attingere omnino aut degustare posse videamur, quae quanquam homine indignae sint, a multis tamen conquiruntur omni studio et ultimum bonorum esse existimantur.

---

545. absenti, sed ne praesenti] presenti, sed ne absenti *G.*
546. strupta *V;* stipia *sic N.*
547. hominum *V.*
548. nullatenus *coni. Sch.*
549. bonum neque architectum *om. P.*
550. preest *codd.;* prodest *coni. Sch.*
551. ad *V.*
552. alii *B.*
553. *in mar. sin.* Tantalus *G¹.*
554. *ann. in mar. d.* De voluptate gustus *F¹.*
555. collocari *B.*

in the Roman curia for reproaching and abusing) no one is spared, whether he is absent or present, and everyone is equally attacked, to the great guffawing and laughter of all. Dinner parties, tavern life, pandering, bribes, thefts, adultery, sexual degradation, and shameful acts are publicly revealed.

[15] From this one acquires not only pleasure but also the greatest utility, since the life and character of all is thus placed before your eyes. No one can escape you when the whole curia is like this. And so, if you ever need a favor from these people, the result is that, almost like a learned doctor, you have your medications ready and prepared. You can apply them as if to some kind of illness, so that, if you know how to use your medications correctly, you are never turned away by anyone. I do not know if there can be any place better or more desirable than the curia for one who wishes to live opportunely among men. [16] After all, who would call a workman or architect who does not know the tools of his trade a good workman or architect? Someone who does not know the character of those with whom he associates in all matters—this man, I say, is not only crude and ignorant in life but, as far as I am concerned, scarcely to be considered a man. Therefore, since the curia is an outstanding place to prevent one's suffering disadvantage, one will have in it the ability not only to hear many things but also to live more wisely and more securely.

A: [17] Well, as you say, it is a good thing to know the characters of the men among whom you live. To be sure, while it is shameful to seem crude in other matters, it is especially disgraceful and ruinous in life to be deceived, to go astray, and to stumble. Certainly, the curia is deservedly praised if it can offer the kind of skill [it takes to avoid this].

L: [18] If any place can, certainly it is the curia. But let us take a look at the other pleasures, lest we seem like that Tantalus whom we hear about in stories; it would be as if we were placed in a condition of great plenty but were completely unable to touch or taste anything. Although these things are unworthy of humankind, still, many seek them out eagerly and even consider them to be the highest of the goods.

[19] Ex iis vero haud mediocris est illa voluptas quae per gustum ex cibo potuque colligitur.[556] Haec[557] enim nascitur cum ipsis hominibus et una cum aetate adulescit et usque ad extremum[558] vitae comitatur. Haec a nobis nunquam discedit,[559] et, cum reliquae vel curis gravioribus cedant vel sedentur satietate[560] vel dissuetudine obliterentur,[561] haec una expleta statim renascitur acrior nec interpellatur negociis nec intermissa tollitur minuiturve, sed magis invalescit. [20] Haec fons et origo est vel, ut[562] verius dicam, parens et procreatrix reliquarum voluptatum. Ex hac plurimae voluptatum libidines maximaeque venereae //81v// excitantur, quae ea sublata refrigescunt, ut est apud Terentium: "Sine Cerere et Libero."[563] Huius denique voluptatis cupiditas[564] adeo insita nobis atque ingenita est[565] ut cum paulo vehementius nos incesserit, ceterae omnes facile contemnantur. [21] Ad hanc igitur titillationem[566] acerrimae voluptatis explendam copia ciborum, potissimum varietas[567] ac lautitia quaeritur, quarum rerum[568] haud pauciores in curia Romana quam[569] olim philosophorum Athenis scholae, gymnasia, praeceptores, discipuli, artifices numerari possent.

A: [22] Credo equidem ita esse. Quam[570] plurimi in[571] curia Romana sunt homines lauti et qui delicate ac molliter vivant, qui et maximis abundant divitiis et, quod sine labore partas[572] possideant, eas profundunt nulla habita ratione utilitatis, nec[573] quid eos deceat, sed quid[574] libeat cogitant impensaeque modum libidinem suam et[575] cupiditatem statuunt. [23] Hi, omissis reliquis omnibus[576] curis, quasi feriati[577] nihil aliud

---

556. colligitur *om. V.*
557. Nec *V.*
558. ad extremum] *om. P.*
559. decedit *B.*
560. societate *B.*
561. oblitterentur *sic F.*
562. ut] ut ut *sic N.*
563. Sine Cerere et Libero] Sine terre et libro *sic V.*
564. Huius denique voluptatis cupiditas] Denique huius voluptatis denique cupiditas *sic B sed recte corr. B¹.*
565. est *om. Sch., N.*
566. titulationem *P.*
567. varietas *om. P.*
568. verum *sic legit Sch.*
569. qua *V.*
570. Quoniam *GB.*
571. in *om. P.*
572. partis *V.*
573. ne *V.*
574. quid] quid eos *B.*
575. et *om. N.*
576. reliquis omnibus] omnibus reliquis *PB.*
577. ferrati *N.*

[19] Now of these things, a considerable pleasure is the one gained through the sense of taste, from food and drink. Really, this pleasure is born with men themselves, matures with age, and remains their companion right up to the end of life. It never leaves us, and even though the other pleasures yield to more serious cares, subside because of satiety, or are blotted out because of lack of use, this one pleasure is immediately reborn more sharply; it is not hindered by business matters, nor, if interrupted, is it ruined or diminished, but rather, it grows ever stronger. [20] This pleasure is really the cause and origin or, if I may speak more truly, the mother and maker of the rest. It stirs up most desires for [other] pleasures and especially those of Venus, which cool down when the [gustatory] pleasure has suffered, just as Terence says, "without Ceres and Liber."[53] Finally, desire for this pleasure is so natural and innate in us that when it comes on us a little more intensely, all of the others are easily despised. [21] Now, for the tickling of this most keen of pleasures one needs a great abundance, variety, and splendiferous assortment of foods. For these subjects there are no fewer schools, secondary schools, teachers, students, and craftsmen in the Roman curia than there were once schools of philosophers that could be counted in Athens.

A: [22] I certainly believe it to be so. In the Roman curia there are quite a few refined men, as well as those who live luxuriously and delicately. Since they abound in great wealth and possess that portion without having to work for it, they squander their fortunes pointlessly; they consider not what is becoming to themselves but rather what pleases them at the moment. They make their lewd desire the limit to their expenditures. [23] Since they have no other worries, these men, almost as

---

53. Ter. *Eun.* IV.5.

agunt, nihil curant, nihil student, nihil cogitant, nisi[578] ut domi preciosissima
vina optima delicatissimaque cibaria, paratissimos[579] etiam coquos habeant,
nec ex una tantummodo natione, sed ex pluribus, quaecumque in ea arte[580]
praestare existimantur. [24] Et ad ea conquirenda atque[581] aucupanda quocunque exquisitores et quasi emissarios[582] dimittunt, formosos etiam ministros ad ministrandas[583] epulas, catamitos[584] quoque et calamistratos stu-
diose quaerunt eosque splendidis vestibus indutos, leves maximeque
inberbes esse volunt, Alexandri, credo, Macedonis auctoritatem secuti, qui
proelium inituris iussit barbas abradi militibus ne veluti ansas hostibus ad se
capiendum praeberent. Sic in parandis probandisque[585] cibis, invitandis
compotoribus,[586] et confabulonibus[587] suis dies totos consumunt.

L: [25] Quae ego ex te //82// audio? Omitte istos, quaeso, cum sua
luxuria, nec enim sunt digni de quibus sermo habeatur, siquidem sunt
omnes ex eo genere hominum quos ante e curia expellendos diximus. Ad
illos potius comme<mo>randos[588] te conferas, qui in[589] maximis divitiis
et opibus ita vivunt ut[590] nihil prorsus sordide acquirere velint, [26] ut
dignitatem suam pontificisque maximi beneficia non tam copiis quam
virtute tueantur, qui sibi parci, aliis modo dignis magnifici sunt, honestate cupiditates suas metiuntur,[591] qui molliter nihil flagitioseve agunt[592]
aut cogitant, cibos splendidos et delicatos pro convivarum[593] dignitate
instruunt, convivia vero ipsa, sumptus, ministros, reliquum omnem cultum et apparatum non ad voluptatem, sed ad sui et curiae totius[594] splendorem et magnificentiam referunt. [27] In horum domos non compotores
et confabulones sui, sed hospites, legati, principes tam curiales quam
peregrini, honestissimi et splendidissimi homines invitantur, qua re apud
omnes exteras gentes curiae illustratur nomen.

578. nisi *om. B.*
579. peritissimos *PG.*
580. parte *B.*
581. aut *V.*
582. quasi emissarios] aucuparios *sic G.*
583. ad ministrandas] ad administrandas *sic legit Sch.*
584. catamitos *om. N cum spatio vacuo.*
585. probandisque *om. B.*
586. compocionibus *sic leg. Sch.*
587. confabulationibus *VPB;* confabulatoribus *G;* cofabulationibus *sic N.*
588. commemorandos *VPGNB.*
589. in *om. VPGNB.*
590. et *P.*
591. mentiuntur *V.*
592. nihil flagitioseve agunt] flagiciose instruunt nichil ve agunt *B.*
593. conviviarum *B.*
594. curiae totius] totius curie *G.*

if they were on constant holiday, pay attention to nothing else, desire nothing else, and think of nothing else but that they should have in their houses the most precious and valuable wines and the most sumptuous food, as well as the most sophisticated chefs, not only from one country but from many—the ones, that is, whom they perceive to be extraordinarily talented in the field. [24] And to acquire and hunt for those things, they send buyers anywhere, almost as emissaries, and zealously seek out beautiful servant boys to serve the meals, as well as catamites and men whose hair is done a little too finely. They want them to be clothed in splendid finery, smooth and, especially, beardless, in which requirement they follow, I believe, the authority of Alexander of Macedon; he ordered his soldiers who were about to enter into battle to shave off their beards, so that they would not offer the enemy handles, as it were, to grab onto.[54] In this way they spend whole days, preparing and trying out foods, and inviting their fellow banqueters and conversationalists.

L: [25] What am I hearing from you? Pass over those men and their licentiousness, for they aren't even worthy to talk about. Indeed, they all are part of that group we said before should be thrown out of the curia. You had better bring yourself to discussing those who, in the midst of the greatest wealth and luxury, live in such a way that they would come by nothing at all in a dishonorable fashion. [26] As a result of their conduct, it is not so much with wealth as with virtue that they look after their own honor as well as the generosity of the pope. With themselves these men are sparing, and only with others who are worthy are they generous; and they measure their desires with probity: they do and think nothing weak or shameful. They prepare splendid and refined foods in relation to the rank of their guests; yet the banquets themselves—the costs, the servants, and the rest of the refinement and pomp—are calculated in relation not to pleasure but rather to their own honor and greatness and to that of the whole curia. [27] They invite into their homes not drinkers and their drinking buddies but rather foreign guests, legates, and princes, curialists as well as pilgrims—most honorable and magnificent men. In this way, among all foreign peoples the name of the curia is made famous.

---

54. In Plut. *Thes.* V.4, it is mentioned that Alexander had his men shave off their beards, so that the enemy could not get a good hold on them.

[28] Cuiusmodi autem ab ipsis curiae principibus exhibeantur⁵⁹⁵ convivia quo apparatu quanta varietate, quanta copia, dicere timore deterreor, ne aut in iis⁵⁹⁶ luxuriam improbare aut ipse hoc genere nimium delectari videar.⁵⁹⁷ Ex his evenit ut quicquid ubique nascitur boni, modo vecturam patiatur, in curiam comportetur, quod ibi⁵⁹⁸ citius vendatur et carius. Itaque quo frequentior in curia Romana multitudo est hominum, eo maior rerum omnium copia et abundantia reperitur, quod fortasse incredibile ac falso a me dictum videatur, si quis huius rei causam ignoret.

A: [29] Sed nihil est quo haec apud me verearis dicere,⁵⁹⁹ qui, cum in curia multum iam temporis verser, testis tibi optimus esse possum. Illud vero ad hanc voluptatem maxime pertinere arbitror, adesse coquos, fartores, pulmentarios,⁶⁰⁰ qui homines (tantum abest ut desiderentur in curia)⁶⁰¹ ut //82v// plurimi etiam⁶⁰² reperiantur qui his curialibus victu⁶⁰³ tantum, alio nullo stipendio suam operam navent idcirco, quod ad sacerdotium omnes intendunt et illis adiutoribus sacerdotalem aliquem in patria ordinem se assequi posse confidunt.

L: [30] Nec eos fallit spes. Nam saepe quos unctos sordidos in media culina, in fumo et nidore volutari videris, eosdem repente⁶⁰⁴ videas non ad sacerdotium modo, sed ad maximos etiam dignitatis gradus evectos in⁶⁰⁵ patriam remigrare.⁶⁰⁶

A: [31] Hanc ob causam ex Gallia, Germania, Britannia, aliisque exteris⁶⁰⁷ nationibus: quod magni apud illas sacerdotibus honores et praemia habeantur, plurimi in curiam confluunt, qui foedissima quaeque⁶⁰⁸ ministeria subeant nec ullam serviendi conditionem recusent, sed in primis coquinariam libenter exercent⁶⁰⁹ eamque probe callent. Quare hoc hominum genus in curia totum fere barbaricum est, Italici nulli aut pauci⁶¹⁰ admodum invenirentur.

---

595. exhibeatur *N.*
596. hiis *B.*
597. videatur *B.*
598. ubi *N.*
599. didere *sic B.*
600. coquos, fartores, pulmentarios] quos factores pulmentaris *V.*
601. curia] curia et *G.*
602. etiam *om. G.*
603. nutu *sic legit Sch.*
604. repetente *sic V.*
605. in *om. V.*
606. migrare *recte corr. B¹.*
607. exteris] ex terris *V.*
608. quaeque *om. G.*
609. libenter exercent] exercent libenter *V.*
610. parici *V.*

[28] In addition, when the princes of the curia themselves throw ban-quets of this sort—well, fear deters me from saying with what pomp, variety, and abundance they are carried out, lest I seem to reprove the extravagance of these affairs or seem myself to take excessive pleasure in this kind of thing. Because of these men it has come to pass that if any-thing good appears anywhere, provided it is transportable, it is carried into the curia so that it can be sold there more quickly and at a higher price. Therefore the larger the crowd of men in the Roman curia, the greater the abundance and plenty of things one discovers. In fact, it might seem unbelievable and falsely asserted by me, if one did not know the reason why this occurred.

A: [29] There is no reason why you should fear telling me these things, since by now I have lived quite some time in the curia and can be the best of witnesses for you. Really, I think it is certainly a part of this pleasure that these cooks, sausage makers, and gourmet food makers are pres-ent.[55] One finds these men in great number (far from being lacking) in the curia, and their only task is to provide food for these courtiers, with no other obligation, since they all aim toward the priesthood. With the help of their curial bosses they are confident of being able to attain some kind of priestly rank in their homeland.

L: [30] And they are not wrong in their hopes. After all, you will have often seen those men covered with grease and grime in the middle of the kitchen, embroiled in the smoke and stench. Then, out of nowhere, you see them move back to their homeland, raised not only to the priesthood but even to the highest degrees of honor.

A: [31] This is why from France, Germany, England, and other foreign countries—since in those nations priests possess great distinctions and rewards—so many men pour into the curia. They take on the most hor-rible jobs and do not refuse any condition of service; rather, they work willingly and primarily at cooking and are quite experienced in it. This is why this sort of person in the curia is almost always foreign and why no Italians, or at least few, are to be found.

---

55. For Lapo's "coquos, fartores, pulmentarios," cf. Ter. *Eun.* 257, cited in Cic. *Off.* I.150: "cetarii, lanii, coqui, fartores, piscatores."

L: [32] Non invideo equidem. Quamquam enim nostra natio haud imperita huius disciplinae sit, concedat tamen licet hanc laudem barbaris,[611] et ea se carere[612] tam aequo animo patiatur quam illi se olim a nobis bellica gloria spoliari passi sunt.

A: [33] Nec[613] vero privatim tantum et alienae domi hoc exequuntur munus, sed qui paulo lautiores sunt, apothecas conductas habent et in publico epulas vendunt. Quocunque accedas, complurima ibi invenias gulae irritamenta parari nec uno tantum ritu, ut ceteris in[614] locis. Quot enim sunt in curia exterae nationes, tot instruendorum ciborum mores ac ritus servantur.

L: [34] Quapropter, si quis est qui hac voluptate vehementius capiatur, duo sibi, ut video, potissimum exoptanda sunt: unum ut sibi in curia vivere liceat, //83// alterum gulam sibi non iam ciconiae, quod olim quendam a diis immortalibus precatum ferunt,[615] sed tuba longiorem dari, ne subito[616] voluptas tanta glutiendi intereat. Hoc igitur in curia voluptatis genus huiusmodi est et ita accurate colitur et tot artifices, magistros,[617] atque studiosos habet.

A: At si quem delectat odorum[618] suavitas, qui hoc assequi in curia poterit, ex fumo, arbitror, ciborum aucupetur sibi eiusmodi[619] voluptatem.

L: [35] Minime. Nam hic quidem odor gulae tantum deditis[620] convenire videtur, qui non odore, sed cibi cuius is est odor desiderio commoventur; veluti leo cum cervae[621] odorem persensit aut lupus[622] balatum ovis exaudit, non vocis odorisve gratia, sed vorandae[623] praedae cupiditate excitantur. [36] Verum sunt alii quoque plurimi[624] suavissimi acerrimique odores ex India, Egypto, Syria Arabiave advecti, quibus in beatorum domibus triclinia, cubicula, aedes totae complentur. Nec enim

---

611. barbarbaris *sic F;* barbaris *codd.*
612. carare *N.*
613. Hec *P.*
614. inde *VG.*
615. fuerunt *V.*
616. subita *P.*
617. artifices, magistros] magistros, artifices *B.*
618. odoris *P.*
619. huiusmodi *B.*
620. deditus *VPB.*
621. carnis *sic legit Sch.*
622. lupum *sic FGN;* lupus *VPB.*
623. devorande *B.*
624. alii quoque plurimi] quoque plurimi alii *P.*

L: [32] I certainly don't envy them. Really, although our people are not unskilled in this art, still, it is fair to concede the barbarians this praise and bear our lack of it with the same equanimity with which they once bore being despoiled by us in the glories of war.

A: [33] But they don't only carry this task out privately or at someone else's place. Those who are a little more well heeled have rented storerooms and sell their feasts to the public. Wherever you go, you will find that there are great numbers of temptations to gourmandizing being prepared—and not only in one style of cuisine, as in other places. There are just as many customs and rituals for preparing foods as there are foreign peoples in the curia.

L: [34] And so if there is someone who is powerfully taken with this pleasure, there are two things he really ought to wish for, as I see it: first, that he be permitted to live in the curia; second, that he be given not the throat of a stork—which they say someone once asked of the immortal gods—but a throat longer than a trumpet, so that the great pleasure of swallowing does not pass away in an instant. This, then, is the sort of gustatory pleasure that there is in the curia; it is cultivated with great precision and has quite a few practitioners, teachers, and students.

A: But if the charm of the aromas pleases someone who could come by it in the curia, then he might, I think, hunt for himself this sort of pleasure from the vapor of the foods.

L: [35] Not at all, since this aroma certainly seems to be adapted only to those gluttons who are moved not by smell but by desire for the food whose smell it is. Just like a lion who senses the smell of a deer, or a wolf who hears the bleating of a sheep, they are aroused not by the sound or smell but by the desire to devour their prey. [36] But there are also many other delectable and pungent aromas drawn from India, Egypt, Syria, and Arabia. All of the dining rooms, sleeping rooms, chambers, and even whole apartments in the houses of the holy are filled with them. Really,

putandum est, qui in ceteris vitae partibus ita lauti sint[625] et splendidi, in hoc uno genere minus accuratos et diligentes esse.[626]

A: Sed de his satis hactenus dictum sit.[627] Iam venerea, quae[628] reliqua sunt, cupio a te explicari.

L: [37] Venereis autem voluptatibus non minor quam superioribus relinquitur in curia Romana campus, quippe quae latissime pateant, nec[629] his curiales homines minus quam illis indulgeant, nec id immerito. Superior enim quanquam maxima est illa quidem, sine hac tamen imperfecta quodammodo[630] et incohata esse videtur. Quid enim prodesset sitim provocasse, si eam sedare non possis? Quid incendisse libidinem, si desit quo nervos intendas et ubi excitatum incendium restinguatur?[631] Itaque huic quoque generi optime prospexerunt prudentes viri et diligentes, ne quid in curia ad cumulatam voluptatem deesset.

[38] Nec vero ego nunc privata stupra nec domestica scorta //83v// nec adulteras matronas nec etiam honestioris loci meretrices prosequar, quae sibi sua[632] quisque in arte pararit,[633] etsi plurima non incognita <co>mmemorare[634] proferreque possem. Non enim id mihi propositum est, ut tecta cuiusquam flagitia detegam, aut mihi[635] invidiam[636] comparem. Si qua latent, ea clausa silentio meo ac tecta esse patiar. Tantum vulgaria prostibula et meritoria oratione complectar,[637] quibus in curia omnes viae, vici, angiporti, balnea, thermae cauponiaeque redundant.

---

625. sunt *B.*
626. esse *om. N.*
627. est *VPGNB.*
628. quae *om. G.*
629. ne *G.*
630. quod admo(dum) *N.*
631. extinguatur *G.*
632. suo *VPNB.*
633. pararet *B.*
634. memorare *V;* commemorare *PGB.*
635. propositum est, ut tecta cuiusquam flagitia detegam, aut mihi *om. V.*
636. iniuriam *VPGNB.*
637. complecta *V (et B?).*

you should not think that those who live luxuriously and magnificently in the other areas of their lives are less exacting and diligent in this one.

A: Well now, enough about these things. Now I want you to explain what remains—the matters related to Venus.

L: [37] Well, in the Roman curia there is no less a place for the pleasures of Venus than for the others. In fact the pleasures of Venus are certainly most apparent there, and the curialists indulge in them no less than in the others and not undeservedly. After all, although gustatory pleasure is certainly the greatest, without this one it seems somehow imperfect and unformed. Really, what good would it do to provoke thirst if you couldn't quench it? What good is it to have fired up your sexual appetite if there is nothing with which you can release your sexual desire, where you can put out the fire that has been ignited? And so, prudent and diligent men have energetically provided for this sort of thing, so that nothing toward the end of filling the cup of pleasure to the full would be lacking in the curia.

[38] Now I shall not go into any detail about private debaucheries, domestic prostitutes, adulterous matrons, or even the courtesans of more honorable status, all of whom have their own specialties—although I could remember and disclose quite a bit of well-known material. Really, it was not my task to blow the roof off anyone's shames or to bring ill will on myself. If there are any disgraces that remain hidden, with my silence I allow them to remain locked up. But let me include in my speech common prostitution and harlotry by saying that in the curia all of the streets, districts, narrow lanes, public baths, hot baths, and taverns are swimming with them.

A: [39] Vera narras,[638] itaque mihi nunquam in iis[639] locis esse aut[640] per ea transire casto licet. Etenim accedenti[641] catervatim omnes apertis pectoribus, nudis mammis ebore ac nive candidioribus longe tibi obviam prodeunt; saltu, gestu ac risu applaudunt[642] cantilenisque salacioribus te salutant; deinde propiores[643] factae mollibus vinciunt complexibus, iungunt basia, obscenas obtrectant partes omnibusque adhibitis blanditiis te in fornicem et in cellulam conantur pertrahere; lacteos etiam catellos habent, quibus uti illas aiunt ad lambendas feminum sordes, ut[644] Nestori et Priamo ac etiam natu grandioribus pruriginem concitare possint. [40] Quibus artibus si Phaedra illa, quondam Thesei uxor, instructa fuisset, pudorem potius posuisset Hipollytus quam se marinis obiiceret monstris et quadrigis dilacerandum committeret. Haec omnia cum ad commodum et oblectamentum curialium sint inventa, una in re parum voluptati consultum est, quod vel minimo precio ea voluptas ematur, siquidem, ut est apud poetam nostrum: "Haec magis oblectant animos,[645] quae pluris emuntur."

L: [41] Perabunde quidem et copiose meum[646] explevisti munus.[647] Sed haec lenonum disputationibus relinquamus, quae eruditorum sermone indigna sunt. //84// Hactenus de curiae commodis non ita accurate fortasse, ut tanta res flagitabat, sed pro facultate[648] mea disserui. [42] Si igitur in curia Romana virtutes plurimae et maximae, si doctissimorum et praestantissimorum[649] virorum necessitudines et amicitiae, si nomen

---

638. narrans *V.*
639. hiis *PG.*
640. atque *G.*
641. accedentes *G.*
642. applaudant *B.*
643. propriores *N.*
644. et *V.*
645. canimos *sic P.*
646. meum] in eum *B.*
647. munus *om. V cum spatio vacuo.*
648. .. verbi ..us.. *in mar. d. B.*
649. prostantissimorum *sic N.*

A: [39] You're right about that. That is why, as a chaste man, I can never allow myself to be in those places or even walk through them. Indeed, as you approach, they all swarm on you with chests revealed, their naked breasts shining like ivory and snow. They strike you, dancing, gesturing, and laughing, and greet you with lewd songs. Then once they have come closer, they encircle you with soft embraces, adding kisses and fondling your privates. Once they have applied all of their flatteries they try to lure you into the brothel and then into their little room. They also have milk white little lapdogs, whom—people say—they use to lick up filth about your loins, so that they could provoke desire in Nestor and Priam and in those who are even older.[56] [40] If Phaedra, who was once the wife of Theseus, had been instructed in these arts, then Hippolytus would have laid chastity aside rather than expose himself to marine monsters and allow himself to be torn to pieces by the chariot.[57] But even though all of these things were invented for the convenience and pleasure of the curialists, since the pleasure is bought at quite a low price then in one respect insufficient thought was given to pleasure, if it is true, as our poet says, that "those things that are bought at a higher price please the spirit more."[58]

L: [41] Well, you have certainly done my job for me, in a more than abundant fashion. But let's leave these things behind as the arguments of panderers, unworthy to be discussed by the learned. Up to this point I have discussed the curia's advantages not, perhaps, as precisely as a great subject called for but in accordance with my own abilities. [42] If, then, there are in the Roman curia the most and the greatest of the virtues, relationships and friendships with the most learned and excellent men, a

---

56. For Lapo's "ut Nestori et Priamo ac etiam natu grandioribus pruriginem concitare possint," cf. Juvenal VI.324–26: ". . . quibus incendi iam frigidus aevo / Laomedontiades et Nestoris hirnea possit. / tunc prurigo morae inpatiens . . ."

57. Phaedra schemed to seduce her stepson Hippolytus, who refused her advances. After the episode, she told Theseus (Phaedra's husband, Hippolytus's father) that Hippolytus tried to seduce *her.* Theseus believed Phaedra and, angered, prayed to Poseidon for revenge. At Poseidon's command a bull came from the sea as Hippolytus was traveling by chariot into exile; and Hippolytus was killed in the ensuing chariot wreck. On this episode, see Ovid *Met.* XV.497–529; Ovid *Fast.* VI.733–62; Seneca *Phaed.;* Hyginus *Fab.* 47; there is also a mention in Apuleius *Apol.* 79. Lapo would have known these texts, with the exception of Hyginus. For Apuleius, see Sabbadini, *Le scoperte,* 2:202; Reynolds, *Texts,* 15–16. For Seneca and Ovid, see Sabbadini, op. cit., 2:250, 238.

58. Cf. Juvenal XI.16: ". . . magis illa iuvant quae pluris ementur." It is interesting that Lapo calls Juvenal, as opposed to Virgil, "our poet." Bruni also called Juvenal *poeta noster,* "our poet"; see his commentary to the *Oeconomica* in Bruni, *Humanistisch-philosophische Schriften,* 130.

magnum et gloria, si divitiae atque opes amplissimae, si cumulatissimae in omni genere voluptates[650] parantur,[651] idque a me locis[652] pluribus et rationibus demonstratum est et a te ultro concessum et comprobatum, quid est quod a quoquam[653] ad honestatem vitae, splendorem, commodum, iucunditatem desiderari[654] praeterea debeat et aut a te in disputatione requiri aut a me in medium afferri possit? [43] In quo si tibi satisfactum est, tuum est iam ab ea, qua dudum eras, sententia et opinione desistere mihique gratias agere, quod opera mea tanto tam veteri errore liberatus sis, nec posthac[655] quempiam a curia deterrere, ne illius commodis invidere videaris. Si quis autem restat scrupulus, percontari quid dubites, et ipse tibi id pro mea consuetudine, ut potero, explanare aggrediar. Statui enim, quantum in me erit, te nulla in re dubium ambiguumve dimittere.

A: [44] Cumulate mihi abs te quod susceperas munus persolutum est, opi<ni>onem[656] vero illam parum commodam[657] de curia quam habebam, aequo libentique animo penitus remitto atque abiicio, tibique me ob id plurimum debere fateor. Sed quoniam hanc mihi potestatem //84v, 85//[658] facis, haud verear[659] quid sentiam dicere, idque non tam arbitratu[660] meo quam aliorum sermonibus,[661] non videri mihi pontificibus reliquisque antistibus tantas divitias atque opes permittendas esse.

[VIII. Defensio divitiarum a religiosis acquirendarum]

L: [1] Non me fugit esse nonnullos suo quidem iudicio valde sapientes, ut mihi autem videntur stultissimi homines, qui huius saeculi, ut ipsi appellant, luxuriam et opulentiam pontificum improbent, priscorum patrum magnopere vitae tenuitatem desiderent. Quam quidem obiectionem tuam

---

650. voluptatis *V.*
651. proparantur *N.*
652. locisis *sic F.*
653. quo( )que *V.*
654. desiderare *B.*
655. posthac] post hanc *V;* posthanc *B.*
656. opinionem *VGN.*
657. commedam *sic V;* commendatam *sic coni. Sch.*
658. *Pagina vacua 84v (codice F) consulto est, sed sine textus interruptione.*
659. *Ann. in mar. sup.* hic incipit rexien... apud nostrum in..... *V.*
660. arbitratuo *N.*
661. *in mar. sin.* hic non *V.*

great name and glory, abundant wealth and riches, and the greatest gathering of pleasures of every sort—if all of these things are furnished (and I have proven this with many cases and arguments, and you have of your own accord conceded and agreed to this)—what could anyone think was missing, as far as probity, luxury, advantage, or happiness of life go? And what can you need, as far as the argument goes, or what can I add? [43] If you are satisfied with this, then it is up to you now to abandon your former thoughts and opinions and thank me, since you have been liberated—thanks to my work—from quite an old error. And do not let yourself be seen afterward deterring anyone from the curia, for fear you might seem envious of his advancement. But if any scruple remains, allow me to investigate your doubts and let me offer an explanation, as is my custom, insofar as I can. After all, I did decide, as far as it is in me, not to leave you in doubt or ambiguity in any way.

A: [44] In my view you have fulfilled in consummate fashion the obligation you took on. And I give up that unsuitable opinion I held about the curia—I abandon it with an even-tempered and willing spirit—and admit that I owe you quite a bit on this account. But seeing that you give me this power, I am not afraid to say what I feel—and this not so much because of my own judgment but thanks to what others say: it seems to me that popes and the other priests should not be allowed to have such riches and wealth.

[VIII. The Defense of Wealth Held by Religious]

L: [1] I am certainly aware that there are some exceedingly wise men who judge this to be the case. But the result of this is that they seem to me the most foolish of men—those who disapprove of the luxury and opulence of the popes of this age, as they term it, and who so earnestly long for the ancient fathers' purity of life. Now certainly, since I uphold the role of

ac ceterorum, quoniam defensoris⁶⁶² et patroni impositam mihi a te personam substineo, refellendam a me summopere atque infringendam puto
teque in eam sententiam traducendum, ut pontificibus divitias non modo
non adimendas esse, sed etiam, si illis⁶⁶³ carerent,⁶⁶⁴ tribuendas ducas.

A: [2] Permagnam ab illis, quantum intelligo, merebis⁶⁶⁵ gratiam si tot
tam assidue in eos coniecta maledicta, probra,⁶⁶⁶ calumnias refutabis; me
autem vereor ne, cum hoc effeceris, vitae huius, quam mihi delegi, sero
nimium penitere incipiat.

L: [3] Conabor efficere. Quare nunc ab illis, si adessent, et⁶⁶⁷ abs te, qui
ades, libenter audirem, nunquid⁶⁶⁸ existimes inopes tantum probos, castos
religiososque esse viros, divites omnes improbos, sceleratos, flagitiosos,
nefarios? Quod ni⁶⁶⁹ ita putas, quaero, cur⁶⁷⁰ pontificibus divitias adimi
velis? Si <ita> putas, cur reliquos non⁶⁷¹ quoque homines pauperes
censeas⁶⁷² esse oportere? An quia unus tantummodo ex omnibus vir bonus
existere debeat, reliqui pro arbitrio⁶⁷³ vivere, cum una tantum via omnibus
per virtutem ac bonos mores ad beatitudinem contendendum⁶⁷⁴ sit?

A: [4] Nunquam istuc⁶⁷⁵ ego dixerim inopiam bonos, copias malos
efficere, sed magnas ad vicia ac flagitia in divitiis illecebras atque irritamenta esse.

L: Pontificibus an etiam caeteris?

A: Omnibus.

L: Quid,⁶⁷⁶ si caeteris maiora quam illis?

A: //85v// Quonam pacto?

L: [5] Quoniam ii liberiores omnium voluntates⁶⁷⁷ rerum habent et
eorum vita minus⁶⁷⁸ multis oculis observatur. Obscuriori enim loco con-
stituti sunt, pauci vident, pauci audiunt, pauciores quaerunt, paucissimi
curant, itaque sua facinora perfacile occultare possunt. Nacti etiam

---

662. defensores *V.*
663. illis *om. VPGB.*
664. carerem *V.*
665. nubis *VPB;* merebis *coni. Sch., recte;* mihi *G;* imbis *sic N.*
666. proba *B.*
667. ut *N.*
668. nunquid] nunc quid *B.*
669. in *sic P.*
670. quaero cur] quero, curia Romana *P;* que ro(mana) cu(ria) *G.*
671. reliquos non] non reliquos *PBNG.*
672. senteas *sic P.*
673. arbitro *N.*
674. contempnendum *V.*
675. istud *V.*
676. Quod *B.*
677. voluptates *coni. Sch.;* volumptates *sic G.*
678. nimis *sic legit Sch.*

defender and protector that you have placed on me, I think I should expend the utmost effort to rebut this objection of yours and others and then shatter it. I think you should be persuaded to come over to this opinion: that wealth not only should not be withheld from high priests but also should be given them, should they lack it.

A: [2] Well as far as I can tell, you will certainly deserve a great deal of thanks from them, if you refute all the abuses, reproaches, and sophistries that have been so incessantly flung against them. But I *am* afraid that I shall begin to repent all too late of this life I have chosen for myself, should you fail to carry it off.

L: [3] I'll try to do it. Well then, I would gladly hear from them if they were here and from you since you are: do you really think that only the poor are respectable, chaste, and religious and that all of the wealthy are rogues, corrupt, disgraceful, and nefarious? Because if you don't think so, I ask, why do you want to take wealth away from the high priests? If you do think so, why wouldn't you suppose that everybody else should also be poor? Or is it because out of all men, only one good one should exist and the rest should live by his judgment, since there is only one way to pursue happiness for all: through virtue and good character.

A: [4] I would never tell you that poverty produces good men and wealth bad men, but I would say that in wealth there are great temptations and enticements to vice and disgracefulness.

L: For high priests or also for everybody else?

A: For everybody.

L: But what if there were greater temptations for others than for them?

A: In what way?

L: [5] In that they have wills that are freer of all things and that their life comes less under the observation of many eyes. Really, they are set up in a place that is barely visible, few see them, few hear them, fewer ask, and barely anybody cares. And so they can hide their shameful deeds very easily. They have also acquired greater resources for fulfilling their lewd desires, as well as an easier way. In public and in private, at home and

maiorem sunt⁶⁷⁹ facultatem et proniorem viam ad suas explendas cupiditates. Nam et in publico et in privato et domi et foris et cum aliis et
secum et die noctuque ut libet sine cuiusquam reprehensione versantur,
quae quidem libertas vitae maiores etiam⁶⁸⁰ concitationes habet. Multa
enim quottidie et vident et sentiunt, quibus eorum excitentur libidines, et
quasi inviti ad facinus rapiantur. [6] Habent praeterea socios, amicos,
familiares, conscios⁶⁸¹ complures⁶⁸² ad quorum vitam ac mores, nisi rustici atque inhumani existimari volunt, conformari eos oporteat, quibus
multa concedere, quorum suasionibus multa facere, quae ipsi saepe
improbent et sibi interdum permolesta sint. Qui quidem, si inquinati⁶⁸³
sunt homines et corrupti, difficillimum est in eorum⁶⁸⁴ consuetudine
decorum honestatemque retinere. Nec illam parvam illecebram⁶⁸⁵ ad⁶⁸⁶
peccandum esse arbitror habere exploratum⁶⁸⁷ fore ut delictis suis, nisi
detestabilis aliqua insit⁶⁸⁸ improbitas, omnes ignoscant et in oblivionem
celeriter adducantur.⁶⁸⁹ [7] Nemo enim eorum facta ad vim summae religionis exquirenda esse arbitratur.⁶⁹⁰ Exuberantibus igitur copiis, stimu-
lante voluptate, urgente furore, suadente libidine nihil est praeterea, nisi
eximia aliqua et divina vis animi virtusque obsistant, quo a scelere,
improbitate, audacia revocari et contineri queant.

[8] Pontifices autem—pontifices cum dico, reliquos quoque antistites
intelligi volo—pontifices, inquam, multa sunt quae etiam⁶⁹¹ natura pro-
cliviores //86// in vicium peccare non sinant, quae eos dies noctesque
absterreant. Persona primum an⁶⁹² nomen ipsum quod sustinent,⁶⁹³
quibus, ne ex eorum vita aliqua nota et ignominia inuxta⁶⁹⁴ esse videatur,
necesse est illos, si quis sensus humanitatis aut ratio inest, religionis quot-

---

679. maiorem sunt] sunt maiorem *G.*
680. et *V.*
681. consocios *V.*
682. complures] quam plures *P.*
683. inquinati] iniqus nati *sic N.*
684. rorum *sic V;* rerum *sic legit Sch.*
685. illecebrem *VP.*
686. ad *om. V.*
687. habere exploratum] haberi et exploratum *B.*
688. visit *sic G.*
689. abducantur *P.*
690. arbitrantur *P.*
691. et *V.*
692. ac *P.*
693. Persona primum an nomen ipsum quod sustinent *om. G.*
694. immixta *V;* mixta *P.*

outside, with others and with themselves, and day and night as you please they are engaged in these things without being blamed at all. Certainly, this liberty of life also comes with greater excitements, since every day they see and hear things that stimulate their sexual appetites and they are almost unwillingly dragged into shame. [6] Besides, they have quite a few companions, friends, intimates, and associates. If they do not want to be considered rude and barbarous, they have to conform to the lives and characters of these men. They have to yield many things to them and do many things on account of their persuasion, things that they themselves often disapprove of and that—sometimes—are personally very troublesome. Of course if these men are polluted and corrupt, it is tremendously difficult in their company to hold on to decorum and integrity. I think it has also been determined that it is no small temptation to sin when no one knows about their crimes—unless there is some execrable shamefulness—and when the crimes quickly pass into oblivion. [7] Really, no one thinks their deeds should be investigated with the force of the highest religious standard. Therefore, with wealth abounding, with pleasure as a stimulus, with frenzy urging them on and lust persuading them, there is nothing with which they can be checked or withheld from wickedness, disgracefulness, and insolence, unless some extraordinary and divine spiritual power and virtue prevent them.

[8] However, the high priests—and when I say, "high priests," I mean [not only the pope but] also the rest of the bishops—as to the high priests, I say, there are also many things that prevent them from falling into sin and vice, even if they are naturally rather inclined to do so. Indeed, many things deter them day and night. First of all there is the person, or the name itself, that they maintain. Because of this, if they have any human sense or reason at all, they must be careful every day when it comes to religion, lest it seem that any mark of disgrace be imprinted on them

tidie solicitos esse. [9] Deinde ordo ipse, qui ita⁶⁹⁵ expositus est atque⁶⁹⁶
editus in altum ut ab omnibus undique circunspici et observari possit,
itaque, si quid temere administrarint, si qua in re a virtute atque ab
officio declinarint, effertur statim et in oculos⁶⁹⁷ omnium ac voces
maledicorum incurrit; ex quo manifesto perspicere possint id sibi non
ad⁶⁹⁸ exigui temporis calumniam futurum, sed ad <de>decus⁶⁹⁹ atque
infamiam⁷⁰⁰ sempiternum,⁷⁰¹ nec sibi soli, sed reliquis etiam⁷⁰² omnibus
qui post se in eum locum successuri sunt. [10] Quid? Quod occlusi⁷⁰³
quottidie continentur domi, nec eis prodire unquam⁷⁰⁴ sine multitudine
licet⁷⁰⁵ nec ad ea videnda, quibus reliqui et oblectantur et
incend<unt>ur,⁷⁰⁶ accedere, nihil sine arbitris agere licet, ut, etiam si⁷⁰⁷
caetera omnia caeci cupiditate contempserint nec famae suae nec
hominum futuris de se sermonibus consulendum⁷⁰⁸ putent, pudore
tamen praesentium et verecundia, nisi haec ipsa quoque abiecerint, pro-
hibentur, postremo nullis sermonibus, nisi de rebus gravibus seriisque
interesse itaque, cum pauciora videant paucioraque audiant, pauciora
etiam appetant necesse est?⁷⁰⁹ [11] Accedit etiam, ut secessus ipse, ocium,
cessatio⁷¹⁰ a labore, austeritas vitae et perpetuus, ut sic dixerim, carcer
non modo debilitet infringatque corporis vires, sed langorem⁷¹¹ quoque
animis afferat, ex quo remissiores et sedatiores fiunt animi motus. Quare
cum nec cupiant nec servata existimatione cupiditates exequi possint,
haud sane video quantum in iis⁷¹² valeant divitiarum illecebre.

    A: [12] Caetera tibi facile concedo, sed in illo extremo a te vehementer
dissentio, quod dixisti ocio ac vacatione cupiditates imminui, cum ex iis
consensu omnium plurimae et nequissimae gignantur cupiditates.

    L: [13] Est hoc aliqua ex parte verissimum, sed de ocio distinguendum
videtur. //86v// Est enim animi et corporis ocium, quorum alterum, id est

---

695. ita *om. V.*
696. atque] atque ita *G.*
697. *emendavi ego ex* inoculos; in ortulos *V.*
698. ad *om. G.*
699. dedecus *PNB.*
700. infamiam] infamiam magnam *B.*
701. sempiternam *GN;* sempiternamque *B.*
702. reliquis etiam] etiam reliquis *B.*
703. inclusi *coni. Sch.*
704. usquam *G;* nunquam *B.*
705. licet *om. VB.*
706. inceduntur *V;* incenduntur *PNB.*
707. etiam si] etsi *V.*
708. de se sermonibus consulendum] etiam sermonibus de se consulendum *G.*
709. est *om. N.*
710. cessans *sic legit Sch.*
711. languorem *PB.*
712. hiis *P.*

thanks to their lifestyle. [9] Next there is the rank itself, which has been set apart and put on a pedestal to such an extent that everyone everywhere can inspect and observe it. So if they handle anything rashly or fall short of virtue and duty in any way, it is found out immediately, comes into everyone's view, and enters into the talk of slanderers. Thanks to this they can see clearly that this will lead not just to short-term defamation but rather to shame and eternal infamy—and not just for themselves alone but for all those who remain to succeed them in their position. [10] What of the fact that they are secluded every day at home and never allowed to go out in public without a big crowd or to go see those things that delight and arouse everybody else? That they are allowed to do nothing without chaperones? Even if they were blind with desire, scorned everything else, and came to think they should not care for their own reputation or about what men would say about them in the future, still, out of shame and respect for those who are present—unless they cast these very things aside too—they are hemmed in; and finally, they are prohibited from taking part in any conversations that are not about grave and serious things. Since they see and hear less, must they not also desire less? [11] And you can add that solitude itself, leisure, respite from work, severity of life, and perpetual imprisonment, so to speak, not only debilitate and weaken their bodily powers but even inject their souls with sloth, so that the soul's movements become slacker and calmer. Since, then, they do not desire and—if they want to preserve their reputation—are unable to pursue pleasures, I really do not see how much power the temptations of wealth can have over them.

A: [12] The other things I shall readily concede you, but I disagree strongly with that last argument you made, that is, that desires are diminished by intellectual leisure and exemption from work. Everybody agrees that these things beget the greatest number and the wickedest of desires.

L: [13] Very true, on the one hand. But it seems that when it comes to leisure one has to make distinctions. There is leisure of the spirit and

corporis, cum nimis[713] assiduum est, corpus ipsum enervat[714] et conficit. Animi autem vacatio pravas cogitationes inducit quibus corrumpitur animus et ad scelus flagitiumque impellitur. [14] Sed cum ad ocium animi ac vacationem commoda corporis valitudo accedit, tum maxime efficitur illud quod dicis; cum autem[715] feriato omnino corpore assiduis laboribus distinetur[716] animus, quod in pontificibus evenit, naturalis deficit vigor et ad internitionem[717] statim perducitur. Itaque videmus huiusmodi homines vel brevi vitam finire vel in lepram, podagram, hydropsim aliosque incurabiles morbos incidere.

A: [15] Fieri aliter non potest. Cum enim distrahitur animus curis maioribus et a sensibus[718] cogitatione abducitur et quasi separatur nec corpus fovet, ut debet, corpus desidiosum per se languidum et animi ope destitutum aut interire propediem aut aegrotare necesse est.

L: Non sunt igitur, ut ostendimus, perniciosae illis divitiae.

A: Minime, verum aliis.

L:[719] [16] Quid? Si ne[720] aliis quidem, nisi improbis, intemperatis, flagitiosis perniciosae, quin potius salutares et ad bene vivendum maxime necessariae? Sunt enim non privatis modo hominibus,[721] sed etiam civitatibus universis et in bello et in pace et domi et foris adiumenta et ornamenta maxima, sine quibus nec domestica res bene constitui nec publica[722] administrari nec magnum aliquid et praeclarum fieri potest. [17] His enim geruntur bella, his propulsantur hostes, his fines patriae, his salus, his libertas defenditur; his pax et ocium comparatur civibus, his iniuriae potentium et factiosorum occurritur, his oppressi, inopes, afflicti, perditi[723] in civitate retinentur; his freti ducibus ad omnia quae cupimus aditum habemus; his nihil est tam difficile atque arduum quod non facillime superetur,[724] //87// quibus qui et[725] honeste affluunt et recte sapien-

---

713. minus *sic legit Sch.*
714. enarvat *P.*
715. aut *B.*
716. destinetur *VP.*
717. interemcionem *sic legit Sch.*
718. assensibus *G.*
719. L *om. VPGN (et F?), ubi est in parte textus quae abradatur;* L *coni. Sch. et ego id accepi.*
720. Si ne] Sine *FVGN;* Si ve *B.*
721. modo hominibus] hominibus modo *B.*
722. publicari *N.*
723. prediti *P.*
724. superentur *B.*
725. qui et] et qui *G.*

leisure of the body. The latter, leisure of the body, weakens and diminishes that very body if there is too much of it. But exemption from spiritual work brings distorted thoughts that pervert the soul and incite it to crime and shameful deeds. [14] Yet when an advantageous health of body is added to leisure of spirit and exemption from work, then what you suggest comes about and greatly so. Moreover, since one's spirit is drawn apart when the body has been given leave from all continuous labor—which happens with the high priests—then one lacks natural energy and is quickly destroyed. And so we see that men of this sort either end their life in a short time or come down with leprosy, gout, dropsy, and other incurable diseases.

A: [15] It can't happen otherwise, since when the soul is distracted by greater cares and removed and almost separated from the senses because of thought and does not take care of the body as it should, then the body—idle and sluggish in itself and deprived of the soul's assistance—must either die very soon or become ill.

L: Wealth, then, as we have shown, is not dangerous for them.

A: Not at all, but for others.

L: [16] What, then? If wealth certainly isn't dangerous for others, unless they are dishonest, intemperate, and shameful, why don't we just come out and say that it is advantageous and integrally essential to live well? Wealth is a great aid and ornament not only to men of the private sector but also to all cities, both in war and at peace, at home and away. Without it the household cannot be well established, public affairs cannot be managed, and nothing great or outstanding can happen. [17] After all, with wealth wars are waged, enemies are beaten back, and the country's borders, security, and liberty are defended. With wealth, the citizens acquire peace and leisure, you can meet head-on the injustice of the powerful and seditious, and the oppressed, the poor, the put-upon, and the hopeless are taken care of in the city. With the confidence of wealth as our leader we have access to everything we desire; with wealth, there is nothing so difficult or arduous that it can't be easily overcome. Those who abound in wealth and use it justly and wisely—well, we are rightly

terque utuntur, beneficos, praeclaros, splendidos magnificosque viros merito appellare solemus. [18] Sunt enim virtutes quaedam quae divitias quasi materiem quam tractent et in qua versentur requirant, ut benignitas, liberalitas, munificentiaque[726] absque[727] divitiis nullae omnino esse possunt. Itaque non temere, tametsi fortasse non vere, philosophi quidam illis beatitudinem contineri, alii[728] verius augeri atque illustrari dixerunt.

A: [19] Retexis,[729] ut videris, orationem[730] et pugnantia inter se se[731] contrariaque loqueris, et quae ante incitamenta libidinum esse concesseris,[732] eadem nunc hominibus ac civitatibus utilia et salutaria esse dicis et ad beatitudinem etiam pertinere!

L: [20] Vehementer erras! Non enim quicquam muto quod superius a me positum est, divitias quibusdam esse viciorum materiem. Nam malis mala sunt omnia. Sed nego idcirco perniciosas aut fugiendas esse.[733] Nam sic paupertas multo perniciosior magisque fugienda foret. Ad maiora enim ac detestabiliora scelera homines impelluntur inopia quam divitiis adducuntur. Difficilius est enim[734] res asperas et incommodas firmo constantique animo ferre nec ab honestatis ratione discedere, quam in secundis et optatis se continere sibique moderari, quinetiam[735] divitiis affluentes, si victi cupiditate a virtute deflexerint, in minora tamen erumpunt vicia. [21] Molliores enim qui sunt, gulae, somno, desidiae luxuriaeque se dedunt, qui paulo erectiore sunt animo, ad pompam, ad luxum, atque ad dominatum spectant et ad largiendum et corrumpendum pecuniis abutuntur. Quae peccata etsi reprehendenda sunt, non tamen penitus ab humanitate remota. Ex inopia vero furta, praedae rapinaeque oriuntur, ex eadem insidiae, proditiones, caedes, exitia hominibus importantur. [22] Necessitas enim et[736] bonorum quibus indigemus carentia violentissima omnino res est, quae sanctos interdum atque integros viros peccare etiam invitos[737] ac renitentes cogit et animalia saepe natura man//87v//sueta ferocia immaniaque efficit et in alio-

---

726. magnificentiaque *P.*
727. atque *V.*
728. aliis *V.*
729. Retexisti *G.*
730. orationem] orationem tuam *VG.*
731. se *om. PB.*
732. censeris *V*; censuisti *coni. Sch.*
733. Sed nego idcirco perniciosas aut fugiendas esse *om. G;* esse *om. N.*
734. enim] *hoc vocabulum illegibile in F.*
735. quinetiam] quiin et *V;* quin immo et *sic legit Sch.*
736. et *om. G.*
737. invictos *V.*

accustomed to call them liberal, outstanding, distinguished, and noble. [18] For there are certain virtues, like liberality, generosity, and munificence, that require wealth as the means that they use and in which they flourish. Without it none of those virtues would even be possible. And so, even if it is untrue, it is not rashly that certain philosophers have said that happiness is located in wealth. Others, more truly, have said that happiness is increased and adorned by wealth.

A: [19] As you'll see, you are unweaving your speech and are saying contrary things that work against one another. The things that you admitted earlier were incentives to sexual desire—now you claim that they are useful and beneficial for men and cities and even lead to happiness!

L: [20] You are so very wrong! Really, I am not changing what I argued before, that wealth is for certain people the stuff of vice. After all, for bad men all things are bad. But I deny that wealth is dangerous because of this or that one should flee it. Poverty, for instance, would be so much more dangerous and something one would have to flee from even more. Really, men are pushed to greater and more detestable crimes by poverty than they are led to by wealth. For it is harder to bear harsh and disagreeable things with a firm and constant spirit and not fall away from a system of honor than it is to contain and limit oneself when favorable and desirable things are at hand. Also, as a matter of fact, if men who overflow with wealth turn away from virtue, then at least the vices they break out into are only lesser ones. [21] After all, there are those who are more delicate, who devote themselves to gourmandizing, sleep, idleness, and extravagance. There are also those who are a little more lively in spirit, who look toward ostentation, debauchery, and power and use up money both for payoffs and bribes. And even if these sins are to be disapproved of, still, they are not so far from the human condition. But thefts, plundering, and robbery are born of poverty; poverty brings men treachery, betrayals, slaughter, and destruction. [22] Really, the necessity and privation of the goods we lack is altogether a very violent thing and compels those who are normally sacred and pure to sin even when they are unwilling and resistant. This necessity also often makes naturally gentle animals turn ferocious and savage, inciting them to mur-

rum necem incitat. Deinde ad ea omnia quae facillime conficiuntur divitiis,[738] quae maxima et preclarissima sunt aditus intercluditur plurimaque subeuntur inopibus[739] incommoda, quae a divitibus leviter declinari possunt.

[23] Quis igitur non videt hac ratione paupertatem, si eam non ex natura ipsius, sed ex hominum viciis spectare velimus, rem unam omnium capitalissimam esse summaque ope ab omnibus repellendam, quam tamen plerisque scimus salutarem fuisse, multos etiam[740] ex illa sibi nomen maximum et gloriam comparasse?

[24] Non sunt igitur pernitiosae cuiquam per se nec[741] fugiendae divitiae—etsi ab illis quidam deteriores fiant—nisi iam robur formae, dignitatem, ad haec ingenium, mentem, orationem, tum genus, cognationem, necessitudines, amicitias, clientelas, affinitates pernitiosas ac fugiendas putamus, quae cum per se optima sint[742] nobisque ad salutem et conservationem nostri vel a natura vel a fortuna ipsa concessa, tamen improbi eorum pervertunt usum et ad cladem saepe hominum et pernitiem referunt. [25] Quodsi demonstratum est[743] divitias minime fugiendas esse (tametsi habenti interdum noceant), sed contra magnopere expetendas, cum sint utiles et salutares maximamque ad res praeclaras bene gerendas afferant facultatem, quid est causae cur eas pontificibus quispiam adimendas aut cur non ultro nec petentibus[744] nec cupientibus deferendas censeat?[745] Etenim si qui improbi sunt, illorum nequitiam bonis viris fraudi esse non decet, sed aut ii[746] non constituendi pontifices aut deprehensi et cogniti pontificio abdicandi. [26] Si probi, nonne satius est[747] illos copiis abundare, quibus multis benefacere possint et[748] dignitatem suam apostolicaeque sedis amplitudinem et maiestatem tueri? Equidem numquam negabo virtutem, integritatem, sanctitatem, religionem in pontificibus primum esse oportere, et haec qui praestare de se //88// nequit, non modo non pontificem, sed ne hominem quidem habendum

---

738. quae facillime conficiuntur divitiis] *om. N.*
739. inopibus] in opibus *codd.*
740. et *V.*
741. per se nec] pernitioso *G.*
742. fine *B.*
743. est *om. Sch.*
744. potentibus *V.*
745. censeatur *N.*
746. hii *P.*
747. abdicandi; si probi, nonne satius est] abdicandi si *[tum vocabulum desiderat]* nonne satius est *V*; abdicandi sunt; nonne sanctius est *sic Sch.*
748. sed *P.*

der others. In addition, [lacking wealth,] one is denied access to all of the great and most outstanding things that wealth so easily brings about; those without it suffer many disadvantages that can easily be avoided with wealth.

[23] So in light of this argument, who does not see that poverty is the one most pernicious thing of all that everyone must by all means avoid— if, that is, we want to look at it not from the perspective of its own nature but from the perspective of men's vices? [This is so] even if we are aware that poverty has been beneficial to many and that many, too, have acquired glory and a great name owing to it.

[24] So wealth in itself is not dangerous to anyone nor should anyone flee it—even though some do slide a little because of it—unless we now think that strength of body and worth, as well as genius, intelligence, and eloquent speech, then noble birth, kindred, relations, friendships, client-age, and marriage relationships are also dangerous and things one should flee. Now in themselves these things are optimal and have been given us for our well-being and preservation, whether they have come by nature or even by fortune. Still, the dishonest employ them perversely and often use them for the damage and destruction of men. [25] Now it is true that it has been demonstrated that one should not in any way flee wealth (although it does at times hurt the one who possesses it) and rather that one ought greatly to pursue it, since wealth is useful and beneficial and greatly assists one's ability to do outstanding things. Still, why would anyone think wealth should be taken away from the high priests or, beyond that, that wealth should not be freely granted to those who seek or desire it? Of course, if there are those who are dishonest, it is wrong that their wickedness makes good men seem fraudulent. But either they shouldn't be appointed as high priests or, once they have been found out and recognized, they should be made to give up their pontifical office. [26] If they are honest, is it not preferable that they abound with riches with which they can benefit many and look after their own worth as well as the greatness and majesty of the apostolic see? Of course I shall never deny that virtue, integrity, holiness, and religion are necessary first of all in high priests and that whoever cannot exhibit these qualities in and of

esse, [27] ea vero cum assint, si ornentur copiis, magis[749] elucescere et plus apud omnes gentes auctoritatis et admirationis habere, praesertim cum summa illis potestate permissa, ea[750] proposita sint quae saepe sine maximis sumptibus recte administrari non possint, ut sublevare inopes et calamitosos dotesque illis ad filias locandas impendere, quae sancti religiosique viri officia sunt, edificare templa, collapsa instaurare et rebus omnibus exornare, cultus, sacra,[751] ceremonias instituere, quae magnificentissimo semper apparatu ac pompa[752] immortalem Deum fieri voluisse sacrae testantur historiae; [28] deinde legationes ad varias regiones[753] transmittere, pecunias erogare, reges ac principes ad pacem, ad unionem, ad religionem[754] traducere,[755] et quoniam eo[756] iam audaciae ac sceleris prolapsa res est, ut a praedonum manibus absque praesidio tuti esse non possint, equites peditesque ad sui corporis tutelam conducere,[757] quorum singula per se vim magnam pecuniarum deposcunt.

[29] Quae[758] igitur hae tantae amentiae sunt, ut pontifices inopes habere quam locupletes malint, cum omnium gentium,[759] omnium sectarum, omnium religionum pontifices summos semper viros eosdemque ditissimos fuisse et legere et audire potuerint? Quaere[760] Romanorum religiones, evolve diligenter[761] eorum monumenta. Invenies[762] apud[763] illos non humilibus et inopibus,[764] sed opulentissimis hominibus, principibus civitatis summum sacerdotium mandari solitum esse. [30] Siquidem legimus Iulios, Scipiones, Marcellos, Emylios, Catones, qui Romae temporibus illis gloria rerum gestarum, opibus, auctoritate, potentia plurimum praestare putabant<ur>,[765] summos saepe sacerdotes fuisse. Quam dignitatem Numam Pompilium a rege ad alios detulisse accepi-

---

749. magisque *V.*
750. et *V.*
751. sacra *corr. ad* sacras *G.*
752. pompa] pompa ac *B.*
753. varias regiones] sacras religiones *V.*
754. ad unionem, ad religionem] ad religionem, ad unionem *G.*
755. traducetur *V.*
756. eo *om. VPGN.*
757. traducere *G.*
758. Quare *G.*
759. gentium] gentium omnium nationum *B.*
760. Quaere] Qua re *N;* Quare *B.*
761. diligenter *om. V.*
762. Iuvenes *G.*
763. apud *om. G.*
764. et inopibus *om. V.*
765. putabantur *B.*

himself should not even be considered a man, let alone a high priest. [27] But when these qualities are present, if they are fitted out with riches, [the high priest] shines forth and has more authority and admiration among all peoples, especially since he has been entrusted with the highest power, and since there are things that often cannot be correctly managed without great expense. [Examples of these things are] helping the poor and afflicted and giving them dowries so that their daughters can be properly placed, which are the duties of a holy and religious man; building churches, restoring ruins, and beautifying all things; instituting worship, rites, and ceremonies—sacred scripture testifies that immortal God wanted this always to happen with the greatest pomp and circumstance; [28] then, sending legations to various regions, formally requesting money, winning over kings and princes to peace, union, and religion; and—since things have slipped to such a point of temerity and crime that the high priests cannot be guarded from the hands of predators without protection—hiring horsemen and foot soldiers for their own bodily protection. Each of these things in itself demands a great deal of money.

[29] And so what kind of mindlessness is it that would rather have the high priests be poor instead of rich? One can read and hear that out of all peoples, all sects, and all religions the high priests have always been the greatest of men as well as the most wealthy. Take a look at the religious practices of the Romans; think diligently about their example. You will find among them that they customarily entrusted high pontifical office not to the humble and the poor but rather to the wealthiest men, princes of the city. [30] [This is so,] inasmuch as we have read that the Iulii, the Scipios, the Marcelli, the Aemilii, and the Catos were often the highest priestly officials (in the Rome of those days they were considered outstanding because of the glory of their deeds, their wealth, their authority, and most of all their power). We have also learned that Numa Pompilius

mus, tantum ne quando rege bellicis rebus occupato divinus cultus inter-
mitteretur. Quaere Persarum sacerdotes qui erant et dicebantur magi;
quaere Egyptiorum, Assiriorum, aliarum nationum quantis divitiis
opibusque extiterint. [31] Quodsi haec te aut illos parum movent, quia
externa et peregrina sunt maximeque a nostris legibus abhorrent,
repetantur[766] summi Hebreorum //88v// sacerdotes, quorum vetustissimi
Aaron, Eleazer, Finees, Heli, Abiathar sic omni copiarum genere abun-
darunt ut dictu incredibile videatur.

A: [32] Non negarent hi Hebreorum sacerdotes fuisse ditissimos, sed
eas ipsas divitias sibi ex decumis, primitiis donisque quotannis
provenisse, proprium nihil fuisse convincerent.

L: Velim ita fuisse ab initio constitutum. Quid tum?[767] Num quae
semel eis data erant auferebantur deinde?

A: Nequaquam, sed cumulabantur in dies.

L: Propria igitur fiebant?

A: Sic arbitror.

L: [33] Quid refert igitur pontifices uno tempore acervatim an variis ac
paulatim ditari[768] ex decumis,[769] primitiis, donis quottidianis accipere
divitias an perpetuas et proprias possidere? Hoc fortasse nostrorum
pontificum divitiae iustiores sunt quam illorum, quod hae cultui divino
omnes sacris legibus dicatae sunt, ex iis[770] vero coniuges, concubinae,
liberi, servi alebantur.

A: [34] Quid haec ad rem? Illis enim haec omnia suis legibus licebat
fieri, nostris autem pontificibus Christi legibus non licet. Eo enim nato,
priores leges vel abrogatae penitus vel immutatae sunt ac pro illis novae
constitutae. Non igitur Hebreorum, sed Christi institutis et moribus uti
debent, quem pauperrime natum per omnem vitam pauperrimum fuisse
comperimus.

---

766. reputantur B.
767. quid tum] *om.* V; quid tum nonne B.
768. diatari *sic* F; ditari VG.
769. decimis G.
770. his G.

transferred this duty from the king to others, so that divine worship would not be interrupted in case the king were busy with the affairs of war. Take a look at the priests of the Persians, who were magicians and were called such, or the priests of the Egyptians, the Assyrians, and the other peoples: they were noteworthy because they possessed such wealth and riches. [31] But it might be that you or others are not moved by these things, since they are extraneous, foreign, and greatly inconsistent with our laws. In that case, then, the highest priests of the Hebrews may once again be called to mind, of whom the oldest were Aaron, Eleazar, Phineas, Eli, and Abyathar; they had so much of every kind of wealth that it seems unbelievable to tell.

A: [32] These priests of the Hebrews would not deny that they were the wealthiest of men, but they would argue that that very wealth had come to them from tithes, first fruits, and quite a few gifts every year and that thus nothing was really their own.

L: I wish this had been set up like this from the beginning. What do you mean then? Surely not that the things once given them were thereafter taken away?

A: Not at all, but rather that these things accumulated as the days went by.

L: Then did they become their own?

A: I think so.

L: [33] So what does it matter, then, whether the high priests become rich all at once and in heaps or little by little from various tithes, first fruits, and daily gifts? What does it matter whether they accept wealth or possess their own lasting wealth? Maybe in this respect the wealth of our high priests is more just than theirs [i.e., the Hebrew priests'], since it is all by sacred law devoted to divine worship, whereas wives, concubines, children, and slaves grew along with their wealth.

A: [34] What does that have to do with anything? Really, in their case all of these things were allowed to happen because of their laws, whereas for our high priests they are not, thanks to the laws of Christ. For when Christ was born, all prior laws were either completely repealed or changed and new ones were founded in their place. So they ought to base their behavior not on the Hebrews' laws and behavior but on those of Christ, who we have learned was born in the poorest of fashions and remained so throughout his whole life.

L: [35] Cur, si ita est, non iubes eosdem miracula edere, liberare aegro-
tos, vita defunctos a mortuis excitare, cur non etiam columnae alligari,
cedi flagellis, spinis coronari, in crucem suspendi, descendere ad inferos
atque inde cum priscis patribus ad superos evolare iubes?[771]

A: [36] Durissima quidem pontificibus vitae conditio proposita est, si
omnia sibi Christi mysteria obeunda sunt, quod homines cum sint, ille
Deus, nulla ratione effici potest.

L: [37] Quid? Si cum impossibile sit hoc[772] fieri, tum ne[773] necessar-
ium quidem est? Cum enim plurima remittantur pontificibus quae a
Christo gesta sunt, //89// quid est cur paupertas ab his[774] tantopere
flagitetur, caetera ne quaerantur quidem? Quia videlicet Christus, cuius
personam gerunt, pauper fuit? Fuerit sane! Nullamne temporum,
hominum, locorum,[775] rationem habendam censent,[776] cum eveniat per-
saepe, ut quod honestissimum sit, variatis[777] illis, commutetur fiatque
contrarium? [38] Quemadmodum fodere agrum honestum est, festis
autem diebus id fieri religio vetat; et apud Cyprios olim puellas in questu
ad parandas dotes prostituere licebat, apud nos[778] probro obicitur;[779]
procreandis liberis operam dare natura nos et leges et humanitas invitat;
idem, si sacro in loco aut publico fiat, iure reprehenditur. Haec enim tantam habent vim ut omnis vitae actio in his tota consistere videatur. Noli
igitur haec tempora ad illorum temporum rationem exquirere. Alios enim
illa mores, alios haec desiderant.

[39] Tunc[780] enim Christo ibi fundamenta novae religionis iacienda
erant, ubi tot exuberabant divitiae, ut nemo esset qui earum copiam
admiraretur, nemo quin[781] satietate defessus foret. Proinde contraria illi
longeque diversa vitae ratio ineunda fuit. Praeterea, cum alii vates ac Deo
pleni praeter admodum paucos res humanas contempsissent et inopem
vitam et sordidam adamassent, ipse quoque, vatum reliquorum max-

---

771. iubes] iubes iubes *sic G.*
772. illud *B.*
773. ne *om. G.*
774. iis *PNB.*
775. hominum, locorum] locorum hominum *B.*
776. censetur *G.*
777. varietatis *recte corr. B¹.*
778. nos *om. N.*
779. abiicitur *N.*
780. Tum *G.*
781. quin] qui in *V.*

L: [35] Well if that is the case, why don't you order them to perform miracles, heal the sick, and raise the dead? Why don't you also bid them to be bound to a post, beaten with whips, crowned with thorns, and hung on a cross and to descend into hell and fly out thence with the ancient fathers into heaven?

A: [36] Certainly the harshest condition of life has been set up for the high priests if they are to undergo all the mysteries of Christ. Since they are men and Christ was God, in no way can this be brought about.

L: [37] What? If, on the one hand, it is impossible that this happen, then, on the other, isn't it necessary? Really, since most of the things Christ did are waived for the high priests, why is poverty so urgently demanded of them while the other things are not? Is it because Christ, whom they represent, was poor? Would that it were! And do they think no account should be taken of the times, men, or places? After all, doesn't it often happen that when these factors are switched around, what is most honorable is changed and becomes the contrary? [38] For instance, it is honorable to dig up a field, but religion forbids it from happening on feast days; and in olden days the Cyprians used to allow young girls to be prostituted in the search for dowries, but we object to this as shameful. Nature invites us to give our attention to procreation, as do the laws and our common humanity, but, again, if it happens in a holy or public place, it is censured and justly so. For these things have such force that every action of life seems to consist in them. Do not, therefore, examine present times on the basis of former ones. Those times required one set of morals, these another.

[39] Really, back then Christ had to lay the foundations of a new religion—there, where wealth abounded. He had to do it in such a way that there would be no one who admired the abundance of wealth or would be weary in [the midst of] the overflow of wealth. Accordingly, he had to embark on a way of life that was contrary to the old one and very different. And especially since the other prophets who were also full of God—with the exception of a few, of course—had shunned humanity and come to admire a poor and squalid style of life, Christ himself, the greatest of

imus, reliquorum institutum retinere debuit. Aliter non[782] movisset homines ad religionem,[783] ut sibi proposuerat, verum etiam deterruisset.[784] [40] Deinde erat sibi cum hominibus peritissimis, calidissimis, pertinacissimis, atque alteri religioni addictis et consecratis ineundum certamen, qui cum ab ea nec vi abstrahi nec metu[785] imperioque absterreri nec rationibus abduci <potuerint[?]>, novitate rei, properatione,[786] admiratione, sanctitatis miraculis permovendi erant atque ita afficiendi ut nullus in eorum mentibus error aut suspitio resideret.[787] [41] Quare, si divitiis aggressus esset, //89v// haud tanta[788] fuisset opinio et admiratio doctrinae, sanctitatis, religionis, sed in varias perditorum hominum calumnias incidisset, quas tamen neque ita effugit, dixissentque alii illum gratia, alii spe, alii promissis, alii largitione capere homines pellicere,[789] delinire,[790] corrumpere, novam superstitionem[791] potentiae suae ampliandae causa introducere. [42] Cum vero pauper humili loco, paupercula ex virgine natus, nullis[792] fretus opibus, tam repente praeter expectationem omnium tantam sapientiam mox puer adeptus foret ut in disputationibus sapientissimos Hebreorum convinceret et prae admiratione mutos atque obstupescentes relinqueret,[793] pauloque post ad divulgandam novam legem, instruendos homines, et sacro baptismatis lavacro lustrandos expiandosque conversus, suscitaret mortuos, morbos incurabiles pelleret, taetris[794] spiritibus vexatos liberaret sola voce, [43] quid aliud suspicari poterant nisi id quod re vera erat,[795] divinum esse hominem vel potius Deum, Deo natum, divinoque[796] spiritu inflatum et e coelo ad salutem ac liberationem generis humani demissum, qui, ut parentibus suis vates cecinerant, homines veteris peccati labe absolveret ad veramque traduceret religionem sublatisque superioribus legibus meliores sanctioresque ferret.[797] Itaque ei nemo non credidit nisi qui invidia, naturae perversi-

---

782. non] non modo non *PGNB*.
783. regionem *N*.
784. decrevisset *B*.
785. metu *om. N*.
786. properatore *N*.
787. resideret *om. V*.
788. tamen *G*.
789. pollicere *VN;* polliceri *coni. Sch.*
790. delimere *VB*.
791. novam superstitionem] superstitionem novam *P*.
792. ullus *B*.
793. relinquere *G*.
794. certis *V*.
795. erant *B*.
796. divinoque] divino quasi *V*.
797. ferent *B*.

the prophets, had to maintain what the rest of them had established. Otherwise, instead of inspiring men to religion as he had intended to do, he would have frightened them off. [40] Thereafter, he had to enter into conflict with the most learned, shrewdest, and most tenacious of men, who were dedicated and even consecrated to another religion! They could not be pulled away from their religion by force or fear or scared off with power or drawn away with reasoned arguments. Because of this, they had to be thoroughly inspired by the newness of the thing, by its speed, by wonderment, and by miracles that smacked of holiness. They had to be so affected that no uncertainty or mistrust remained in their minds. [41] And so if Christ had attempted this with wealth, then his teaching, holiness, and religion would not have had such a great reputation and been the cause of so much admiration. Indeed, he would have incurred the various insults of the godforsaken—which in any case he did not manage to avoid. Some would have said that he took men in with charm, others would have said with hope, others would have said with promises; and others still would have said he took men in with bribes, to seduce, weaken, and corrupt them, and to introduce a new superstition just to widen his power. [42] But he was born a pauper in a humble place, of a poor virgin, supported with no money. As a boy he was endowed so swiftly and far beyond everyone's expectations with such wisdom that in disputations he refuted the wisest of the Hebrews, leaving them mute and stunned in their astonishment. Shortly thereafter, he gave his attention to spreading the new law, to educating men, to purifying them with the holy bath of baptism, and to forgiving the converted. He raised the dead and expelled incurable illnesses. With his voice alone he freed men disturbed by abominable spirits. [Because of all these things,] [43] what else could they suspect, unless it was this (which was really true): that he was a divine man, or rather God, born of God, filled with the divine spirit and sent down from heaven for the benefit and liberation of the human race; that he was one who, as the prophets had sung to his forebears, would absolve men from the stain of ancient sin and lead them to true religion; that he was one who after standing strong under the older laws, would bring better, holier ones. And so, unless someone was held back by envy or by the perversity and ill will of his nature, there was no one who did

tate, ac malignitate retentus est; nemo illum oppugnavit nisi ii[798] qui pri-
vatae utilitatis causa timebant, qui ea institui atque renovari moleste fere-
bant; [44] nemo Deum verum dubitavit esse[799] qui de Deo recte sentiret;
nemo in illius mortem conspiravit atque consensit qui non se morte
dignum iudicaret; postremo nullus contra illum mali quippiam molitus
est quin is iudicio omnium meritas ac debitas suo sceleri poenas per-
solverit.

[45] Nunc autem //90// iactis his fundamentis religionis nostrae patefactaque veritate omnis iam sublatus est error et ambiguitas. De Christo
enim[800] omnes idem volunt, idem loquuntur verissimumque illum et
unicum[801] Dei filium ac solum Deum uno ore, voce, mente consentiunt,
nec superstitione ulla ab hac rectissima et[802] certissima sententia concessuri sunt. [46] Quae quidem Christi religio, cum ita animis hominum
insita atque innata sit ut convelli aut[803] concuti nulla ratione possit, ita
eius miraculis et sectatorum illius fortissimorum virorum et sanctissimo-
rum[804] testimoniis corroborata, eruditissimorum et sapientissimorum litteris monumentisque confirmata atque illustrata ut nullius praeterea
roboris et firmamenti indigere videatur, exornanda est opibus,[805]
excolenda divitiis ut non solum vi sua ad se animos[806] pertrahat, verum
etiam oculos splendore sui et fulgore perstringat; reicidendum[807]
parumper a pristina illa Christi austeritate et acrimonia ac novum aliquid
addendum. [47] Patitur hoc natura, fert ratio, religionis flagitat consuetudo ut non eadem semper maneant quae semel instituta sunt, sed muten-
tur vetustate, temporibus innoventur. Et[808] praeterea eiusmodi[809]
hominum ingenium ut nova atque inusit<at>a[810] appetant probentque,
vetera atque usitata, etsi praeclara sint et preciosa, fastidiant.[811] Est ea

---

798. hii *P.*
799. esse] esse nisi *VPBGN.*
800. autem *B.*
801. et unicum] nuntium *G.*
802. ac *N.*
803. convelli aut] convelleant *P.*
804. sanctissimis *P.*
805. quibus *B.*
806. amicos *V.*
807. recedendum *VPNB.*
808. Est *B.*
809. huiusmodi *B.*
810. innusita *sic F;* inusitata *VPGNB.*
811. fastidiant] ut fastidia *P.*

not believe in him. None opposed him, except for those who were afraid for their own private affairs, who resented what he founded and renewed. [44] No one who believed rightly about God doubted that he was the true God, and no one who conspired and agreed to his death would not later judge himself worthy of death. Finally, no one has exerted himself in any evil way at all against Christ without paying the punishments that he (in the judgment of all) deserves and owes for his crime.

[45] But now that the foundations of our religion have been laid and the truth has been made clear, every error and ambiguity has already been successfully removed.[59] For about Christ everybody means the same; they say the same thing: that he is the truest and only son of God and the only God. With one mouth, one voice, and one mind they agree, and no superstition will lead them to depart from this most correct and certain of sentiments. [46] Certainly, this religion of Christ is so natural and inborn in the spirits of men that it can in no way be overthrown or weakened. It is so well corroborated by his miracles and by the witness of his followers, who were the bravest and holiest men, and—thanks to the writings and proofs of its most learned and wisest men—it is so established and clear that it seems to lack no further strength or mainstay. Because of this it should be adorned with riches and honored with wealth, so that it brings souls to itself not only by its power but also by deeply affecting the eyes with its magnificence and brilliance. One should draw back a bit from that ancient severity and energy of Christ and add something new. [47] Nature permits this, reason supports it, and the custom of religion demands it: that the things that were once established not remain always the same but rather be changed with great age and fashioned anew with the passing of time.[60] And besides, the genius of

---

59. For Lapo's "Nunc autem iactis his fundamentis religionis nostrae patefactaque veritate omnis iam sublatus est error et ambiguitas," cf. Bruni's 1405 preface to his translation of Plato's *Phaedo*: "Qua in re licet Christiana doctrina nullo indigeat adiumento, cum omnia usque adeo plana ac firma sint, ut in neminem penitus nisi omnino insipientem ulla dubitatio iam cadere possit" (Bruni, *Humanistisch-philosophische Schriften*, 4, as cited in Hankins, *Plato*, 1:50 n. 45).

60. Cf. Lucretius V.1275–78: "Now copper lies low, and gold has taken the highest honor. So do the circling years bring about reversals of fortune. What was once prized, then becomes of no account; yes, something else takes its place and emerges from ignominy" [Nunc iacet aes, aurum in summum successit honorem. / Sic volvenda aetas commutat tempora rerum. / Quod fuit in pretio, fit nullo denique honore; / porro aliud succedit et contemptibus exit].

rerum omnium conditio, ut maxima quaeque ab humilibus orsa principiis in dies assumant aliquid crescendoque ad summum perveniant; ea huius aetatis disciplina, ut[812] inopiam cuiusque et tenuitatem despiciamus, copias et opulentiam admiremur.

[48] Quis enim[813] his temporibus est tam religiosus, tam sanctus, tam a vulgi opinione abhorrens, qui pontificem humili veste, paucis comitibus et iis quidem sordidis et[814] nudis pedibus incedentem[815] vel asello insidentem[816] //90v// more priscorum patrum, non dico venerari atque adorare[817] velit, sed adire aut alloqui? [49] Quis qui pontificis nomine et honore dignum putet, qui non risu praetereuntem cavillisque prosequatur? Itaque optime mihi a veteribus institutum[818] videtur, ut deorum[819] simulacra ex auro aut inaurata fierent. Videbant enim sapientissimi viri auri[820] ipsius speciem mentes hominum ad cultum divinum ac religionem magis inpulsuram esse.

[50] Nimis iam multa in hanc sententiam pro defensione pontificum dixisse videor. Quibus de rebus omnes non invidos aut[821] pertinaces arbitror mihi facile assensuros. Desinant[822] igitur maledici[823] et obtrectatores luxuriam et opulentiam pontificibus obiicere! Desinant Christi vicarios, quos colere debent, petulantissimis verbis insectari! [51] Concedant aliquando divitias illis non modo utiles et necessarias esse, sed etiam divinitus traditas et concessas, cum videant tot, tantas, tam varias, tam multiplices undique illis insidias ab impiis hominibus comparari, tot sceleratos nefariosque latrones eorum bonis fortunisque assidue[824] inhiantes, eosdem tamen quottidie opibus, potentia, auctoritate, imperio augeri nec illis quemquam aliquid unquam detrahere aut violare ausum esse quin is statim vel morbo vel morte durissimas poenas et supplicium luerit. Ex quo satis apparet hoc ab hominibus sapientissimis et religiosissimis institutum divino numine[825] comprobatum esse.

---

812. ut *om. N.*
813. enim *om. G.*
814. vel *B.*
815. incendentem *N.*
816. vel asello insidentem] *om. P.*
817. odorare *sic F;* adorare *V;* adorari *B.*
818. *corr. ex* institum *F¹ (aut F³?)·*
819. eorum *P.*
820. auri *om. V.*
821. atque *N.*
822. Designant *P.*
823. maledicti *V.*
824. assidue *om. VPGN.*
825. munere *V.*

mankind is such that man desires and tries new and uncustomary things and tires of the old, customary ones, even if they are admirable and valuable. This is the state of all things: that the greatest things, born from humble beginnings, augment themselves and in growing reach their apex. This is the custom of this era: that we look down on someone's poverty and indigence and admire riches and opulence.

[48] After all, who is there in this day and age who is so religious, so holy, so contrary to public opinion that he would come up and speak to—let alone respectfully and courteously entreat—a high priest who, attired in a pauper's clothes, walked along with only a few companions (and these certainly of the lowest sort), with nothing on his feet, or riding on a donkey? [49] Who is there who would think him worthy of the name and honor of high priest, who would not pursue him as he passed by with laughter and jeering? This is why it seems to me well founded by the ancients that they made their images of gods out of gold or gilded material. Since they were very wise, they saw that the beauty of gold itself would impel the minds of men even more toward divine worship and religion.

[50] Well, I already seem to have spoken quite a bit along these lines in defense of the high priests, and I think that anyone who is not envious or stubborn will readily agree with me. And so away with those cursed naysayers who object to the extravagance and opulence of the high priests! Away with those who heedlessly reproach the vicars of Christ whom they are supposed to worship! [51] Let them concede that wealth is not only useful and necessary for the high priests but also divinely entrusted and allowed, especially since they see how wicked men from all over plot against the priests in such varied ways. They see that there are so very many corrupt and nefarious thieves who look longingly and untiringly at the high priests' property and fortunes but that the priests nonetheless grow daily in riches, power, authority, and empire. And no one has dared in any respect to stand in their way or to disturb them without paying right away the harshest of penalties and punishments: either illness or death. From this it is clear enough that this institution was founded by the wisest and most religious of men and sanctioned by divine command.

A: [52] Verissime istuc⁸²⁶ dictum puto. Nec enim existimandum est
tantum imperium, tam florentes Romanae ecclesiae opes conservari tam
diu incolumes ac retineri invitis numinibus potuisse. Verum tamen
Christi exemplo pauperes pontifices iubentur esse. Qui⁸²⁷ ergo impositam sibi⁸²⁸ ab eo legem sine scelere et piaculo negligere potuerunt?

L: [53] Haud negligenda //91// lex est, sed videndum, ne decipiamur in
verbis. In legibus enim interpretandis maiores nostri semper sententiam,
non verba spectari voluerunt. Neque ego Christum arbitror, cum iussit,
ita plane et aperte⁸²⁹ locutum, praesertim cum nulla esset⁸³⁰ causa cur
verba ut sonant intelligi oporteret,⁸³¹ sed altiorem verbis ipsis⁸³² sensum
subiecisse nec divitiis privare pontifices, sed a cumulandis⁸³³ divitiis
absterrere⁸³⁴ voluisse. [54] Nam qui ita animo se conformarit⁸³⁵ ut in se
uno sua ponat omnia, externum nihil admiretur, nihil concupiscat, nihil
ad se pertinere existimet,⁸³⁶ hic neque pauperior⁸³⁷ neque ditior⁸³⁸ fortuna effici potest. Hac ratione nunquam Aristidem illum⁸³⁹ Atheniensem,
qui Iustus cognominatus est, nunquam M.⁸⁴⁰ Fabritium, Curium,
Cincinnatum, Cn. Scipionem appellabo divites, tametsi Croesum aut
Darium quas contempserant divitiis superassent; nec rursus M. Crassum,
C. Verrem, homines summa cupiditate atque avaritia perditos, etiam si
rerum omnium premantur inopia, idcirco pauperes habendos putabo.⁸⁴¹
[55] Si tamen aut ii⁸⁴² divites sunt dicendi qui nihil habent divitiis
praestabilius, aut pauperes qui⁸⁴³ preciosissimas, optimas, praeclarissi-
masque divitias possident, quae nec fortuna auferri nec⁸⁴⁴ vi⁸⁴⁵ aliqua

826. istud *VP.*
827. Quomodo *V.*
828. impositam sibi] sibi impositam *B.*
829. apte *sic N.*
830. esse *VPG.*
831. oportet *V.*
832. ipsis *om. B.*
833. a cumulandis] accumulandis *V;* accumulandos *G.*
834. absterreri *N.*
835. conformant *VPGN;* conformat *coni. Sch.*
836. existiment *G.*
837. pauperiores *G.*
838. ditiores *G.*
839. illum *om. G.*
840. Marcus *N.*
841. puto *N.*
842. iis *B.*
843. qui *om. N.*
844. ne *V.*
845. in *P.*

A: [52] What you've said is very true, I think. Really, it is hard to imagine how so much imperial power as well as the flourishing wealth of the Roman church could have been safely preserved and maintained up to now if the divine powers had been unwilling. But still, the high priests are enjoined by the example of Christ to be poor. Who therefore could neglect—without crime or guilt—the law that was imposed on him by Christ?

L: [53] It is not that the law should be neglected, but it should be carefully scrutinized, so that words do not deceive us. After all, in interpreting the laws, our ancestors always thought we should look after the spirit, not the letter, of the law. Nor do I think that Christ, when he commanded, spoke all that clearly and openly, especially since there was no reason why the words had to be understood as they sounded. The deeper meaning in his words was that he wished, not to deprive the high priests of wealth, but to deter them from accumulating it immoderately. [54] Really, anyone who spiritually educates himself so that he places all his possessions inside himself, admires nothing external, desires nothing, and thinks nothing belongs to him[61]—he can be made neither richer nor poorer by fortune. This is why I shall never call that Athenian Aristides, who had the cognomen *Iustus,* a wealthy man, nor shall I ever call Marcus Fabricius, Curius, Cincinnatus, or Cnaeus Scipio wealthy men; for even though they were wealthier than Croesus or Darius, they looked down on their wealth. And, on the other hand, I shall never think that Marcus Crassus and Gaius Verres, men wretched with the highest cupidity and avarice, are to be considered poor, even if they were humbled by total poverty. [55] Still, if those who have nothing more outstanding than wealth must be called wealthy, there are also the poor who possess the most valuable, highest, and most admirable wealth, which cannot be taken away by fortune or changed or harmed by any external force.

---

61. A few years later, Valla, too, would emphasize the cultivation of the interior man; cf. Valla, *De professione religiosorum,* X.19: "Non exterior homo sed interior placet deo."

extrinsecus immutari labefactarive queant, divitiae igitur et paupertas animo hominis, non numero metiendae sunt. [56] Quapropter, cum praecipit Christus pauperes esse pontifices, quid aliud praecipit nisi animo libero esse nec ulli minus honestae cupiditati obnoxio, divitias si non habeant, suis ac propriis bonis contentos despicere humana, si habeant, non amare, sed ea sibi conditione datas arbitrari, ut non ad suas exsaturandas libidines, sed ad beneficentiam liberalitatemque[846] convertant. Atque ita qui fecerit,[847] peroptime praecipienti Christo //91v// obtemperasse, et qui sic interpretetur, haud[848] inepte eius praeceptum[849] interpretari videatur.

[IX. Conclusio]

A: [1] Recte tu quidem arbitratu meo interpretatus es. Quare iam cedo tibi meque victum fateor, nec invitus, sed ultro ac lubens[850] in sententiam tuam venio. Sed tamen dicam enim quod sentio. Tantos spiritus, tantum fastidium, tantam insolentiam atque intolerantiam, quantam in plerisque curiae principibus video, probare aut etiam animo aequo ferre nullo modo possum. [2] Sunt enim primum incessu ac reliquo omni gestu motuque corporis elati et tumidi,[851] in cultu morosi, fastidiosi in congressu hominum, arrogantes in sermonibus ac contentiosi in sententia, pertinaces in percontando, breves et obscuri in respondendo, contumeliosi in audiendo, inpatientes in ira, vehementes et amari, iidem tamen in poscendo molesti, in accipiendo prompti, in bene promerendo tardi, in remunerando negligentes. Quibus[852] si accedentibus asurrexeris aut via cesseris aut[853] aliud quidvis[854] honoris gratia[855] feceris, dissimulant se videre[856] conniventibusque oculis[857] praetereuntes non magis honore[858]

---

846. libertatemque *B.*
847. fecerint *sic F et codd.*
848. aut *V.*
849. eius praeceptum] preceptum eius *B.*
850. libens *B.*
851. elati et tumidi] dati etumidi *sic N.*
852. Qui *VGN.*
853. aut *om. VPGN.*
854. quodvis *B.*
855. gratia *om. Sch.*
856. se videre *om. N.*
857. oculis] oculis et *P.*
858. honorar *sic N.*

Wealth and poverty, then, must be measured not in numerical terms but rather in the spirit of man. [56] And so when Christ ordered the high priests to be poor, what else did he order than that they have a spirit that was free and permeated only by honest desire? [He ordered them,] if they do not have wealth, to look down on merely human things, happy with their own goods; if they have wealth, not to love it, but rather that it be given them on this condition: that they apply it not to satisfying their lewd desires but rather to beneficence and liberality. And whoever has done this seems to have obeyed very well the Christ who commands. And whoever interprets Christ's command in such a way seems to have interpreted the command wisely.

[IX. Conclusion]

A: [1] Well you have certainly interpreted correctly in my opinion, and so now I yield to you and confess I have been beaten—and not unwillingly. In fact, on the contrary, I come over to your opinion with pleasure. Still, let me say what I feel. In no way can I approve of or even in good faith put up with the amount of haughtiness, superciliousness, insolence, and intolerance that I see in most of the curial princes. [2] Really, first of all, thanks to their walk, and actually to every remaining gesture and bodily motion, you can tell they are haughty and puffed up with pride. They are peevish when it comes to care of their appearance and supercilious in their dealings with people; they are arrogant in their speech and contentious in their opinions; they are stubborn in their questioning, short and obscure in responding; they are abusive in listening, easy to anger; they are vehement and bitter. And nonetheless, the same men are pests when it comes to asking for things, quick to take, late in doing anyone any good, and negligent when it comes to repaying. If you get up when they approach or if you yield the road to them or do them any courtesy for honor's sake, they pretend not to see you and with appropriate expressions of the eyes

illo⁸⁵⁹ habito quam marmoreae aut aereae statuae moventur nec salu-
tati⁸⁶⁰ resalutant. [3] Si ad eos domum adeas, antequam intromittaris,
rogandus ianitor, tum cubicularius obsecrandus, intimis eorum domesticis, familiaribus, famulis,⁸⁶¹ catulis denique blandiendum, dies totus in
foribus conterendus,⁸⁶² quoad dominus non voce, ne quid spiritus amit-
tat⁸⁶³ frustra, sed tintinnabuli sonitu introire te iubeat; ingressus statim
iuberis paucis⁸⁶⁴ proferre, quid velis, et in media plerunque oratione
indicto silentio praeceps⁸⁶⁵ eiiceris.

L:⁸⁶⁶ [4] Nec probandi, me hercule, nec ferendi, si⁸⁶⁷ qui sunt
principes⁸⁶⁸ qui ista faciant! Verum nonnisi eos facere arbitror, qui cum
per se obscuri sint et ignoti⁸⁶⁹ //92// vel aliis praesidiis destituti, ut inter
principes eminere nequeant, ad⁸⁷⁰ huiusmodi se adiumenta ac perfugia
conferunt, quibus sibi gravitatis, severitatis,⁸⁷¹ sapientiae opinionem
paratum iri existimant, sed tota errant via. Tantum enim abest ut id quod
cupiunt assequantur, ut prudentibus stulti, inepti, rustici, vitae communis
ignari, caeteris autem hominibus superbi, contumaces, stomachosi, et
propterea communi⁸⁷² odio digni esse videantur.⁸⁷³ [5] Sapientis est enim
magnique principis quo clarior sit et maior, eo se omnibus affabiliorem
praestare.⁸⁷⁴ Humanitas enim et affabilitas, cum⁸⁷⁵ in privatis hominibus
laudanda, tum in principibus maxime admirabilis⁸⁷⁶ est; [6] neminem ne
infimum quidem hominem ad se aditu prohibere, quiete interrogare,
patienter audire, sedate ac placide respondere nec efferri iracundia, sed
clementem, mitem⁸⁷⁷ et placabilem esse, in conferendis beneficiis quam in

859. ille *V.*
860. saluti *G.*
861. famulis *om. V.*
862. quonterendus *N.*
863. admittat *V.*
864. paucis *om. GB.*
865. silentio praeceps] scilentio preces *G.*
866. L *om. N.*
867. se *N.*
868. princeps *N.*
869. obscuri sint et ignoti] ignoti sint et obscuri *N.*
870. ab *G.*
871. gravitatis, severitatis] gravitas, severitas *N.*
872. communi *om. G.*
873. videntur *N.*
874. prestatur *N.*
875. tum *B.*
876. laudabilis *VPGN.*
877. autem *N.*

pass on by. Having received that honor, they are no more moved than statues of marble or bronze. And if someone greets them, they do not return the greetings.[62] [3] If you go to them at home, before you are admitted you have to plead with the doorkeeper, beg the valet, and finally fawn over their domestics, servants, and even dogs. You have to waste a whole day outside, until the lord orders you to come in—and not with his voice, lest he should waste a little breath on you in vain, but with the ringing of a bell. As soon as you have entered, you are ordered to tell in a few words what it is that you want, and in the middle of the most important part of your speech, you are told to hush and are thrown out, headfirst!

L: [4] By Hercules, if there are princes who do these horrible things they should not be approved of or even tolerated! But I think the ones who behave that way are doing it as a kind of aid or shelter for themselves, since in themselves they are obscure and unknown or lacking other defenses; the result is that among princes they are unable to stand out. With these tactics they think they will gain themselves a reputation for seriousness, severity, and wisdom. But they have lost the way completely. Really, they are so far from reaching their goal that in the eyes of the prudent they seem foolish, unwise, boorish, and ignorant of everyday life. In the eyes of the rest, moreover, they seem proud, obstinate, irritable, and, because of this, worthy of everyone's hatred. [5] After all, it is characteristic of the wise and great prince that the more admirable and great he is, the more he comes across as approachable to everyone. Truly, although kindness and approachability are praiseworthy in men of the private sector, in princes they are greatly admirable. [6] To prohibit no one from seeing him, even if it were the lowest of men; to ask questions in a reserved manner; to listen patiently; to respond in a sedate and placid fashion, and not to break out into anger but rather to be kind, gentle, and

---

62. This description is similar to Theophrastus's *Char.* XXIV (ed. Jebb no. IV), ὑπερηφανίας (Arrogance).

accipiendis et in referenda quam[878] in exigenda gratia proniorem, provo-
cantem officio non despicere, blande appellare homines, obvios salutare,
salutanti cumulatam salutationem reddere, demum in factis[879] dictisque
omnibus cum dignitatis suae, tum decori<s>, gravitatis, modestiae, facil-
itatis rationem habere. [7] Hae sunt artes principibus congruentes, hae
principibus dignae,[880] hae a principibus excolendae ac retinendae sunt,
his capiuntur omnes, his oblectantur et eos, quibus illas inesse cernunt,[881]
non ut homines modo et observant et diligunt, sed ut divinos quosdam
viros vel[882] potius deos stupidi admirantur, et eis servire quam aliis dom-
inari malunt,[883] iis si serviant, beatos se esse existimant. Talis in curia
Romana principes nonnullos agnosco, et eos in primis qui in ea plurimum dignitate, potentia, opibus, auctoritate pollent, quibuscum etiam
mihi magnus usus et plurimis suis maximisque[884] officiis constituta[885]
necessitudo est et in quibus summam spem habeo futurae dignitatis et
amplitudinis collocatam.

A:[886] [8] Non mediocrem tibi //92v// felicitatem obtigisse arbitror si
principibus eiusmodi, quales perpauci admodum reperiuntur, adeo famil-
iariter uteris; in quo minime tibi invideo, sed ut haec spes illorum
beneficiis firma rataque sit, vehementer exopto.

L:[887] Spero ita fore. Sed estne aliud quod desideres?

A:[888] [9] Copiosissime omnia quae pro curia dici poterant a te modo
explicata probataque sunt. Nec, quantum intelligo, aliquid praeterea
restat, nisi ut et[889] nobis invicem gratulemur, quibus his tantis bonis
Romanae curiae praesentibus frui conceditur, hortemurque[890] caeteros,
quorum honori,[891] dignitati, et commodis studemus, ut si per industriam
et solertiam celeriter se humo attollere[892] atque illustrari cupiunt, in hunc

---

878. referenda] referenda magis *V.*
879. factis] factis suis *B.*
880. dignae *om. V.*
881. cernuntur *V.*
882. vel *om. G.*
883. volunt *VN.*
884. suis maximisque] maximisque suis *B.*
885. consuetudo *B.*
886. A *om. N.*
887. L *om. N.*
888. A *om. N.*
889. et *om. G.*
890. hominemque *N.*
891. honorari *N.*
892. humo attollere] hunc tollere *N.*

easily appeased; to be more likely to give favors than accept them, and to be more likely to show gratitude than demand it; not to look down on someone who appeals to his sense of duty; to deal with men in a flattering fashion; to greet those whom he meets, and to greet in turn someone who has greeted him; and finally in everything he does or says to look not only toward his own sense of worth but also toward seemliness, gravity, modesty, and courteousness—[7] these are the arts appropriate for princes, these are the arts that are worthy of princes, these are the arts that must be cultivated and preserved by princes, and with these arts everyone is captivated and delighted. Everyone respects and loves those in whom they see these arts present, and not only as men. Rather, they are astounded and wonder at them as if they were divine, or rather gods; and they prefer to serve them rather than dominate others. If they serve them, they think themselves blessed. I know some such princes in the Roman curia and those first of all who are powerful thanks to dignity, power, riches, and authority. I am also greatly familiar with them and linked to them by their very many great kindnesses, and I have placed in them the highest hope of worth and distinction in the future.

A: [8] I think you have hit on not just a middling happiness, if you have become friendly with princes of this sort, of whom there are very few. I cannot say that I envy you, but I do wish with all my heart that this hope of yours be strengthened and confirmed by their favors.

L: I hope it will be so. But is there anything else you desire?

A: [9] You have explained and demonstrated absolutely everything that could be said for the curia. And as far as I can tell not much remains, really, save that we congratulate each other, since we have been allowed to enjoy all the goods that are ready to hand at the Roman curia. As to the others for whose honor, dignity, and advantage we are zealous proponents, let us urge them that if, through industry and skillfulness, they wish to raise themselves up swiftly and to become famous, they turn to

celeberrimum totius orbis terrarum locum, in hoc amplissimum gentium et nationum omnium domicilium, in hunc frequentissimum clarissimorum virorum et illustrissimorum cetum et conventum, in hanc curiae Romanae lucem se transferant. [10] Nec iis artibus et disciplinis freti, quibus utuntur plerique, se id quod cupiunt assequi posse confidant, sed illis praeclarissimis et optimis, quibus hominum vita excolitur, instructi et ornati sperent se in ea honestatem, laudem, nomen, existimationem, opes praeterea, divitias, ornamenta plurima, commoda amplissima cum voluptate maxima habituros.

L.:[893] [11] Sapienter illos admones, si modo viri esse aut te audire volent. Verum illud quoque peroptandum est et ab immortali Deo votis ac precibus deposcendum, ut seditiosissimos et turbulentissimos[894] homines ulciscatur,[895] qui pacem et ocium ecclesiae suae tot iam per annos turbare eamque funditus delere gestiunt, aut—quod est fortasse et precari iustius et impetrare[896] facilius—illis in animum ponat, ut depositis simultatibus, abiectis inimicitiis, sopitis contentionibus, reconciliatis animis aliquando errores suos recognoscant, [12] se[897] peccasse fateantur veniamque supplices orent et cum pontifice maximo ac patribus in gratiam redeant eorumque se[898] //93// potestati[899] et auctoritati submittere malint quam intemperanter et temere abutentes[900] licentia ac viribus[901] se ipsos una cum illis summo cum dedecore et probro in certissimum[902] periculum discrimenque immittere.

[13] Quod quidem etsi difficile putatur esse ob multa quae[903] adversa impendere videntur, tamen divina ope non despero fore ut haec nostra impleantur vota. Sic autem compositis rebus Romanaque curia in amplitudinem et dignitatem pristinam restituta, faciliorem video et honestiorem iis quas dixisti[904] artibus vitae[905] conditionem futuram.

---

893. L *om. VG.*
894. et turbulentissimos *om. Sch.*
895. ulciscantur *N.*
896. impetrari *N.*
897. sese *N.*
898. se *om. N.*
899. portati *N.*
900. abeuntes *VN.*
901. iuribus *V.*
902. *hoc modo* incertissimum *scribunt FPGB;* incestissimum *V.*
903. quae *om. N.*
904. dixi *B.*
905. vitae] vite et *N.*

this, the most famous place in the whole world, the grandest home of all peoples and nationalities, this most populous assembly and congress of most excellent and famous men—to this, the light of the Roman curia. [10] And let them be assured that they can attain what they desire relying not on those skills and branches of learning that most others employ. Rather, instructed and distinguished in those skills and branches of learning that are the most outstanding and the highest and that ennoble the life of man,[63] let them hope that in the curia they will have honor, praise, and esteem, as well as riches, wealth, great distinction, and the most splendid of benefits as well as the greatest pleasure.

L: [11] You advise them wisely, if only they wish to be men and listen to you. But with vows and prayers we must hope and beseech from immortal God that he strike down the most factious and seditious men, who gleefully try to throw the peace and leisure of their own church into disorder and who now for so many years have tried to destroy the church completely. Or—and this is perhaps something more just to pray for and easier to accomplish by prayer—[we must hope and pray] that God at some time puts it into their spirit to recognize their own errors, after their jealousies have been put away, their enmities set down, their arguments put to rest, and their spirits reconciled; [12] that they admit they have sinned; and that, humbly, they beg forgiveness, come back into grace with the pope and the fathers, and choose to submit themselves to their power and authority, rather than insolently and rashly abusing uncontrolled power (as well as the law) and placing themselves as well as the others—with the greatest shame and disgrace—in most certain danger and conflict.

[13] To be sure, one thinks this is difficult thanks to the many things that seem to weigh against it, but still, I am not without hope that with divine aid these prayers of ours might be fulfilled. Further, once things have been set in order in this way and the Roman curia has been restored to its old distinction and dignity, it looks to me like there will be a more prosperous and more honorable way of life for those skills you were talking about.

---

63. I.e., the humanities.

[14] Sed de his ad praesens satis multa[906] disseruimus et[907] alias, cum voles, plura etiam disseremus.[908] Nunc, quoniam sol medio orbe confecto ad[909] occasum declinare videtur, iam tempus est ut cardinalem meum[910] salutatum abeam.[911] Nam illum post meum reditum non dum vidi et videre vehementer cupio. Quare sermoni huic nostro fine[912] imposito consurgamus et[913] quae instant potius curemus.

[15] Sic ille domi remansit, ego, egressus ad cardinalem ipsum, me in pontificale palatium contuli.[914]

θεῷ χάριν. Absolvi Lapus in Ferariensi concilio, in palatio maiori, vii Kl. septembris, die lunae, post iii horam noctis, anno domini Mccccxxxviii.[915]

---

906. multa *om. N.*
907. et *om. N.*
908. dixerimus *N.*
909. ad *om. V.*
910. modum *B.*
911. habeam *VGN.*
912. finem *V.*
913. ut *P.*
914. contuli] contuli. *[abbreviatio illegibilis P];* contuli. Explicit de commodis curie romane per Lapum Castelliunculum *P¹;* contuli. FINIS. Amen *G;* contuli. Finis est. Amen *N;* contuli. Finis. huius translationis non tam perfecte scripte quam correcto *[sic]* per *B.*
915. θεῷ χάριν. Absolvi . . . anno domini Mccccxxxviii *om. VPGNB.*

[14] But we have discussed these things quite thoroughly for now and, when you wish, shall discuss others even more. But now that the sun has turned and seems to be setting, it is already time that I go, to greet my cardinal, for I haven't yet seen him since my return and would really like to do so. With this, since we have ended this discussion of ours, let us get up and take care of more pressing matters.

[15] And so Angelo stayed home and I went out and made my way to the pontifical palace, to that very cardinal.

Thanks be to God. I, Lapo, finished this at the Council of Ferrara in the Palazzo Maggiore on Monday, the seventh day before the calends of September [26 August], after the third hour of the night, in the year of our Lord 1438.

Bibliography

Alberti, Leon Battista. *Dinner Pieces*. Trans. D. Marsh. Medieval and Renaissance Texts and Studies, 45. Binghamton, N.Y., 1987.

———. *The Family in Renaissance Florence: A Translation of . . . I libri della famiglia*. Trans. R.N. Watkins. Columbia, S.C., 1969.

———. *Opera inedita et pauca separatim impressa*. Ed. G. Mancini. Florence, 1890.

———. *Opere volgari*. Ed. C. Grayson. 3 vols. Bari, 1960.

Aliottus, Hieronymus [Girolamo Aliotti]. *Epistolae et opuscula*. Ed. G.M. Scarmatius. Arezzo, 1769.

Augustine. *Traités anti-Donatistes*. 5 vols. Paris, 1963–65.

Baron, H. "Franciscan Poverty and Civic Wealth as Factors in the Rise of Humanistic Thought." *Speculum* 13 (1938): 1–37.

———. *In Search of Florentine Civic Humanism: Essays on the Transition from Medieval to Modern Thought*. 2 vols. Princeton, 1988.

Becker, M. *Florence in Transition*. 2 vols. Baltimore, 1967–68.

Belloni, G. "Intorno alla datazione della *Vita civile* di M. Palmieri." *Studi e problemi di critica testuale* 16 (1978).

Bertalot, L. "Forschungen über Leonardo Bruni Aretino." In *Studien zum italienischen und deutschen Humanismus*, ed. P.O. Kristeller, 2:375–420. Rome, 1975.

———. *Initia humanistica latina*. Vol. 2, pt. 1. Ed. U. Jaitner-Hahner. Tübingen, 1990.

Berti, E. *La filosofia del primo Aristotele*. Padua, 1962.

Birkenmajer, A. "Der Streit des Alonso von Cartagena mit Leonardo Bruni Aretino." *Beiträge zur Geschichte der Philosophie des Mittelalters* 20, no. 5 (1922): 129–210.

Bisticci, Vespasiano da. *Le vite*. Ed. A. Greco. 2 vols. Florence, 1970–74.

Black, R. *Benedetto Accolti and the Florentine Renaissance*. Cambridge, 1985.

Boyance, P. "Les méthodes de l'histoire littéraire: Cicéron et son oeuvre philosophique." *Revue des études latines* 14 (1936): 288–309.

Bracciolini, Poggio. *Opera omnia*. Basel, 1538. Reprint, with a preface by R. Fubini, Turin, 1964.

———. *Poggio Bracciolini, 1380–1980: Nel VI centenario della nascita*. Istituto Nazionale di Studi sul Rinascimento, Studi e Testi 8. Florence, 1982.

Brandmüller, W. *Das Konzil von Konstanz, 1414–1418.* 2 vols. Paderborn and Munich, 1991–97.

Bresslau, H. *Handbuch der Urkundenlehre für Deutschland und Italien.* 3d ed. 2 vols. Berlin, 1958.

Brucker, G. *Renaissance Florence: Society, Culture, and Religion.* Goldbach, 1994.

Bruni, Leonardo. *Epistolarum libri VIII.* Ed. L. Mehus. 2 vols. Florence, 1741.

———. *The Humanism of Leonardo Bruni.* Ed. G. Griffiths, J. Hankins, and D. Thompson. Binghamton, N.Y., 1987.

———. *Humanistisch-philosophische Schriften.* Ed. H. Baron. Berlin, 1928. Reprint, Stuttgart, 1969.

Camporeale, S. "Lorenzo Valla tra medioevo e rinascimento, *Encomium Sanctae Thomae.*" *Memorie Domenicane,* n.s., 7 (1976): 3–190.

———. *Lorenzo Valla, umanesimo e teologia.* Florence, 1972.

Carlini, A. "Appunti sulle traduzioni latine di Isocrate di Lapo da Castiglionchio." *Studi classici e orientali* 19–20 (1970–71): 302–9.

Castelli, G. "Nuove lettere di Lapo da Castiglionchio il Giovane." Tesi di laurea, Università Cattolica Milano, 1966–67.

Castiglionchio, Lapo, the Elder. *Epistola o sia ragionamento di Messer Lapo da Castiglionchio.* Ed. L. Mehus. Bologna, 1753.

Celenza, C.S. " 'Parallel Lives': Plutarch's *Lives,* Lapo da Castiglionchio the Younger (1405–1438), and the Art of Italian Renaissance Translation." *Illinois Classical Studies* 22 (1997): 121–55.

———. "The Will of Cardinal Giordano Orsini (ob. 1438)." *Traditio* 51 (1996): 257–86.

Chroust, A.-H. "*Eudemus* or *On the Soul:* A Lost Dialogue of Aristotle on the Immortality of the Soul." *Mnemosyne,* 4th ser., 19 (1966): 17–30.

Commendone, G.F. *Discorso sopra la corte di Roma.* Ed. C. Mozzarelli. Rome. 1996.

Copenhaver, B. "Translation, Terminology, and Style." In *CHRP,* 77–110.

Cortesi, M. "Umanesimo greco." In *Lo spazio letterario del medioevo.* Pt. 1. *Il medioevo latino,* vol. III: *La ricezione del testo,* 457–507. Rome, 1995.

D'Amico, J. "Humanism in Rome." In *Renaissance Humanism: Foundations, Forms, and Legacy,* ed. A. Rabil, Jr., 1:264–95. Philadelphia, 1988.

———. "Humanism and Pre-Reformation Theology." In *Renaissance Humanism: Foundations, Forms, and Legacy,* ed. A. Rabil, Jr. 3:349–79. Philadelphia, 1988.

———. *Renaissance Humanism in Papal Rome: Humanists and Churchmen on the Eve of the Reformation.* Baltimore and London, 1983.

Decembrio, Pier Candido. *De vitae ignorantia.* Ed. E. Ditt. *Memorie del R. Istituto lombardo di scienze e lettere* 24 (1931).

Douglas, A.E. "Cicero the Philosopher." In *Cicero,* ed. T.A. Dorey, 135–70. London, 1964.

Dover, K.J. *Greek Homosexuality.* 2d ed. Cambridge, Mass., 1989.

Düring, I. *Aristotle's "Protrepticus": An Attempt at Reconstruction.* Göteborg, 1961.

Dykema, P. A., and H. A. Oberman. *Anticlericalism in Late Medieval and Early Modern Europe*. Studies in Medieval and Reformation Thought 51. Leiden, New York, and Cologne, 1993.

Eleuteri, P. "Francesco Filelfo copista e possessore di codici greci." In *Paleografia e codicologia greca: Atti del II Colloquio internazionale (Berlino-Wolfenbüttel, 17–21 ottobre 1983)*, ed. D. Harlfinger and G. Prato, 1:163–79, 2:107–14. Alessandria, 1991.

Eleuteri, P., and P. Canart. *Scrittura greca nell'umanesimo italiano*. Milan, 1991.

Field, A. *The Origins of the Platonic Academy of Florence*. Princeton, 1988.

Fink, K.A. "Eugene IV and the Council of Basel-Ferrara-Florence." In *Handbook of Church History*, ed. H. Jedin, 4:473–87. New York, 1970.

Flamini, F. "Leonardo di Piero Dati." *Giornale storico della letteratura italiana* 16 (1890): 1–107.

Fraser-Jenkins, A.D. "Cosimo de' Medici's Patronage of Architecture and the Theory of Magnificence." *Journal of the Warburg and Courtauld Institutes* 33 (1970): 162–70.

Frulovisiis de Ferraria, T. Livii de. *Opera hactenus inedita*. Ed. C.W. Previté-Orton. Cambridge, 1932.

Fubini, R. "All'uscita dalla Scolastica medievale: Salutati, Bruni, e i 'Dialogi ad Petrum Histrum.'" *Archivio storico italiano* 150 (1992): 1065–99.

———. "Castiglionchio, Lapo da, detto il Giovane." *Dizionario biografico degli Italiani* 22 (1979): 44–51.

———. *Umanesimo e secolarizzazione: Da Petrarca a Valla*. Rome, 1990.

Garin, E. "Leon Battista Alberti: Alcune intercenali inedite." *Rinascimento*, 2d ser., 4 (1964): 125–258. Reprinted as *Intercenali inedite*, ed. E. Garin. Florence, 1965.

———. "L'età sforzesca dal 1450 al 1500." *Storia di Milano*. Vol. 7, no. 4 (1955–56): 540–97.

———. "Le traduzioni umanistiche di Aristotele nel secolo XV." *Atti dell'Accademia fiorentina di scienze morali "La Colombaria"* 16 (1951): 55–104.

Garin, E., ed. *Prosatori latini del Quattrocento*. Milan and Naples, 1952.

Gauthier, R.A., ed. *Aristoteles Latinus, XXVI 1–3, fasciculus tertius, Ethica Nicomachea: Translatio Roberti Grosseteste Lincolnensis sive "Liber Ethicorum"* A. *Recensio Pura* (Leiden, Brussels, 1972) and B. *Recensio recognita* (Leiden, Brussels, 1973).

Gigon, O. "Prolegomena to an edition of the *Eudemus*." In *Aristotle and Plato in the Mid-fourth Century*, ed. I. Düring and G.E.L. Owen, 19–33. Göteborg, 1960.

Gill, J. *The Council of Florence*. Cambridge, 1959.

———. *Personalities of the Council of Florence*. Oxford, 1964.

Goldthwaite, R.A. *Wealth and the Demand for Art in Italy, 1300–1600*. Baltimore and London, 1993.

Grabmann, M. "Eine ungedruckte Verteidigungsschrift von Wilhelms von Moerbekes Übersetzung der Nicomacheischen Ethik gegenüber dem Humanisten Leonardo Bruni." In *Mittelalterliches Geistesleben*, 1:440–48. Munich, 1926.

Grafton, A. *Commerce with the Classics: Ancient Books and Renaissance Readers.* Jerome Lectures 20. Ann Arbor, 1998.

Grauert, H. *Magister Heinrich der Poet in Würzburg und die römische Kurie.* Abhandlungen der Königlichen Bayerischen Akademie der Wissenschaften, Philosophisch-philologische und historische Klasse 27. Munich, 1912.

Gualdo, G. "Francesco Filelfo e la curia pontificia: Una carriera mancata." *Archivio della Società Romana di Storia Patria* 102 (1979): 189–236.

Hankins, J. "Cosimo de' Medici as a Patron of Humanistic Literature." In *Cosimo "il Vecchio" de' Medici, 1389–1464: Essays in Commemoration of the Six Hundredth Anniversary of Cosimo de' Medici's Birth,* ed. F. Ames-Lewis, 69–94. Oxford, 1992.

———. *Plato in the Italian Renaissance.* 2 vols. Leiden, New York, 1990.

Harlfinger, D. *Die Textgeschichte der pseudo-aristotelischen Schrift Περὶ ἀτόμων γραμμῶν: Ein kodokologisch-kulturgeschichtlicher Beitrag zur Klärung der Überlieferungsverhältnisse im Corpus aristotelicum.* Amsterdam, 1971.

———. "Die Überlieferungsgeschichte der eudemischen Ethik." In *Akten des 5 Symposium Aristotelicum,* ed. P. Moreaux and D. Harlfinger, Peripatoi I, 1–50. Berlin, 1971.

Hody, Humphrey. *De graecis illustribus.* Ed. S. Jebb. London, 1742.

Hoffman, W. von. *Forschungen zur Geschichte der kurialen Behörden vom Schisma bis zur Reformation.* 2 vols. Rome, 1914.

Holmes, G. *The Florentine Enlightenment, 1400–1450.* Oxford, 1969.

IJsewijn, J. *Companion to Neo-Latin Studies.* Amsterdam, New York, and Oxford, 1977.

Jones, P.J. "Florentine Families and Florentine Diaries in the Fourteenth Century." *Papers of the British School at Rome* 24 (1956): 182–205.

Kent, F.W., and P. Simons, eds. *Patronage, Art, and Society in Renaissance Italy.* Oxford, 1987.

King, M.L. *Venetian Humanism in an Age of Patrician Dominance.* Princeton, 1986.

Knox, D. *Ironia: Medieval and Renaissance Ideas on Irony.* Columbia Studies in the Classical Tradition 16. Leiden, New York, 1989.

Kohl, B.J. "The Changing Concept of the *Studia Humanitatis* in the Early Renaissance." *Renaissance Studies* 6 (1992): 185–209.

König, E. *Kardinal Giordano Orsini †1438: Ein Lebensbild aus der Zeit der großen Konzilien und des Humanismus.* Studien und Darstellungen aus dem Gebiete der Geschichte, vol. 5, pt. 1. Freiburg im Breisgau, 1906.

Krakow, Matthew of [Mateusza z Krakowa]. *De praxi Romanae curiae.* Ed. Władysław Seńko. Breslau, 1969.

Kraye, J. "Moral Philosophy." In *CHRP,* 303–86.

Kristeller, P.O. *Iter Italicum: A Finding List of Uncatalogued or Incompletely Catalogued Humanistic Manuscripts of the Renaissance in Italian and Other Libraries.* 6 vols. Leiden and London, 1963–95.

———. *Renaissance Thought and Its Sources.* New York, 1979.

Lambert, M.D. *Franciscan Poverty: The Doctrine of the Absolute Poverty of Christ and the Apostles in the Franciscan Order, 1210–1323.* London, 1961.
———. *Medieval Heresy: Popular Movements from Bogomil to Hus.* London, 1977.
Lauer, P., ed. *Catalogue général des manuscrits latins.* Vol. 2 (nos. 1439–2692). Paris, 1940.
Lawner, L. *Lives of the Courtesans: Portraits of the Renaissance.* New York, 1987.
Leff, G. *Heresy in the Later Middle Ages.* 2 vols. Manchester and New York, 1967.
Lehmann, P. "Zur *Disputatio Ganfredi et Aprilis de statu curiae Romanae.*" *Historische Vierteljahrschrift* 17 (1916): 86–94.
Ludwig, W. *Schriften zur neulateinischen Literatur.* Ed. L. Braun. Munich, 1989.
Luiso, F.P. *Studi su l'epistolario di Leonardo Bruni.* Ed. L. Gualdo Rosa. Studi storici, Istituto storico italiano per il medio evo, fascicles 122–24. Rome, 1980.
———. "Studi su l'epistolario e le traduzioni di Lapo da Castiglionchio iuniore." *Studi italiani di filologia classica* 8 (1899): 205–99.
Marsh, D. *The Quattrocento Dialogue: Classical Tradition and Humanist Innovation.* Cambridge, Mass., 1980.
———. *Lucian and the Latins: Humor and Humanism in the Early Renaissance.* Ann Arbor, 1998.
———. "Xenophon." In *Catalogus Translationum et Commentariorum,* 7, ed. V. Brown. Washington, DC, 1992.
Martellotti, G. "Barzizza, Gasparino." *Dizionario biografico degli Italiani* 7 (1965): 34–39.
Martines, L. *The Social World of the Florentine Humanists, 1390–1460.* Princeton, 1963.
Masson, G. *Courtesans of the Italian Renaissance.* London, 1975.
Mathes, F.A. "The Poverty Movement and the Augustinian Hermits." *Analecta Augustiniana* 32 (1968): 5–154; 33 (1969): 5–116.
McManamon, J. *Pierpaolo Vergerio the Elder: The Humanist as Orator.* Tempe, 1996.
Mehus, L. *Historia litteraria florentina.* Florence, 1769. Reprint, with an introduction by E. Kessler, Munich, 1968.
Mercer, R.G.G. *The Teaching of Gasparino Barzizza.* London, 1979.
Michel, A. *Rhétorique et philosophie chez Cicéron: Essai sur les fondements philosophique de l'art de persuader.* Paris, 1960.
Miglio, M. "Vidi thiaram Pauli papae secundi." *Bullettino dell' Istituto Storico Italiano per il Medio Evo* 81 (1969): 273–96.
———. *Storiografia pontificia del Quattrocento,* Bologna, 1975.
Monfasani, J. "The Fraticelli and Clerical Wealth in Quattrocento Rome." In *Renaissance Society and Culture: Essays in Honor of Eugene Rice, Jr.,* ed. J. Monfasani and R. Musto, 177–95. New York, 1991.
———. *Fernando of Cordova: A Biographical and Intellectual Profile.* Transactions of the American Philosophical Society 82, no. 6. Philadelphia, 1992.

————. "A Theologian at the Roman Curia in the Mid-Quattrocento: A Bio-Bibliographical Study of Niccolò Palmieri, O.S.A." *Analecta Augustiniana* 54 (1991): 321–81; 55 (1992): 5–98 (printed separately with continuous pagination).

Montaigne, Michel de, *The Complete Essays*. Trans. M.A. Screech. New York, 1987.

Müllner, K. *Reden und Briefe italienischer Humanisten*. Vienna, 1899. Reprint, with an introduction by H.B. Gerl, Munich, 1970.

O'Malley, J.W. *Praise and Blame in Renaissance Rome: Rhetoric, Doctrine, and Reform in the Sacred Orators of the Papal Court, c. 1450–1521*. Duke Monographs in Medieval and Renaissance Studies 3. Durham, N.C., 1979.

Onians, J. "Alberti and ΦΙΛΑΡΕΤΗ: A Study in Their Sources." *Journal of the Warburg and Courtauld Institutes* 34 (1971): 96–114.

Otis, L.L. *Prostitution in Medieval Society: The History of an Urban Institution in Languedoc*. Chicago and London, 1985.

Pade, Marianne. "Revisions of Translations, Corrections and Criticisms: Some examples from the Fifteenth-century Latin Translations of Plutarch's 'Lives'." In *Etudes classiques IV: Actes du colloque "Méthodologie de la traduction: de l'Antiquité à la Renaissance,"* ed. C.M. Ternes. Luxembourg, 1994.

————. "The Latin Translations of Plutarch's *Lives* in Fifteenth-century Italy and Their Manuscript Diffusion." In *The Classical Tradition in the Middle Ages and the Renaissance*, ed. C. Leonardi and B.M. Olsen. Spoleto, 1995.

Palma, M. "Castiglionchio, Lapo da." *Dizionario biografico degli Italiani* 22 (1979): 40–44.

Palmieri, Matteo. *Della vita civile*. Ed. F. Battaglia. Bologna, 1944.

Partner, P. *The Pope's Men: The Papal Civil Service in the Renaissance*. Oxford, 1990.

————. "Ufficio, famiglia, stato: Contrasti nella curia Romana." In *Roma capitale (1447–1527)*, ed. S. Gensini, 39–50. Pisa, 1994.

Pelzer, A. *Codices Vaticani Latini*. Vol. 2, pt. 1, *Codices 679–1139*. Vatican City, 1931.

Pesce, L. *Cristoforo Garatone trevigiano, nunzio di Eugenio IV*. Rome, 1975.

Petrarca, Francesco. *Il "De otio religioso" di Francesco Petrarca*. Ed. G. Rotondi and G. Martellotti. Vatican City, 1958.

————. *Le Familiari*. Ed. V. Rossi. 4 vols. Florence, 1933–42.

————. *Le traité "De sui ipsius et multorum ignorantia."* Ed. L.M. Capelli. Paris, 1906.

————. *Petrarcas "Buch ohne Namen" und die päpstliche Kurie: Ein Beitrag zur Geistesgeschichte der Frührenaissance*. Ed. P. Piur. Halle an der Saale, 1925.

————. *Petrarch's Book without a Name: A Translation of the "Liber sine nomine."* Trans. N.P. Zacour. Toronto, 1973.

Piccolomini, Aeneas Silvius. *De curialium miseriis epistola*, ed. W.P. Mustard. Baltimore and London, 1928.

————. *De gestis concilii Basiliensis commentariorum libri duo*. Ed. D. Hay and W.K. Smith. Oxford, 1967.

———. *Der Briefwechsel des Eneas Silvius Piccolomini*, I, ed. R. Wolkan, 453–87. Vienna, 1909.

Poncelet, P. *Cicéron traducteur de Platon.* Paris, 1957.

Prodi, P. *The Papal Prince, One Body and Two Souls: The Papal Monarchy in Early Modern Europe.* Trans. S. Haskins. Cambridge, 1987.

Quint, D. "Humanism and Modernity: A Reconsideration of Bruni's *Dialogues*." *Renaissance Quarterly* 38 (1985): 423–45.

Rabil, A., Jr. "Humanism in Milan." In *Renaissance Humanism: Foundations, Forms, and Legacy*, ed. A. Rabil, Jr., 3:235–63. Philadelphia, 1988.

Rabil, A., Jr., ed. *Renaissance Humanism: Foundations, Forms, and Legacy.* 3 vols. Philadelphia, 1988.

Reynolds, L.D., ed. *Texts and Transmission: A Survey of the Latin Classics.* Oxford, 1983.

Re, N. del. *La curia Romana: Lineamenti storico-giuridici.* 3d ed. Rome, 1970.

Robin, D. "A Reassessment of the Character of Francesco Filelfo (1398–1481)." *Renaissance Quarterly* 36 (1983): 202–24.

———. *Filelfo in Milan, 1451–1477.* Princeton, 1991.

Rocke, M. *Forbidden Friendships: Homosexuality and Male Culture in Renaissance Florence.* Oxford, 1996.

Rosenthal, M.H. *The Honest Courtesan: Veronica Franco, Citizen and Writer in Sixteenth-Century Venice.* Chicago, 1992.

Rosmini, C. de'. *Vita di Francesco Filelfo da Tolentino.* 3 vols. Milan, 1808.

Rossiaud, J. *Medieval Prostitution.* Trans. L.G. Cochrane. Oxford and New York, 1988.

Rotondi, E. "Lapo da Castiglionchio e il suo epistolario." Tesi di laurea, Università di Firenze, Facoltà di magistero, 1970–71.

Sabbadini, R. *Storia del ciceronianismo e di altre questioni letterarie nell'età della Rinascenza.* Turin, 1886.

———. "Tito Livio Frulovisio: Umanista del sec. XV." In *Giornale storico della letteratura italiana* 103 (1934): 55–81.

———. *Le scoperte dei Codici latini e greci ne' Secoli XIV e XV.* 2 vols. Florence, 1914. Reprint, 1967.

Sammut, A. *Unfredo Duca di Gloucester e gli umanisti italiani.* Umanesimo 4. Padua, 1981.

Saxonia, Jordanus de, O.S.A. *Liber Vitasfratrum.* 3:2. Ed. R. Arbesmann and W. Hümpfner. New York, 1943.

Schlenker, B.R. *Impression Management: The Self-Concept, Social Identity, and Interpersonal Relations.* Monterey, Calif., 1980.

Schmitt, C.B., and Q. Skinner, eds. *The Cambridge History of Renaissance Philosophy.* Cambridge, New York, 1988.

Scholz, R. "Eine humanistische Schilderung der Kurie aus dem Jahre 1438, herausgegeben aus einer vatikanischen Handschrift." *Quellen und Forschungen aus italienischen Archiven und Bibliotheken* 16 (1914): 108–53.

———. "Eine ungedruckte Schilderung der Kurie aus dem Jahre 1438." *Archiv für Kulturgeschichte* 10 (1912): 399–413.

Schuchard, C. *Die Deutschen an der päpstlichen Kurie im späten Mittelalter*

(1378–1447). Bibliothek des deutschen historischen Instituts im Rom. Tübingen, 1987.

Schuster, B. *Die freien Frauen: Dirnen und Frauenhaüser im 15. und 16. Jahrhundert*. Frankfurt and New York, 1995.

Schwarz, B. *Die Organisation kurialer Schreiberkollegien von ihrer Entstehung bis zur Mitte des 15. Jahrhunderts*. Tübingen, 1972.

Seigel, J. *Rhetoric and Philosophy in Renaissance Humanism: The Union of Eloquence and Wisdom, Petrarch to Valla*. Princeton, 1968.

Sidwell, K. "Il *De curialium miseriis* di Enea Silvio Piccolomini e il De mercede conductis," in *Pio II e la cultura del suo tempo*, ed. L.R.S. Tarugi, 329–41. Milan, 1991.

Stieber, J.W. *Pope Eugenius IV, the Council of Basel, and the Secular and Ecclesiastical Authorities in the Empire: The Conflict over Supreme Authority and Power in the Church*. Leiden, 1978.

Stump, H. *The Reforms of the Council of Constance*. Studies in the History of Christian Thought 53. Leiden, New York, and Cologne, 1994.

Sullivan, P.A. "The Plan of Cicero's Philosophical Corpus." Ph.D. diss., Boston University, 1951.

Thomson, J.A.F. *Popes and Princes, 1417–1517: Politics and Polity in the Late Medieval Church*. London, 1980.

Torre, A. Della. *Storia dell' accademia platonica di Firenze*. Florence, 1902. Reprint, Turin, 1968.

Trexler, R.C. "La prostitution florentine au XVᵉ siècle: Patronage et clientèles." *Annales* 6 (1981): 983–1015.

Trinkaus, C.M. *"In Our Image and Likeness": Humanity and Divinity in Italian Humanist Thought*. 2 vols. London, 1970.

Valla, Lorenzo. *De professione religiosorum*. Ed. M. Cortesi. Padua, 1986.

———. *Epistole*. Ed. O. Besomi and M. Regoliosi. Padua, 1984.

———. *Opera omnia*. Ed. J. Vahlen. Basel, 1540, Reprint with additions, Turin, 1962.

Verona, Gaspare da. *De gestis Pauli secundi*. In Muratori, *Rerum italicarum scriptores*, III:XVI (Città di Castello, 1904), 3–64.

Vickers, K.H. *Humphrey Duke of Gloucester*. London, 1907.

Voigt, G. *Die Wiederbelebung des classischen Althertums oder das erste Jahrhundert des Humanismus*. 2 vols. Berlin, 1960.

Walser, E. *Poggius Florentinus: Leben und Werke*. Leipzig and Berlin, 1914. Reprint, Hildesheim, 1974.

Walther, H., ed. *Lateinische Sprichwörter und Sentenzen des Mittelalters in alphabetischer Anordnung*. 5 vols. Göttingen, 1963–67.

———, ed. *Lateinische Sprichwörter und Sentenzen des Mittelalters und der frühen Neuzeit in alphabetischer Anordnung*. 3 vols. Göttingen, 1982–86.

Watkins, R.N. "Mythology as Code: Lapo da Castiglionchio's View of Homosexuality and Materialism at the Curia." *Journal of the History of Ideas* 53 (1992): 138–44.

Watson, A.G. "Thomas Allen of Oxford and His Manuscripts." In *Medieval Scribes, Manuscripts, and Libraries: Essays Presented to N.R. Ker,* ed. M.B. Parkes and A.G. Watson, 279–314. London, 1978.

Weiss, R. *Humanism in England during the Fifteenth Century.* 2d ed. Oxford, 1957.

———. "Per la biografia di Antonio Beccaria in Inghilterra." *Giornale storico della letteratura italiana* 110 (1937): 344–46.

West, M.L. *Textual Criticism and Editorial Technique.* Stuttgart, 1973.

Witt, R.G. *Hercules at the Crossroads: The Life, Work, and Thought of Coluccio Salutati.* Durham, NC, 1983.

———. "Medieval Italian Culture and the Origins of Humanism as a Stylistic Ideal." In *Renaissance Humanism: Foundations, Forms, and Legacy,* ed. A. Rabil, Jr., 1. Philadelphia, 1988.

Index of Manuscripts

Index of Names and Subjects

In this index, references to the introductory study, i.e., chapters 1–5, are by page numbers; references to the text and translation are by section numbers. The entry for Lapo da Castiglionchio the Younger covers only separate prose works of his, excluding translations. Angelo da Recanate is not indexed when he appears or is discussed as an interlocutor in the *De curiae commodis*. Modern scholars are indexed only if their names appear in the text.